THE TROUT ANGLER IN
SHETLAND
PAST & PRESENT

KEITH HARWOOD

MMXVII
THE MEDLAR PRESS
ELLESMERE

Published by The Medlar Press Limited,
The Grange, Ellesmere, Shropshire.

ISBN 978-1-907110-70-2

Text © 2017 Keith Harwood
Design © 2017 The Medlar Press

Keith Harwood has asserted his rights
under the Copyright, Design and Patents Act, 1988,
to be identified as Author of this work.

All rights reserved. Without limiting the rights under copyright reserved above, no part of this publication may be reproduced, stored in a retrieval system, or transmitted in any form or by any means (electronic, mechanical, photocopying, recording or otherwise) without the prior permission of both the copyright owner and the Medlar Press Limited.

The author and publisher would like to thank those who have given permission for copyright material to be reproduced in this book. If any have been inadvertently overlooked they will be pleased to make the necessary arrangements.

*Cover design by The Medlar Press
from an image by the Author.*

Typeset in 12 on 14 point Garamond Roman.
Produced in England by The Medlar Press Limited, Ellesmere, England.

Contents

Introduction 9
Map of Shetland 12

1 - The Trout Angler's Quarry 13
2 - The Development of Angling in Shetland 27
3 - Shetland Angling Clubs 43
   Colour plates 56
4 - Angling Guide Books 57
5 - Edward Charlton : Angler & Traveller 73
6 - John Russell : The Angling Minister of Whalsay 83
7 - 'Old Wick' on Angling 93
8 - Mr Gaskell's Fishing Excursion 105
9 - Sir Edward Grey on Shetland 113
10 - Fishing with the Doctor in Shetland 121
11 - Sir George Aston on Shetland 127
12 - Trout Fishing in Shetland by 'Black-Beetle' 135
13 - Fishing with the Professor on Unst 143
14 - A Sea Trout Courtesy of a Seal 151
15 - Heather Moss in Shetland 155
16 - An Old Etonian on Unst 167
17 - The Buchans in Shetland 173
18 - John Leslie - An Angling Member of Parliament 183
19 - Negley Farson on Shetland 191
20 - The Petersons 199
21 - Moray McLaren & the Simmer Dim 205
22 - The Brown Trout Era 213
23 - Flies for Shetland : Past & Present 221
   Colour plates of flies 224
24 - Piscator Non Solum Piscatur 239

Appendix : Selected Fly Dressings 251
Bibliography 257
Index 259

[5]

Acknowledgements

This book would not have been possible without the generous help and cooperation of a number of people on Shetland. Paul Bloomer, angler and artist, has been a constant source of encouragement and has provided me with a great deal of material in his possession and has read through my draft chapters. Fellow Shetland Anglers' Association member, Mark Sandison, has also been very generous with his time and has provided me with written and photographic material. Big fish expert David Pottinger kindly supplied me with a set of his flies and, in a number of telephone conversations, passed on his valuable advice. Graeme Callander, too, very kindly dressed a number of flies that were photographed for this book. Alec Miller, secretary of the Shetland Anglers' Association, has been extremely helpful and has read through many of my draft chapters and provided me with a great deal of material, especially concerning the history of the Shetland Anglers' Association which will be celebrating its centenary year in 2020. Dr Ian Tait, curator of the outstanding Shetland Museum, has read through a number of draft chapters and stopped me from making too many errors regarding aspects of Shetland's history. He has also generously given permission for the use of photographic material in the museum's collection. Archivists, Brian Smith and Dr Mark Smith, have kindly provided answers to my many queries and have allowed me access to material in the archives' collection. Angling historian, John Austin, has also read through some of my draft material and made a number of suggestions.

However, my greatest debt of gratitude is to my wife Helen who has ventured up to Shetland with me and put up with me while writing and researching this book. Her knowledge of computers and their ways is far better than mine and on several occasions she has magically retrieved material that I had accidentally deleted.

Clitheroe, September 2017.

*For all members of the
Shetland Anglers' Association
past and present.*

John Manson and J.P. Henderson fishing on Loch of Spiggie.
Courtesy of Shetland Museum & Archives.

Introduction

It was Negley Farson who wrote, 'See the Shetlands once, and they will haunt you for ever' (*The Way of a Transgressor*, 1935). Writer and broadcaster, Moray McLaren expressed similar feelings when he wrote, 'I have acquired for Shetland an affection that haunts me; it is the kind of affection which comes upon people in middle life, and is different from the ardours and endurances of youthful love' *(A Singing Reel*, 1953). I agree wholeheartedly with the sentiments expressed by both authors. I must confess that I am a fairly recent visitor to the islands and dearly wish I had come to this remote and most northerly area of Britain much earlier in my life. On the very first day of our arrival on Shetland several years ago, my wife and I drove down towards Sumburgh Head to view the lighthouse and visitor centre. Along the way, we stopped in a layby overlooking the sea near the airport. Almost at once we caught sight of an otter swimming among the bladder-wrack in search of its next meal. We were both entranced by the spectacle and immediately fell in love with the place. Since that first morning we have travelled (and I have fished) extensively throughout the islands in the archipelago and have been captivated by the islands' beauty, dramatic coastal scenery, wildlife, archaeology and most of all, by the friendliness of the people we have come across. There is a real sense of community in Shetland, which, alas, is now rarely encountered elsewhere in the British Isles.

As an angler, archaeologist and lover of natural history, Shetland has everything that I desire in a holiday destination. After buying my fishing licence in the tourist information office in Lerwick, I was amazed at how much fishing there was available

- and for less than the price of a day ticket on some southern reservoirs. It was not long before I took myself off to the Loch of Tingwall and managed to tempt some of its hard fighting brown trout for which the loch is justly famous. However, when I ventured into the Shetland Times Bookshop in Lerwick and the bookshop in the Shetland Museum at Hay's Dock, I was surprised to find that very little had been published on the trout and sea trout fishing in the islands. As an angling historian I resolved to put that right - hence this book was born. I returned to Shetland the following summer and spent a number of mornings in the excellent archives searching through the material on angling. Since then I have lived and breathed angling on Shetland and have managed to track down many of the elusive volumes containing material on its trout and sea trout fishing.

During the latter half of the nineteenth century, following improvements in rail and sea transport, Shetland became a fashionable destination for well-to-do anglers in search of peace and tranquillity where they could pursue their sport in pristine waters. Not surprisingly, Shetland soon became renowned as one of the top venues in Europe for its sea trout fishing and anglers would venture from mainland Britain and even further afield for the opportunity of catching these hard-fighting fish in the saltwater voes, a type of fishing rarely encountered elsewhere. From the late nineteenth century through to the mid twentieth century, Shetland attracted a number of distinguished visitors who have left behind accounts of their battles with sea trout. This same period witnessed the heyday of angling tourism on Shetland and brought about a notable boost to the local economy. During the later decades of the nineteenth century a number of local entrepreneurs opened hotels to cater for the needs of visiting anglers and their companions. Sadly, as the twentieth century wore on, sea trout numbers began to decline, so much so that by the mid-1980s numbers had declined to such an extent that barely a dozen fish were caught in a season. Fortunately, Shetland is home to well over 300 lochs containing wild brown trout and, as sea trout stocks collapsed, anglers turned their attention to devising flies and techniques to tempt the large brown trout lurking in their depths. Nowadays, Shetland is justly famed for the excellence of its wild brown trout fishing and for anglers from the south, tired of catching ragged finned hatchery reared rainbow trout, Shetland is an angler's paradise and if the fish are not taking on one loch it is a simple matter to move to another one. The sea trout fishing, too, has also begun to show signs of improvement in recent years, thanks largely to the effort of the Shetland Anglers' Association and similar clubs on the outer islands.

This book charts the development of fishing for trout and sea trout in Shetland from the mid-nineteenth century to the present day and includes the accounts of the angling experiences of a number of well-known and not so well-known figures who have fished these islands. Also included are chapters on the angler's quarry and on the flies used to catch them, as well as the clubs that have grown up to cater for the angler's needs. The Shetland Anglers' Association will shortly (2020) be celebrating its centenary year and I would like this book to serve as a fitting tribute to an association that has done so much to maintain and improve the quality of fishing in these islands.

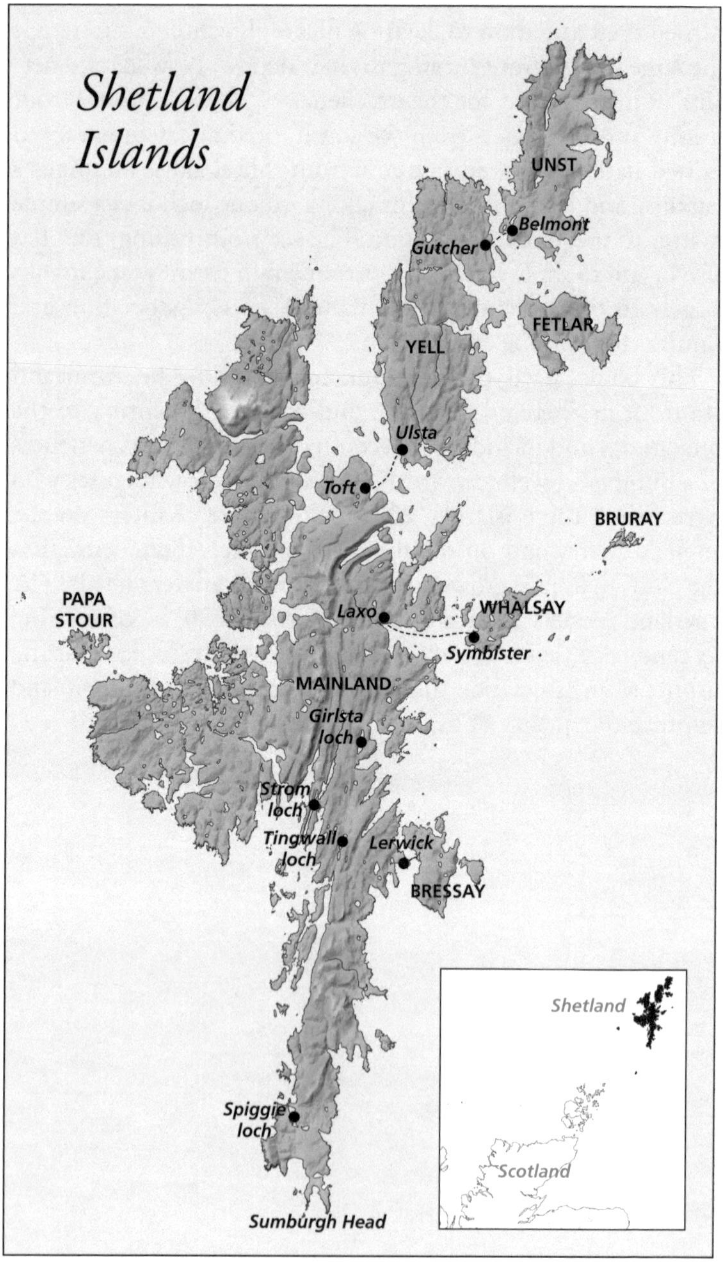

Shetland
Islands
UNST
Belmont
Gutcher
FETLAR
YELL
Ulsta
Toft
BRURAY
PAPA
STOUR
Laxo
WHALSAY
Symbister
MAINLAND
Girlsta
loch
Strom
loch
Tingwall
loch
Lerwick
BRESSAY
Shetland
Scotland
Spiggie
loch
Sumburgh Head

CHAPTER 1

The Trout Angler's Quarry

Shetland is an archipelago of around 100 islands, only 16 of which are inhabited today, although in the early part of the nineteenth century around 40 were occupied. The islands form the most northerly part of the United Kingdom, located 200 miles north of Aberdeen, and 230 miles west of Bergen, Norway. For several hundred years Shetland was under Norwegian rule and the capital, Lerwick, is nearer to Bergen than it is to London. Shetland lies at the same latitude as southern Greenland and St Petersburg but the warming effects of the Gulf Stream mean that it has a temperate maritime climate and, over the course of a year, the temperature typically varies from 3°C to 15°C and is rarely below -1°C or above 17°C. The general character of the climate is windy and cloudy with at least 2mm of rain falling on 250 days a year. Due to the islands' latitude the northern lights can sometimes be seen on clear winter nights and in the summer there is almost continual daylight, referred to locally as the 'simmer dim'.

Due to its complex and varied geology, Shetland has a great diversity of lochs, ranging in size from less than an acre to the large lochs of Girlsta and Cliff. The five most important types of loch are as follows:

Dystrophic: these are small, nutrient poor lochs, sometimes little more than a hole in the peat filled with water. The majority of these lochs are of very little interest to anglers as the vast majority hold no fish. Red-throated divers, on the other hand, often choose these lochs for their nesting sites.

Oligotrophic: these lochs are generally larger and deeper than the dystrophic ones and are commonly found on the ice-scoured granite of the Ronas Hill plateau. Many of these lochs have very clear water, which deepens quickly from the shore and this is coupled with a mainly rock or shingle bottom. Aquatic plant life is scarce and the lochs are populated by mostly small trout, although some of the lochs do produce trout of considerable size.

Mesotrophic: these lochs are relatively common on the West Mainland and some of them lie on limestone, which can give rise to a large variety of aquatic plant life. Such lochs often hold good stocks of quality trout although fishing, especially in late summer, can be difficult due to prolific weed growth.

Eutrophic: lochs of this nature are generally small, with the exception of Spiggie Loch, and are the most fertile. Such lochs are rich in mineral and organic nutrients and promote a proliferation of algae and aquatic plants, resulting in a reduction of dissolved oxygen.

Brackish: most of these lochs are small with the exception of Strom Loch, which is over a mile long. Some of these lochs have relatively high salt content and may contain seaweed and species of marine fish such as coalfish and flounder. They are of interest to the angler for the sea trout found in them.

Shetland has no rivers as such, only streams and burns, which contain small brown trout. Several of the larger burns have runs of sea trout and small numbers of salmon, mostly under ten pounds in weight.

Shetland is truly an angler's paradise with its numerous lochs and burns. During the latter half of the nineteenth century and first half of the twentieth century the sea trout was the angler's main quarry and Shetland had the reputation of having some of the finest sea trout fishing in Europe. Anglers from far and wide visited Shetland for the opportunity to fly fish for these hard-fighting fish in the saltwater voes, a type of angling rarely encountered elsewhere in the British Isles. Now that sea trout numbers have declined, although there are signs of a comeback, brown trout fishing predominates and in recent years some specimen brownies have been caught in the islands. The angler in Shetland is certainly not short of choice. If one loch is not producing, it is an easy matter to move on to another one, as John Tudor wrote in the following verse from *The Orkneys and Shetland: Their Past and Present State* (1883):

Lochs to the right of him
Lochs to the left of him
Lochs in front of him
Glisten'd and gleam'd.

There are two main species of game fish that are of interest to the game angler in Shetland - the ubiquitous brown trout and the sea trout. Char are also present in the Loch of Girlsta (in Central Mainland), the deepest loch in Shetland (max. depth 22.5m or 74 ft). Small numbers of salmon, both wild fish and escapees from fish farms are found in the voes and burns, and are occasionally caught by the angler fishing for sea trout.

Brown Trout

With 526 lochs over one hectare (according to Walter Scott's *Shetland,* 2011), most of which contain brown trout and receive little fishing pressure, the angler on Shetland is certainly not short of choice of where to fish. In fact, should he/she so wish, an angler could fish a different loch every day of the brown trout fishing season which runs from the 15th of March to the 6th of October. Most of the lochs on Shetland are controlled by the Shetland Anglers' Association, which publishes a map and guide to over seventy of the most popular lochs entitled *Trout Fishing in Shetland (*available from outlets in Shetland or directly via the

Brown trout

association's excellent website), which contains a wealth of information for the visiting angler.

The brown trout (*Salmo trutta*), sometimes referred to in older books as the yellow trout, to distinguish it from the more silvery sea trout, is a very adaptable fish and is found in practically all Shetland lochs. The species *Salmo trutta* includes the resident brown trout and the migratory sea trout. The Shetland brown trout has to be adaptable to survive the many different environments found within Shetland. Shetland lochs vary a great deal both in size and depth and in water quality from dark peaty moorland lochs to rich fertile limestone lochs. Most lochs in Shetland contain trout averaging six to twelve ounces but fish of more than three pounds in weight are not uncommon and much larger fish are occasionally encountered. The front cover of the April 2003 edition of *Shetland Life* magazine displays a photograph of proud angler Michael Tait from Lerwick with a magnificent 20lb brown trout caught by spinning on Loch Brouster on the opening day of the season. A number of fish cages were sited in Loch Brouster several

[16]

years ago and it appears that this trout grew fat on a diet of fish pellets and, as a result, this fish cannot be said to be a truly wild fish. One of the largest fly-caught wild brown trout recorded in recent years was a 9lb 4oz specimen caught on Whalsay by Dodie Irvine on the 8th of April, 1981. The fish was taken on a Zulu fly.

Few other creatures can adapt to match their environment and available food supply as successfully as the trout. The trout has been around for a long time. Its ancestor, *Eosalmo driftwoodensis*, was swimming around the waters of what is now North America around 50 million years ago. *Eosalmo* is the earliest known salmonid and is the ancestor of all today's trout and salmon. It derives its name *Eosalmo driftwoodensis* from an ancient lake bed in the Driftwood Canyon in British Columbia, where its fossilised remains were first discovered in 1977. It is believed that originally *Eosalmo* was a freshwater fish and only learned to feed in saltwater at a later stage. This is confirmed by the fact that all salmonids, even those like the sea trout that spend a considerable time at sea, return to freshwater to spawn. The brown trout (*Salmo trutta*) shares the *Salmo* genus with the Atlantic salmon (*Salmo salar*). Apparently, these two species split from their common ancestor around 4.5 million years ago and the brown trout first appeared in the area we know as the Balkans, while the salmon evolved in the Atlantic.

The diet of Shetland trout varies a great deal depending on the type of loch it inhabits but midges or buzzers (chironomids) form an important part of the diet of most loch trout and the angler is well-advised to carry a variety of artificial patterns imitating the life cycle of this important creature. Caenis, caddis, olives, corixae, snails, beetles, terrestrials, sticklebacks etc. all form part of the diet of Shetland trout at various times in the season and the angler is advised to get to know a water well and build up a picture of where and when the seasonal food source is available to the trout.

Although most of the brown trout on Shetland are truly wild fish, attempts have been made over the years to improve and stock various lochs. In the early decades of the twentieth century Sir William Watson Cheyne (1852-1932), the eminent surgeon and pioneer of antibiotics, stocked Loch Funzie (pronounced 'Finnie') on Fetlar with trout. Nowadays, Loch Funzie is best known as one of the most important breeding sites for the red-necked phalarope but trout can still be caught from its waters. Since 1995, aided by grants from various bodies, the Shetland Anglers' Association has been carrying out a comprehensive stocking programme of both sea trout and brown trout, principally in waters on the Mainland and Yell. All these fish have been reared in Shetland and, in recent years, fish numbers have increased as has the average weight of fish.

Sea Trout

Sea trout and brown trout are the same species (*Salmo trutta*) but a combination of genetics and environmental factors mean that some trout go to sea to feed before returning to their native burn or loch to spawn. The sea trout of Shetland do not confine spawning to streams or burns but also use areas of shingle in shallow water around the edges of lochs. This is probably due to a lack of suitable spawning grounds in the streams and burns.

During the late nineteenth century and the first half of the twentieth century the sea trout of Shetland were highly prized by well-to-do visiting anglers who made the long journey to these remote islands specifically to fish for them. However, it appears that sea trout were less well prized by the native crofter-fishermen who set their nets in the voes and caught sea trout along with a variety of other fish. A good-sized haddock was much preferred for the table over a sea trout. In late autumn crofters took quantities of sea trout from the spawning burns with the *høvi*. A *høvi* was a fish trap made of the stalks of dock, wide at one end and narrow at the other. A dyke was built across a suitable burn, leaving an open space in the middle sufficient to admit the wider end of the *høvi*. After the *høvi* was firmly placed in the open space, a crofter, stick in hand, would wade

Sea trout

the burn and drive the sea trout before him into the *høvi*, from which they could not escape. A more modern form of *høvi*, made out of netting and a barrel hoop at the mouth end, was still in use until comparatively recently. Shetland angler David Pottinger recalls seeing such fish traps in use in the 1950s and 1960s. These fish were then salted and dried, a standby if times were hard, but a poor substitute for other salted fish such as cod or ling. Such fish were also smoked in crofts to preserve them. Quite often, however, these autumnal sea trout ended up being dug into the ground to serve as a fertiliser.

By the 1960s serious concerns were being expressed regarding the decline of these magnificent fish, as evidenced by a couple of articles in *The New Shetlander* magazine in 1964 (numbers 68 & 69), written by John Peterson:

> *Today the shoals of trout have gone. Listen at night and you will be fortunate to hear a single fish jump; examine the burns, whose pools were once rich in young fish, and hardly a fish can be found. Memory can of course be deceptive, but I feel confident that there is not now one-tenth of the sea trout that existed in our waters fifty years ago!*

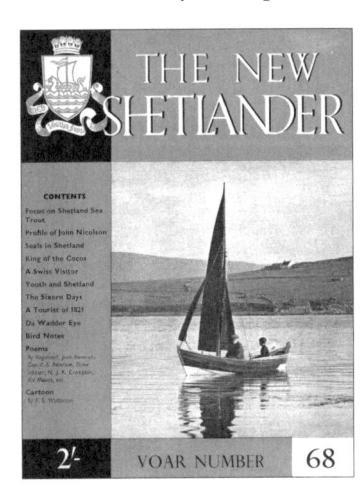

John Peterson gave a number of reasons for the decline in sea trout numbers, the main one being over-fishing. Increasing numbers of motor cars in the islands enabled people in towns and villages to take up angling and to travel to hitherto inaccessible areas in search of their quarry. The car also allowed net-fishers to travel farther afield in search of sea trout. Modern fibres made nets more deadly and less bulky and modern freezers, in which summer and autumn caught sea trout could be preserved for winter consumption, made netting more profitable. Peterson claimed that many fishermen were unaware of the harm they were doing by catching large numbers of immature fish and killing them. Peterson also believed that the season for sea trout, which started on the 1st of February and ended on the 15th of November was much too long and that Shetland sea trout were in poor condition up to the end of March. Nowadays, the sea trout season runs from the 25th of February to the 31st of October, but still too long by Peterson's standards. In some years, if the annual Viking festival, the Up-Helly-Aa, fell on the last Tuesday in January, some anglers would celebrate all night and then go straight 'ta da troots' in the morning. Sea trout at that time of the year would be out of condition and some would still have been spawning. In order to improve matters Peterson advocated setting up conservation areas where fishing for sea trout would be banned for a number of years. In support of this idea he noted that in deep-sea fishing grounds, which were 'rested' during the two world wars, the fish stocks greatly increased and he saw no reason why sea trout stocks should not respond correspondingly.

Unfortunately, Mr Peterson's ideas appear not to have been taken up and by the 1980s and 1990s sea trout numbers had declined to such an extent that in some seasons fewer than ten fish were caught by anglers. A more recent article, written by angler and artist Paul Bloomer, on the reasons for the sea trout's demise was published by *Shetland Life* magazine in January, 2008 (Issue number 327). The reasons for the decline in sea trout numbers are complex and multifarious and anglers themselves have a role to play in halting this decline. Although most anglers would only take the odd fish for the pot, Bloomer refers to stories of others taking large baskets of undersized fish.

Illegal netting is another major problem faced by the sea trout and this is compounded by the very nature of sea trout themselves, as Bloomer says:

> *The unique lifestyle of sea trout coupled with the unique geography of Shetland means that they are very vulnerable to exploitation. The myriad of small burns around the isles are not capable of carrying large numbers of fish unless they are in spate, meaning that sea trout gather in the vicinity of the burn mouth awaiting heavy rain, which could be weeks or months away. This is when they are at their most vulnerable to excessive angling pressure, seals and nets.*

Restocking by a number of Shetland angling clubs seems to have led to a corresponding increase in illegal netting and Bloomer refers to an incident at Cunningsburgh. Following the landslides of 2003, both burns in Cunningsburgh were restocked and a good head of sea trout was quickly established. In 2005 and 2006 stocks declined rapidly and some fish were caught that were heavily net-marked. By 2008 there were so few fish left that it was pointless even to set a net. In 2007, there was a report of 50 sea trout netted at Hamnavoe in Yell, which were then photographed by their captor.

During the 1980s a number of fish farms for rearing salmon were established by several native Shetlanders and others, the majority of whom have since sold out to multi-national Canadian and Norwegian firms. In recent decades fish farming on Shetland has become an important industry and although the farms provide much needed jobs in remote rural communities their environmental impact is great. Warnings have been sounded for some time that the enormous proliferation of sea lice from open-net cage salmon farming are decimating wild migratory sea trout and salmon populations. Salmon cages are a magnet for sea lice, which breed in their billions. Sea lice are free swimming and move on tidal currents and, as wild fish swim past, they are confronted with clouds of these lice. Sea trout can survive with up to six sea lice on them but fish in Shetland have been captured with as many as 300 on them. Although numerous attempts have been made at controlling sea lice, all have met with varying degrees of success and the problem still continues. In the early days of fish farming large amounts of concentrated chemicals were thrown into the fish-rearing cages in an attempt to control the sea lice problem. Unfortunately, if wind and tides were adverse it could result in large quantities of chemicals being concentrated in the heads of voes and killing off the invertebrate life on which sea trout feed. The late well-known Scottish angler and author, Bruce Sandison, reported in 2016 (*Fly Fishing & Fly Tying*, April) that Marine Harvest, the Norwegian-owned largest factory salmon farmer in the world, was planning to introduce fully-enclosed salmon pens at a number of Norwegian sites as a means of reducing the impact of a growing sea lice problem. Unless a similar scheme is introduced in Shetland, the sea lice problem will persist.

According to Bloomer, the gradual degradation of spawning burns caused by agricultural run-offs has made it difficult for sea trout to reproduce successfully and their needs have rarely been considered during any kind of change to freshwater courses. Changes in agricultural drainage in Shetland have also led to the canalisation of once healthy free-flowing burns. The Loch of Strand was once one of the cleanest brackish sea trout lochs in Shetland, but, following the building of a silage pit a mile upstream in the 1970s, the water quality has deteriorated considerably. Large concentrations of cattle around burns can break down banks, leading to the loss of spawning areas through changes in flow pattern and increased silting and any attempt at restocking is doomed to failure unless the environment is restored.

When at sea, a large part of the sea trout's diet consists of sand-eels and a decline in their numbers has not only affected sea trout populations but also populations of sea birds such as Arctic terns and kittiwakes. Various reasons have been put forward for the decline in the sand-eel population including: industrial fishing of sand-eels to make fish meal for animal feed and pellets for farmed fish; and global warming leading to a change in ecosystems. Both these factors are ultimately the result of man's impact on the natural environment.

If sea trout had feathers there would be a public outcry at the decline in their numbers but, since they are out of sight, they appear to be out of mind and research is desperately needed to establish the key reasons for their decline before any realistic conservation measures can be put in place.

Although most of what I have written concerning sea trout stocks seems overwhelmingly negative, there are signs in some areas of Shetland that the restocking work carried out by the Shetland Anglers' Association and other angling clubs in the islands is bearing fruit. A recent article by Jon Beer, which appeared in *Trout and Salmon* magazine (December 2015), records the capture of a number of sea trout in various burns and voes throughout Shetland. It is clear that sea trout can still be found in Shetland but not in the prolific numbers of the nineteenth and early twentieth centuries but, if the angler should come across a shoal, exciting sport is guaranteed.

Girlsta Char

The Arctic char (*Salvelinus alpinus*) is a member of the salmonid family and in Shetland, as in the Faroes, it is found in only one loch - the Loch of Girlsta. In the British Isles, the char is found in some of the deep lakes in Scotland, Wales, Ireland and the English Lake District. As its name implies the Arctic char is a cold-water species and has the most northerly distribution of any fish. In Britain, the populations of char are at the extreme south of their range and are particularly sensitive to environmental change. Whether the char of the Loch of Girlsta can adapt to changes in temperature brought about by global warming

Arctic char

only time will tell. In the Arctic, the char is anadromous, i.e. a fish, like the salmon and sea trout, that feeds in the sea and enters freshwater to spawn. It is generally believed that the Girlsta char evolved from the migratory form but became landlocked in Girlsta's cold, deep water following the retreat of the ice at the end of the last ice age around ten thousand years ago.

The char is a delicate, but very beautiful fish and in overall shape resembles the brown trout. Unlike the trout, however, it is at its most beautiful in its spawning colours. Its breeding livery can be stunning; dark sea-green back, flanks with a slight silvery shade which pass into a beautiful deep red on the belly. The female, at this time, is less brightly coloured and more silvery than the male. The char derives its name from the Gaelic word *caera*, meaning red. The Girlsta char spawn in October and November when they frequent the gravelly shallows at the north end of the loch.

Since it swims deep the char is rarely encountered by anglers. However, char are occasionally caught on fly but the rise of a char is unlike that of a trout. Whereas the trout will sometimes rise with a splash, the char gently breaks the surface of the water.

Writing in *The New Shetlander* magazine in the summer of 1964 (number 69), Dr M. A. Swan reports that four Girlsta char are held in the collection of the British Natural History Museum in London. One of them was acquired in 1873 and the other three were sent in 1909 by Mr J. S. Tulloch to Tate Regan, a noted ichthyologist, who worked at the museum.

During the early 1950s, amid concerns that the Girlsta char might have become extinct, Dr Swan was granted permission by the Shetland Anglers' Association to net the loch. On the 25th of September, 1955, Dr Swan with the help of Charles Arthur who lived at the south end of the loch, set out a herring net in deep water near a gravelly beach at the north end. On lifting the net, it was found to contain fifty-seven char and three trout. The largest of these char was nearly ten and a half inches long (25cm). Girlsta char do not grow large and are akin to the herring in size. The current British record for a char stands at 9lb 8oz, and was captured by W. Fairbairn in Loch Arkaig, near Inverness. It seems likely, however, that Arkaig char grow big by living near the salmon cages and taking advantage of the free food supply! Migratory char grow much larger than their non-migratory cousins and fish up to thirty pounds have been taken in Canada.

Girlsta char are still occasionally caught on fly during the summer months by anglers fishing for trout, and anglers are requested to return them to the water.

Other Freshwater Fish Species

There are very few species of freshwater fish in Shetland, mainly due to the lack of any suitable rivers and the lack of sufficiently large water bodies (only four of Shetland's lochs have a surface area greater than a square kilometre). In addition to the species mentioned above, the eel (*Anguilla anguilla*) is widespread throughout Shetland waters as is the three-spined stickleback (*Gasterosteus aculeatus*). The ten-spined stickleback (*Pingutius*

Three and ten spined sticklebacks.

pingutius) has apparently been recorded in the Loch of Cliff on Unst and it is believed that the lamprey (*Petromyzon marinus*) may be present in some of the larger burns. Flounders, too, are sometimes encountered by anglers fishing in the lochs. Although flounders are primarily a species of sea fish they occasionally make their way up feeder streams and burns into freshwater.

The Loch of Cliff.

CHAPTER 2

The Development of Angling in Shetland

The words 'angling' and 'fishing' are frequently transposed and can lead to confusion. The term 'angling' is derived from the Old English word 'angle', meaning a hook, and generally refers to fishing with hook and line, and angling itself has come to be defined as a recreation or pastime. Although some anglers do kill and eat the fish they catch, their primary purpose when angling is not to put food on the table, but to fish for pleasure and pit their wits against the fish. Fishermen, on the other hand, go fishing to catch fish either for their own consumption or to sell at a profit. Fishing in Shetland has been carried out for thousands of years, whereas angling is a relatively recent phenomenon.

The first settlers to inhabit Shetland arrived around six thousand years ago when the climate was somewhat warmer and drier than it is today. These early settlers were primarily hunters and gatherers who relied on the natural resources they found nearby for food, tools, clothes and housing. As they became more established, they learned to cultivate the land with primitive ploughs and grow cereal crops, primarily barley. Remains of these early farms, field systems and burial cairns are scattered throughout Shetland, especially the hills of the west side. Not surprisingly, since nowhere in Shetland is more than three miles from the sea and the land itself is dotted with myriad lochs, these early inhabitants soon learned how to fish.

Unfortunately, there is very little archaeological evidence of prehistoric fishing in Shetland. This is partly due to the acidic soils which cover much of the islands and inhibit the preservation of fish, or indeed, of any bones. Furthermore, it is only relatively recently that archaeologists have undertaken large-scale soil sieving on archaeological sites. Without sieving the soil, only the bones of large fish such as cod, coalfish and ling are likely to be recovered. However, from excavations elsewhere, both in Britain and the rest of Europe, it is possible to gain some idea of prehistoric fishing methods. Spearing or harpooning fish was a method commonly used in prehistoric times. Harpoons or fish spears were fashioned out of bones carved with projecting barbs and attached to a wooden shaft, similar in many ways to the leisters used in historic times in Scotland for spearing salmon and eels. In the acidic soils of Shetland bone harpoon heads have not survived.

Another method that would almost certainly have been used in prehistoric Shetland was fishing with a line and gorge. Double-pointed gorges made out of wood or bone, were attached to a line made of plant fibre and baited with worm or other live-bait. The idea behind this method was to allow the fish to swallow the baited gorge, then to strike and fix the gorge across its throat. This principle, too, lived on into historic times when needles baited with worms were used for sniggling eels.

Fish traps or 'weels' made out of suitable plaited plant material would almost certainly have been employed by our prehistoric ancestors. Such traps would have been set in the feeder streams and burns issuing out of the many lochs on Shetland. They could be kept in position by stone weights and were used to catch many different kinds of fish, salt- or fresh-water, with or without bait.

The most effective of all devices for catching fish is the net, and there is evidence from archaeological sites throughout Europe that this method has been in use since Mesolithic times. The most primitive type of net is the drag or sweep net designed to surround and enclose surface-swimming fish, mainly in shallow water. Evidence for such nets might include the floats designed to keep the upper edge on the surface, the weights needed to sink the lower edge, and fragments of the net itself.

Prehistoric fish gorges from Clickimin.

The only element most likely to survive in Shetland are the weights, which are not easy to recognise unless found as a series in position. The net themselves may have been constructed out of nettle-fibre, which is unlikely to survive in the archaeological record although impressions of nets have been found on handmade pottery, but not, as far as I know, in Shetland.

The fish bones found so far on archaeological sites in Shetland have come from sea fish but I find it hard to believe that our Iron Age ancestors who built their brochs on the shores of lochs like Clickimin or Houlland did not avail themselves of the trout and sea trout found in the lochs and feeder burns. Fish gorges, unusually made out of bronze, were found during excavations at Clickimin, and may have been used to capture trout from the loch. The Neolithic settlement of Skara Brae on Orkney has yielded evidence in the form of bones that trout formed part of the inhabitants' diet and that fish vertebrae were actually used as beads of a necklace.

The Broch of Clickimin.

The arrival of the Vikings around AD 800 marked a significant change in the way of life of the Shetland islanders. Shetland now became part of Norway and the Shetlanders spoke a Scandinavian language, Norn. New methods of farming and fishing were brought by the Norse settlers from their Norwegian homeland. Fishing for coalfish became increasingly important during the Viking era and formed the staple diet of these Norwegian settlers on Shetland. Evidence for this can be found in the fish-rich middens excavated in Shetland at Sandwick on Unst and at Old Scatness. Before the Viking era there is no direct evidence for the use of boats in Shetland, although boats constructed out of seal skin are thought to have been used. Such boats would have allowed the early settlers to get to and from Shetland and to travel among the islands which make up the archipelago. Fishing, too, would have been carried out from such boats although fishing beyond the confines of the shore was a dangerous activity. The Vikings introduced better boats constructed from wood, imported from Norway in kit form, since there was very little wood in Shetland with which to build boats. Wooden boats would have given the fishermen confidence to venture further afield in search of their quarry. Long lengths of fishing line would have been difficult to manufacture in Shetland given the natural fibres available - horse hair, human hair and nettle - and the Vikings introduced better fibres such as hemp, suitable for the construction of long lines. The *høvi*, a type of fish trap placed in streams (see page 18), was probably a Viking introduction since the word itself is derived from the Old Norse.

Shetland remained part of Norway until 1468/9 when Christian I, the King of Norway and Denmark, had to mortgage Shetland and Orkney to King James III of Scotland as part of his daughter's marriage dowry. The pledge was never redeemed and Shetland became part of Scotland. Under Norse rule fishing had become increasingly important and fish became a staple part of people's diet. Some of the fish that were caught were eaten fresh, while others were cured by salting and drying and others by drying alone and it was a common sight to see lines of drying fish hanging outdoors or inside a croft above the hearth.

Shetland has increasingly been dependent on imports to sustain its population and from the mid-fifteenth century until the early part of the eighteenth century German merchants from the Hanseatic towns of Bremen, Hamburg and Lübeck came to Shetland each spring and set up trading booths all over the islands. From May to September each year they did business with the Shetlanders, exchanging goods such as fishing lines, hooks, hemp, tar, salt, flour, linen cloth, beer, shoes etc., in return for fish, principally cod and ling, that was air dried (stockfish) or part air dried and salt cured (klippfish). This trade with German merchants continued until 1712 when a tax on foreign salt imports put an end to it and proved a blow to the Shetland economy.

From the late sixteenth century the Shetland economy was boosted by the annual arrival in mid-summer of Dutch herring 'busses' (boats) which anchored in Bressay Sound. The Dutch fishermen lived on board their boats and salted the fish they caught on-board. Local women sold them knitwear in exchange for money, gin or tobacco. Although the majority of these transactions were individually on a small scale, when added together, they accounted for a large amount of money coming into the Shetland economy.

During the seventeenth and eighteenth centuries Shetland experienced difficult times, partly caused by the cooling of the climate sometimes referred to as the 'little Ice Age'. This resulted in the white fish stocks moving further off shore and failing harvests which brought about several periods of famine, accompanied by epidemics such as smallpox. White fish, principally ling and cod, were important commercially and the Shetland fishermen had to venture further afield in search of them. This led to the establishment in the early 1700s of the 'far haaf' or deep sea fishery, which operated from May till August each year. By the late eighteenth century it is estimated that fish stocks had moved thirty miles off shore and by the second half of the nineteenth century fifty miles off shore.

Fortunately, the coalfish population appears not to have been affected by the deterioration in the climate and fish stocks remained within easy reach of the shore and continued to form an important part of the Shetlanders' subsistence diet until well into the twentieth century. Various methods were devised for catching these fish from both boat and shore. Piltock (juvenile coalfish up to two years old), as well as being eaten, were frequently used to bait the long lines used by the haaf fishermen. Mackerel were also used to bait the long lines for cod and ling. Fishing from boats of between 15 and 17 feet in length, the fishermen used long rods or 'piltock wands' equipped with a fixed line and flies made of pony-tail hair or from the bleached fibres from the tail of dogfish. Another method involved the use of a hand line with a 1½lb weight on the end and hook baited with crushed limpet. The line would be lowered over the side of the boat and was quickly hauled when hitting the bottom. Sillocks (juvenile coalfish up to one year old) and piltocks could also be caught from the shore from a 'bergset'. The term 'bergset' is derived from Old Norse and refers to a fishing rock, a popular fishing spot used for generations. Fishing from a 'bergset', or 'craig-seat' in English, the fisherman would use a rod of around 11 feet in length equipped with a fixed line with flies or bait attached. If the fish were in a feeding frenzy they could often be caught on a bare hook or bent pin. A line and float was sometimes used to catch these fish. This method involved using a strong line several fathoms long with a cork float on the end. A line of around 6 feet in length with a limpet baited hook was attached to the cork. The shore end of the line was secured to a rock where the fisherman would wait until the cork indicated the bait had been taken. A final method involved the use of a 'pokk' or net, which was suspended from a long pole and lowered into the water in order to net the fish. The mouth of the net was held open by an iron ring.

The period from 1880-1920 witnessed a boom in the herring fishing industry when workers flocked to Shetland to catch and process the fish. Following the decline in herring stocks, the white fish industry developed with the introduction of better gear and navigation equipment. Sadly, due to declining fish stocks, this fishery collapsed in the 1990s. Nowadays, Shetland still has an important fishing industry and its herring boats are among the largest in Britain but its importance to the Shetland economy has been superseded by the offshore oil industry which developed during the 1970s and brought prosperity to the islands.

Although the first angling book to be written in English, *The Treatyse of Fysshynge with an Angle*, was published in 1496 and Izaak Walton's, *Compleat Angler*, in 1653, angling, as opposed to fishing, was a relative latecomer to Shetland and it wasn't until the second half of the nineteenth century that it started to develop in popularity. At the beginning of the nineteenth century most Shetlanders were too busy scraping a living to take part in any sporting or leisure activities. It was only the wealthy few, who had the time and money to buy the equipment, who could indulge in such activities. The remoteness of the islands, the difficulties of transport and the lack of suitable accommodation tended to deter visiting anglers from the British mainland and elsewhere. Transport to and within the islands was mostly by sea and it wasn't until the great potato famine in the 1840s that a road network was built to provide employment for the starving population. The coming of the railway to Aberdeen in the middle of the nineteenth century made it easier for the angler in the south to visit Shetland and it became possible for the well-to-do visiting angler to board an overnight mail train from Euston or King's Cross to Aberdeen and then to proceed by boat to Lerwick.

One of the earliest illustrations that I have come across, which seems to me to depict anglers in Shetland, is Thomas Woore's painting 'The Lakes of Tingwall' *(colour plate opposite page 56)*. Thomas Woore was born in Londonderry in 1804 and joined the navy as a midshipman in 1819, aged fifteen. He worked his way up the ranks and in 1828 he took command of the *Woodlark*, which was engaged in a hydrographic survey of Shetland.

As well as being a ship's captain, Woore was an accomplished artist and during his time on Shetland he produced a number of sketches of scenes throughout the islands. Woore retired from the navy in 1834 and emigrated to Australia where he married, bought a station and became a leading pastoralist. In addition to farming, he carried out some survey work for the railways in Australia and died in 1878.

His painting of the Tingwall Valley is interesting for a number of reasons. The small island in the foreground, connected to the shore by a causeway, is the site of Shetland's oldest parliament, the Alting. At the left-hand side of the painting, a woman is hanging out fish (probably piltock, or coalfish) on the wall of the cottage to dry in the wind. Piltock (juvenile coalfish) formed an important part of the Shetlanders' diet in the nineteenth century and scenes such as this would have been a familiar sight throughout Shetland. In the centre of the picture, which depicts the Loch of Tingwall, an angler is clearly shown fishing from the end of a promontory while two other anglers are shown fishing from a boat. Whether they are fly fishing or not, it is difficult to say, but judging from the angle of their fishing rods, it is certainly possible. It could be argued that the persons fishing are not anglers at all but subsistence fishers trying to catch their next meal. However, the fact that Tingwall is a trout loch and that there are more productive methods of taking these fish other than by rod and line convinces me that they are anglers. Beyond the Loch of Tingwall is the Loch of Asta and beyond that is the sea at Scalloway with a couple of ships lying at anchor.

Edward Charlton was one of the earliest visitors and anglers to write an account of his time on Shetland and, on one occasion in 1852, he took refuge from a storm at a cottage at Hamna Voe where his fishing tackle attracted a great deal of attention. It seems clear that the locals had never seen fishing tackle like it, which suggests that angling was not widely practised in the area at that time. During that same visit Charlton called at the house of a Mr Charles Duncan whom he describes as 'one of the few good fly-fishers in Shetland'. This too suggests that angling, and fly fishing in particular, was not widely practised at this time. Charlton also complains of the lack of hotels in Shetland and, on this occasion and during his travels, he stayed at the houses of friends and acquaintances, sometimes arriving unannounced. John Tudor, too, who visited the islands during the 1870s complains about the lack of accommodation for visiting anglers and, even worse, south of Lerwick there was no place where the visiting angler could buy alcohol and he advises the angler to take his own supplies with him.

Fortunately, this situation began to change in the last two or three decades of the nineteenth century. Increasing prosperity brought about by the Industrial Revolution in the rest of the country and by the herring boom in Shetland, meant that people now had more money and more leisure time. The growth of the road and rail network and better shipping links both to and within Shetland (the *Earl of Zetland* came into service in 1878) made it much easier for wealthy tourists and anglers to visit the islands. Throughout the country, angling as a leisure activity became increasingly popular, as witnessed by the growth of the fishing tackle industry and the establishment of hundreds of angling clubs up and down the country. The *Fishing Gazette*, one of the most popular angling magazines ever published, was established in 1870 and continued to flourish until 1966 and it wasn't long before it started carrying articles and advertisements to entice anglers to venture further afield, including Shetland.

On Shetland, too, a number of local entrepreneurs, realising the growing importance of tourism and especially angling tourism, established a number of hotels and guest houses to cater for this growing demand. The Clousta Hotel, the Spiggie Hotel, the St Magnus Hotel, the Bridge of Walls Hotel, the Queen's Hotel in Lerwick and the Queen's Hotel on Unst were all built during the last three or four decades of the nineteenth century and they were not slow at advertising their attractions to the angler contemplating a visit to Shetland. The Loch of Spiggie was, and still is, one of the most productive lochs in Shetland and proved a magnet for local and visiting anglers alike. During

The Spiggie Hotel and advert.

the late 1870s, the Henderson family built not one but two hotels adjacent to each other, the Spiggie Hotel and Henderson's Hotel, to cater for the needs of anglers and tourists. The brothers Robert and Thomas Henderson were the first proprietors. In the early days, both hotels attracted wealthy visitors from mainland UK and Europe who would travel by steamer from Leith and disembark at the Spiggie beach. The gentlemen would fish for trout on the loch or shoot seals, while the ladies would read, play music, embroider or even learn to spin and weave. Two photographs, (shown opposite) now in the collection of the Shetland Museum photographic archive, show the first tourist party, equipped with fishing rods, to stay with the Hendersons at their hotel. Both images show advocate and politician Andrew Constable, later Lord Constable, clad in kilt and rivlins (shoes made of untanned hide).

One of the unique (almost) features of angling in Shetland, which attracted anglers from all over the country and elsewhere, was the excellence of its sea trout fishing and the fact that these hard-fighting, sporting fish could be caught on fly in the salt-water voes. During the later decades of the nineteenth century

Spiggie Loch Trout Fishing, 1884

Above: The first party of tourists to stay with the Hendersons at Spiggie. Second from left is Andrew Constable (later known as Lord Constable) in kilt and rivlins. Below is another photo of the same party. The boatman on the left in the 'Island Queen' is Peter Sinclair of Royal Houll. Standing in the stern of the other boat is Andrew Constable, standing in the bows is Davie Kinman. Photographs by J. P. Isbister. Courtesy of Shetland Museum & Archives.

St Magnus Hotel and tariffs.

a number of distinguished anglers, including Sir Edward Grey, visited Shetland and left accounts of the superlative sea trout and brown trout fishing to be had in the islands and, no doubt, their enticing accounts of the fishing attracted even more anglers.

There is evidence, too, that on Shetland itself during the latter half of the nineteenth century, angling was growing in popularity. The 20th of August, 1879, saw the establishment of the Lerwick Angling Club by a group of wealthy professional and business men. The club was formed with the purpose 'of encouraging angling in Shetland, and of preserving the lochs, voes and streams throughout the islands' (for details see Chapter Three). One would think that with so much water to go at there would be no need for an angling club in Shetland to promote angling.

However, one of the problems that anglers visiting Shetland frequently complained of was the prevalence of poaching. Many of the inhabitants of Shetland, it seems, were not averse to taking trout and sea trout by traditional methods such as nets, *høvis* (fish traps), set lines or otter boards.

Although the use of otter boards was made illegal in 1861, this does not appear to have hindered their use in the more remote areas of the British Isles until comparatively recent times. Shetland was a long way from London and the prevalent attitude was that the use of such traditional equipment was not a crime. It seems to have been a culture clash of traditional subsistence versus bureaucratic curbs. Basically the otter board is a wooden board (or two joined together by pegs or dowels) with chisel-shaped ends attached to a main fishing line with 6 to 12 flies attached. The board is set in the water, usually a loch, and a weight holds it vertically in the water. As the person controlling the otter starts to walk, the board moves from the land (because of the chisel-shaped ends), dragging the line outwards towards

Otter board in the Shetland Museum.

the centre of the loch, allowing the trout to seize the flies and hook themselves. This proved to be a very effective method of taking fish. Otter boards are still used in some of the large Scandinavian lakes and I have seen them for sale in Norwegian tackle shops. The author of the *Anglers' Guide for the Shetlands*, published in 1902, states that fishing with an 'Otter' was very common in many parts of Shetland as was catching trout in nets. John Tudor, in his series of articles for *The Field* (1878), complains that the Loch of Brouster was regularly raked with a drag net at spring tides and even some of the locals expressed concern at this practice since it could drive away angling tourists. Tudor also complains of the use of otter boards and night lines

Fine catch of trout, 1936. Courtesy of Shetland Museum & Archives.

on Spiggie, and was appalled that the trout caught were used as bait for long lines to catch cod and ling. He also witnessed a 4½lb trout caught on a night line.

Gradually, however, the inhabitants of Shetland began to appreciate the value of angling tourism to the islands' economy and illegal and unsporting methods of catching fish were actively discouraged. Angling and angling tourism continued to flourish during the twentieth century and a number of famous anglers, including John Buchan and Negley Farson, visited the islands to sample the delights of its superlative sea trout fishing. However, from the latter half of the nineteenth century until the first two or three decades of the twentieth century angling in Shetland was very much the preserve of the local gentry and wealthy visitors. A number of wealthy landowners built their angling lodges on Shetland and in the early decades of the twentieth century the distinguished surgeon, Sir William Watson Cheyne, built a concrete fish ladder in the Houbie Burn on Fetlar to provide holding pools for sea trout. According to Dr Richard Shelton of the Freshwater Fisheries Laboratory in Pitlochry, the gradient of the burn itself was more than adequate to provide easy passage for sea trout without the need for an elaborate ladder and the holding pools were created for the benefit of the angler rather than the fish. During the First World War it was only the naval officers who were based in Shetland that went fishing, the ordinary ratings played team sports. Today, angling is a sport enjoyed by everyone and increased prosperity, better transport links, accommodation, and car-hire facilities mean that many more anglers can appreciate what the lochs and voes of Shetland have to offer.

Unfortunately, by the 1960s sea trout numbers began to decline as a result of a number of environmental and man-made factors and by the 1980s and 1990s numbers had declined to such an extent that in some seasons as few as ten fish were caught by anglers. The Shetland Anglers' Association, formed in 1920, was well aware of the situation and began a programme of restocking sea trout in lochs and burns. It appears that this programme is beginning to pay off and recent years have seen an increase in the number of these magnificent fish caught. The Association, through its various publications, also began to promote the wonderful brown trout fishing to be had in the islands and many of today's anglers, tired of fishing for farm-reared rainbow trout in heavily stocked waters further south, are venturing north to sample the delights of catching truly wild brown trout. Judging by the size and quality of the brown trout featured on the Association's website Shetland lochs hold great potential and, with over five hundred lochs to explore, what more could the serious trout angler desire?

CHAPTER 3

Shetland Angling Clubs

The Lerwick Angling Club

As angling became a more popular leisure activity in Britain during the second half of the nineteenth century, hundreds of angling clubs and associations were formed throughout the length and breadth of the country. Not surprisingly, as angling in Shetland began to develop, calls were being made for the formation of their own angling club, as the following notice from the *Shetland Times* of 21st of October, 1876, indicates:

MEMO. FOR LERWICK ANGLING CLUB
(When it is formed)

One of our Lerwick Anglers while fishing with fly from a boat, at Quarff, the other day, hooked two sea trout at one time, and after some difficult navigation through stones and seaweed, succeeded in landing them both. One weighed 2½ lbs, the other 2¾ lbs.

And a Lerwick Angling Club was formed - three years later on the 20th of August, 1879. The Club was set up with the avowed purpose 'of encouraging angling in Shetland, and of preserving the lochs, voes and streams throughout the islands'. The Club's founding members were: Major Cameron, Convenor of the County, Sheriff Rampini, Commander Hotham R.N., C.G. Duncan, Esq., Procurator-Fiscal, Dr Skae, J. Kirkland Galloway, Esq., Procurator-Fiscal, A. Cunningham Hay, Esq., and Andrew

Smith Esq. A committee meeting held on the 4th of September decided that there should be three classes of membership:

1. Ordinary (residing in Lerwick or vicinity).
2. Honorary.
3. Temporary.

Visiting anglers were enrolled as temporary members and were permitted to participate in the privileges of the Club during their residence in Shetland. Ordinary members were expected to pay an entrance fee of one guinea, plus an annual subscription as decided by the committee 'to defray the expense of the current year'. Honorary members were admitted free of the entrance fee and were not liable to any expense whatsoever. Temporary members were admitted without an entrance fee but were expected to pay a subscription of half-a-guinea to the funds of the Club, at the time of receiving their ticket. In addition, it seems that the committee could limit the right of fishing granted to temporary members, both as regards time and place. All classes of member were admitted by ballot and 'ordinary members shall be balloted for at meetings of the whole Club - honorary and temporary members at meetings of the committee. At all ballots two black balls shall exclude.'

Rule XIX sets out the role of the committee - 'It shall be the duty of the Committee to decide on such waters as they may think it desirable for the Club to preserve, and to take the requisite steps for acquiring the fishing therein, to appoint watchers and to fix their remuneration, to resolve upon and instruct the prosecution of trespassers, to order the putting up of Notice-boards and advertisements in the newspapers, to frame Rules and regulations for the management of the Club, to fix the amount of annual contribution payable by the members and, generally, to regulate the affairs of the Club'.

A notice in the *Shetland Times* dated the 18th of August, 1879, two days before the actual formation of the Club, shows that the founding members had already been active in acquiring fishing rights:

> **NOTICE**
>
> THE FISHINGS in the LOCH OF STRAND and LAXFIRTH VOE *having been let to the* LERWICK ANGLING CLUB, *all Persons fishing in these waters, from and after this date, without permission,*
> **WILL BE PROSECUTED.**
>
> E. HOTHAM, *Secretary and Treasurer.*
> *Lerwick, August 18, 1879.*

As well as acquiring fishing rights, the committee organised an annual fishing competition for its members, the first of which was held on the 30th of July, 1881. The *Shetland Times* of the 6th of August carried this report of that first competition:

> *LERWICK ANGLING CLUB*
>
> *This club, we understand, held the first of their annual competitions on Saturday the 30th ultimo, on the Loch of Girlsta. The weather was propitious and a fair number of members appeared. We are glad that a number of ladies were on the scene, showing thereby their appreciative interest in the inaugural competition. The lure used was artificial fly, competitors wading from sides of the loch. At 5 o'clock all assembled to partake of a tea-dinner, at Mr Murray's lodging-house, when, besides the liberal supply of good things, the events of the day were discussed. Although the members mostly fished again in the evening, the*

sport was really over by five o'clock. Notwithstanding the apparent suitableness of the day, the baskets were but light. The two Club prizes were awarded as follows: 1ˢᵗ to Dr Skae for highest basket viz. 12 fish weighing 7 ½ lbs - a book of flies; 2ⁿᵈ to Mr Cunningham Hay for heaviest fish, weighing 2 lbs. - a sportsman's steel yard.

It is noticeable that the two prize winners in this inaugural competition were two of the original founders of the Club and it would be interesting to know how many members the Club actually had in its early years since it appears to have been relatively short-lived. The Club is listed in *Manson's Almanac and Directory* from its first edition in 1892 through to 1894 but is missing from the 'Local Societies' section from 1895 onwards. It appears, therefore, that the Club ceased to exist around 1894. Looking at the Club's Rules and Regulations, it seems to me that it was just too exclusive to survive and was more like a gentleman's club than a fishing club. The original members who set up the Club were all well-to-do professional or business men and I suspect that the entry fee of one guinea plus an annual subscription may well have deterred a good many anglers in Lerwick and the surrounding area from joining. One guinea in 1879 was a considerable amount of money and equivalent to at least two or three times the annual subscription of today's Shetland Anglers' Association. Furthermore, the arcane balloting system, where a person being 'black-balled' was excluded from membership, probably deterred a number of others from putting their names forward. In addition, with so many fishable lochs in Shetland, many in remote areas, there was no need for Shetlanders to join a club to partake in their sport. As the original members of the Club died off, I suspect that it might have become increasingly difficult to recruit new members. The Shetland Anglers' Association, founded in 1920, was and still is, a much more democratic and inclusive organisation with the aim of benefitting all Shetland anglers and visiting anglers, not just a privileged few.

The Shetland Anglers' Association

The Shetland Anglers' Association, under the guidance of its dedicated secretary Alec Miller, is a thriving organisation that currently boasts over 300 members, including ladies and juniors and will shortly (in 2020) be celebrating its centenary. The Association has its own clubhouse in Burns Lane, Lerwick, which was officially opened on the 5th of December, 1977. The building work on the club was carried out by a contractor while the internal fitting was completed by volunteer members. Visiting anglers are welcome to drop in and find out the latest fishing information and the club is open on most Tuesday and Friday evenings throughout the angling season. With so much fishing available it is a good idea for the visiting angler to pay a visit and seek advice on the best places to start. The Association owns outright the fishing rights on some of the best Mainland lochs and rents or has permission to fish on most other Mainland waters. Since 1995 the Association has been pursuing a comprehensive re-stocking programme of both sea trout and brown trout, principally in waters on the Mainland and Yell, aided by grants from the Shetland Islands Council, Shetland Enterprise, Shetland Community Councils and European funds. During the last five years, as grant funding has dried up, the re-stocking programme has been entirely funded by the Association itself. All the fish that are stocked in Shetland waters have been reared in Shetland and it is hoped that the increase in numbers of fish in the lochs and burns which have been stocked will continue and that angling in Shetland will have a bright future.

The Association must surely offer the best value trout fishing in the whole of the British Isles. For the price of a day ticket on a southern reservoir both the local and visiting angler has access to around 300 lochs, set amidst stunning scenery and teeming with wildlife, for the whole season. For a small additional fee, the angler has access to the Association's seven well-maintained fibreglass boats situated on some of the more popular lochs. In addition, the Association maintains its own excellent website (www.shetlandtrout.co.uk), set up by Malachy Tallack several years ago and regularly updated by stalwarts Paul Bloomer and Mark Sandison. The website provides practical information on all aspects of fishing in Shetland, including a very useful section on recommended flies, which is a must for the angler who dresses his own flies. Permits, and a map giving details and notes on over seventy angling locations throughout Shetland, can be purchased via the website. For the angler who enjoys competitive fishing, the Association runs a programme of competitions throughout the season and an annual brown trout festival held in May with the occasional celebrity guest angler(s) in attendance.

The Association was originally founded as the Zetland Angling Club (its name was changed to the Shetland Anglers' Association in 1953) and its inaugural meeting was held on the 22nd of September, 1920. At the meeting D. G. K. Hunter was elected President with Laidlaw MacDougal and J. T. T. Sinclair being elected Joint Vice Presidents. John R Browne was elected to the dual role of Secretary and Treasurer. A week after the initial meeting, another meeting was held to formulate the rules and regulations of the club. The main object of the Association was:

> *To promote the interests of trout angling as a sport in fresh and salt water in Shetland. To take all steps necessary or advisable to protect the interests of its members and to conserve the sport of angling in all waters in Shetland.*

It was decided that there should be three classes of membership:

1. Honorary.

2. Life.

3. Ordinary.

The following were elected Life Members: Jas A. Jamieson, Renfrewshire, and G. Leslie & Son.

The membership fee was agreed and size limits for the taking of fish were set - 7 inches for brown trout and 8 inches for sea trout. Furthermore, a list of potential patrons was drawn up and the secretary was tasked with writing to these landowners to procure their consent:

> Proposed patrons: Sir Robert Hamilton, J. Cathcart Watson, N. O. M. Cameron, Watson Cheyne, J. W. Robertson, Sir A. J. Nicolson, H. F. Anderton, Col E. H. Foster, Lord Ronaldshay, Thos Johnston.

From its very beginning the Association organised angling competitions for its members and the first one was held on the Loch of Tingwall on the 30th of May, 1921. Since that date, the competition scene has grown and now includes a Bank League, held on a number of lochs throughout the season, other bank fishing

> THE
> SHETLAND
> ANGLERS'
> ASSOCIATION
>
> ★
>
> CONSTITUTION

competitions for various trophies, a boat fishing competition and a pairs' competition. Inter-island competitions are held against Whalsay and an annual inter-county boat fishing competition, involving teams of six, against Orkney was instituted in 1951, with the competition being fished in Orkney or Shetland in alternate years. A trophy is awarded to the winning team and two trophies are awarded for the heaviest basket of fish caught over the two days of the competition. In 1998, an annual inter-club competition against Dounreay Angling Club was inaugurated, with the competition being held in Caithness or Shetland in alternate years. This is a bank fishing competition for teams of six anglers and is fished over two days with trophies for the winning team, the heaviest individual basket over two days' fishing and the heaviest fish over two days. Such has been the success of the competition scene on Shetland that over the years it has produced a number of anglers who have represented Scotland in international competitions.

Throughout its history the Association has carried out an active policy of improving the quality of fishing on Shetland and part of this work has involved stocking. Over the years many thousands of trout, salmon and sea trout fry have been stocked in Shetland waters and in recent years, as we have seen, much effort has gone into improving sea trout stocks following the decline of these sporting fish. As early as January 1925 the Association's minute book records an order for 2,000 salmon and 4,000 Loch Leven ova, together with a hatching trough complete with grill, from Mr McNicol of Ardgay. A month later the secretary reported that the ova had arrived in good condition and had been laid down in hatching boxes. Unfortunately, no mention was made of the location of the hatchery. However the ova appear to have hatched successfully and in November 1925 the committee agreed to close fishing on the Loch of Strand from the 15th of May to the 1st of August, 1926, to protect the juvenile salmon that had been stocked into it.

During the winter of 1928/9 it appears that the Association enquired about the possibility of using a hatching house at Girlsta but it seems to have been in a poor state of repair and there is no further mention of it in the minutes.

A report in the *Aberdeen Journal* of the 27th of November, 1936 records the stocking of 10,000 young trout in 'the historic Loch of Tingwall, near Lerwick'. The following year the Association purchased 10,000 ova from Messrs McNicol of Ardgay, Sutherlandshire, which were hatched out at Burnside, Lerwick by members of the Association. This attempt appears not to have been successful and in 1938 the minute book records a proposal to purchase yearling fish to stock the Bressay lochs.

Not surprisingly, during the Second World War and its immediate aftermath, little mention was made of stocking or hatcheries. However, on Saturday the 25th of December, 1948, the *Aberdeen Journal* carried the following dramatic headline:

Mass Killings of Shetland Trout Alleged
Nets and Explosives Used in Raids, Council Told.

Allegations have been made that bag nets, cod nets, seine nets, drag nets, and even gelignite and acetylene gas, have been used in the illegal capture of sea and brown trout in Shetland voes, lochs and burns. Making these claims to Shetland County Council, Major R. Winton and Mr Charles E. Mitchell asked that Shetland should be included in the scope of the commission appointed to inquire into salmon and sea trout poaching in Scottish waters.

Their plea was made, they said, in view of the great slaughter of fish.

After inquiring where these explosives and detonators came from, Mr Mitchell said a large number of sea trout had recently been exported and that on one occasion a box marked lobsters burst on the wharf at Aberdeen. Its contents were found to be sea trout.

The report went on to state that the wholesale slaughter of sea trout could seriously affect Shetland as a resort for anglers. In view of this and other more recent incidents, the Shetland Anglers' Association has had a continual battle on its hands to eradicate poaching and to educate a certain element of the population to act more responsibly. Such incidents also highlight the need for continuous stocking to replenish depleted fish stocks brought about by illegal netting. In November 1949 the Association established its own hatchery in a building owned by the Town Council at Staney Hill water plant. The hatchery was operated by volunteers from the Association who operated on a rota system. Unfortunately, things did not always go to plan and in 1951 no fish were produced due to rats eating the ova. Despite the setbacks, almost a quarter of a million fry were released during the period from 1950 to 1955. It is interesting to note that, unlike a number of clubs elsewhere which stock with grown-on fish, the Association's policy has always been to stock with fry which can grow on naturally in the waters into which they are introduced.

During the 1960s, as rainbow trout fisheries became more popular further south, the Association decided to stock the Loch of Benston and Whitelaw Loch with rainbow trout, which came from the Howietoun Hatchery in Stirling. Although these fish did grow on, concerns were expressed as to whether stocking with rainbow trout was value for money and about the possibility of introducing disease to the Shetland environment. As a result of these concerns rainbow stocking faded out, a wise decision in view of the excellent wild brown trout fishing to be had in Shetland. In more recent years the Association acquired the lease of a hatchery building at Kergord in Weisdale, which served the Association well until its lease was terminated in 2013. Not to be deterred, the Association continued its

Stocking undertaken by the Shetland Anglers' Association.

programme of stocking, especially with sea trout fry, and as recently as March 2016 the Association planted out around 100,000 sea trout fry in the burns and lochs under its control. However, following recent changes in government legislation with regard to stocking, the Association made the decision in April 2016 to cease its stocking programme. What effect this will have on fish stocks and fishing in the future, only time will tell.

On a more positive note, in May 1992, the Association held its first ever annual Trout Festival, sponsored by Glenmorangie and Highlands and Islands Enterprise, and anglers from all over the country were invited to participate. The festival, which ran from the 23rd to the 29th of May was a resounding success and was officially opened by Chris Dawn, the editor of *Trout Fisherman* magazine. The following day Chris demonstrated his considerable angling ability by taking a 5lb 13oz brown trout from the Loch of Clingswater. During the week-long festival a number of angling competitions took place, together with talks

Glenmorangie Shetland Brown Trout Festival 23rd–29th May 1992

Participate in Scotlands friendliest fishing competition.

365 loch to fish, 3 fishing competitions, 3 trophies to be won, also prizes for heaviest fish in competition, whisky tasting, celebrity launch, Prizegiving ceremony and social evening in anglers clubrooms.

Free competition entry.

Bank or boat fishing.

Programme of events available.

Inclusive trout fishing holidays organised by Viking Holidays include:

- Travel by British Airways
- Self-drive car
- Bed & Breakfast in qualit...
- Packed lunch and full eve...
- Local fishing companion
- Guide to Shetlands 100 l...
- Angling Permit
- 6 recommended hand-ti...
- Cancellation and delay i...

Sponsored by: Glenmorar... and Highl...

Organised by: Shetland A... Shetland I... Viking Isl...

Entry Form Overleaf.

The Glenmorangie Shetland Brown Trout Festival, 1992.

and fly-dressing and casting demonstrations from leading anglers such as Bruce Sandison. The festival culminated with a dinner and prize-winning ceremony at the Association's club rooms in Burns Lane. The name of Brian Watt seemed to feature quite prominently in the list of prize winners. Glenmorangie generously sponsored the festival for the first six years of its existence. Nowadays, the festival is slightly shorter and is held over a period of four days and with a variety of different sponsors. In 2015, the event got under way with a fly tying demonstration by Barry Orde Clarke, followed by three evening competitions and an all-day competition with prizes for various categories.

All associations, be they angling clubs or other, rely very heavily on the support of their members and the dedication and enthusiasm of a number of individuals who are prepared to give up their time and energy to serve on committees and to organise events. Fortunately, the Shetland Anglers' Association is a thriving club with some very talented anglers among its members and a very dedicated team at the helm, ably led by long-serving secretary, Alec Miller. The Association will shortly be celebrating its centenary year and let us hope that it will still be flourishing in another hundred years' time.

Unst Angling Club

In addition to the Shetland Anglers' Association, the more northerly isles of Unst and Whalsay are served by their own angling clubs. The Unst Angling Club was originally formed as a sea-angling club in the 1960s but it has since widened its remit to embrace angling for brown and sea trout, which became increasingly popular during the 1980s when local anglers were joined by angling enthusiasts from the RAF base at Saxa Vord. During the 1980s and early 1990s, as sea trout numbers began to decline partly as a result of the massive expansion of fish farming throughout the West Highlands and Island areas, members of the Unst Angling Club decided to do something about it. The Club realised that the future of its fishing was in its own hands and its members embarked on a programme of cleaning up the burns and streams through which sea trout travel to their natal spawning grounds. The Club also developed its own hatchery and began re-stocking with sea trout fry raised from brood-stock taken from their native streams. The result of this stocking programme has been an increase in sea trout numbers of over 25% and more sea trout have been seen around the island for more than two decades. The Club also operates a catch and release policy and every sea trout caught is returned to fight another day. Like their mainland cousins, the Club organises an annual 'simmer dim' fishing festival held in June each year.

Anglers visiting Unst are requested to join, for a small fee, the Unst Angling Club and it produces a brochure giving details of fishing on the island and advice on suitable tackle and flies.

Whalsay Anglers' Association

Like Unst, Whalsay is a relatively small island with a population of around one thousand. The main settlement on the island is Symbister where its fishing fleet, which is the main form of employment on the island, is based. The Whalsay Anglers' Association was formed on the 25th of April, 1955. That same evening, Mr L. Pearson, the secretary, wrote to the Shetland Anglers' Association requesting a supply of brown and sea trout fry to help replenish fish stocks on the island. On the 3rd of May, the secretary of the SAA replied and offered 5,000 sea trout fry gratis and wished the newly-formed association every success. From its humble beginnings, the Association has continued to thrive and has worked hard to improve fishing on the island. In 1974 the Association purchased the fishing rights to the lochs, burns and spawning redds on the island for the sum of £100, thus ensuring sport for future generations of anglers on the island. Nowadays, the Association counts a number of very talented anglers and fly dressers among its members and the Shetland record fly-caught brown trout, which weighed 9lb 4oz, was caught on the Loch of Huxter by Dodie Irvine on a Black Zulu on the 8th of April, 1981. The Association continues to flourish and income from its modest membership fees go towards improving the fishing on the island.

Dodie Irvine's record fly-caught brown trout.

CHAPTER 4

Angling Guide Books

Even though I own a Kindle and an iPad and can download books electronically, I much prefer to read from a physical book printed on paper. However, I have to admit that electronic books do have their place in the greater scheme of things. When I go on holiday I like to download a number of novels, books I would otherwise dispose of once read, on to my Kindle without their bulk and weight filling my suitcase. I also have to admit that electronic devices are making certain kinds of book virtually obsolete and these include the regional angling guides, which were once so prolific. Ownership of waters, contact details and prices of day tickets are constantly changing and, as a result, these angling guides are soon outdated. Nowadays, it is much easier for angling associations and owners of fisheries to create a website for this information and to update it regularly. One of the best websites I have come across, which contains a vast amount of information for the visiting angler, is that of the Shetland Anglers' Association (www.shetlandtrout.co.uk). The site was initially set up by Malachy Tallack, author of *60 Degrees North (2015)*, several years ago. More recently, Paul Bloomer and Mark Sandison have done a great deal of work on it to keep it up to date.

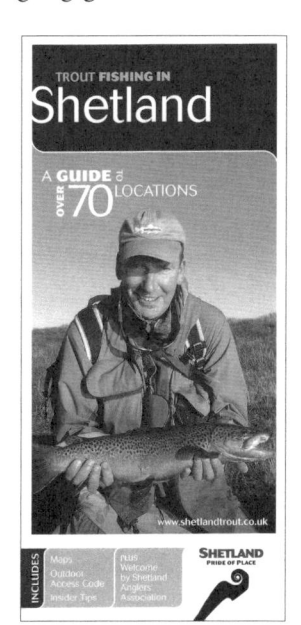

The website contains a preliminary section on the Shetland archipelago and its climate, as well as contact details for airline and ferry services to and from the islands. Links are also available to accommodation websites and local tackle shops where the visiting angler can buy permits and tackle, although it is even possible to buy a permit online, as well as a very hand map and guide to over seventy angling locations throughout Shetland, published by Promote Shetland. Details of the most popular lochs together with hints at the most productive areas on those lochs make the website extremely valuable for the visiting angler. During the late nineteenth century and up to the 1960s Shetland was noted for the excellence of its sea trout fishing, especially in its saltwater voes, but, due to a combination of factors (see Chapter One) the sea trout fishing declined and the main focus of the angler's attention turned to brown trout. Now, however, thanks to the efforts of the Shetland Anglers' Association, the sea trout are making something of a comeback and the website gives excellent advice on some of the best sea trout locations, together with the flies needed to catch them. With regard to flies for brown trout on the numerous lochs, the website has a section entitled *Cast of the Month*, in which local anglers recommend flies and provide details of dressings for a particular month. On the occasions when I have visited Shetland I have found this section particularly useful and, before venturing up there, I dressed a number of the patterns recommended, some of which I have also found useful on my local waters. A number of Shetland anglers, including Colin Wiseman, David Pottinger and others noted for their catches of big trout, have contributed some of their favourite fly patterns to the website. Details of the annual brown trout festival, angling competitions, trout food and imitations, and the availability of boats are also included on the website, which is updated regularly.

The modern angler wanting to fish on Shetland is certainly well catered for by way of information, although this was not always the case. As angling in Shetland grew in popularity during the latter half of the nineteenth century there was an increasing demand from angling tourists for some sort of brochure or angling guide to the islands. Seeing an opportunity for increased business, this demand for information was met by the recently built St Magnus Hotel at Hillswick, which in 1901 published *An Angler's Guide*, written by C.J.H. Cassels. The author himself penned a number of books of Shetland interest including: *In the Island of Unst*, *The Sports of Spiggie* and *Whales and Whale Hunting in Shetland*.

The guide, which cost sixpence, consisted of eight pages of text plus adverts and, unsurprisingly, focuses on the fishing in the Northmavine area. In the introductory section, the author states that due to the lack of decent accommodation in the area for visiting anglers (the St Magnus Hotel was only built in 1900) the lochs have been almost totally neglected and he states that:

> There is nothing so much to the detriment of the glorious sport of trout angling as overfishing; and of the lochs in the neighbourhood of the commodious, comfortable, and up-to-date Hotel, recently erected at Hillswick, it most assuredly cannot be said that -
>
> > 'The Cockney angler up-to-date
> > To loch and river hies,
> > Till northern trout begin to hate
> > The sight of London flies.'

The author goes on to say that many of the Northmavine lochs have never seen an angler apart from himself and he claims to have fished all the unpreserved lochs in the area, some of which yielded excellent sport with both brown and sea trout. According to the guide there are about one hundred lochs in the parish of Northmavine and all those north of the Roer Water Burn, in the neighbourhood of North Roe, are preserved and can only be fished by permission of the proprietor. In addition, many of the preserved lochs are inaccessible. Anglers visiting the St Magnus Hotel had access to over twenty unpreserved lochs and an angler staying for three weeks could fish a different loch every day, if he so wished. The guide also states that none of the lochs in the Eshaness district contain any trout. This is no longer the case as a number of lochs in this area have been stocked by the Shetland Anglers' Association.

The guide then describes the various lochs in the area commencing with those nearest to the hotel. Urafirth Loch and Urafirth Vadals, the area lying immediately below, are recommended for sea trout with fish ranging from 1 up to 8lb in weight. Queyfirth Loch in the Ollaberry district is described as one of the best places in Shetland for sea trout but is difficult and dangerous to wade and a boat is recommended. Eela Water is particularly singled out for the quality and quantity of its brown trout and 15 to 20lb may be taken on a good day. Punds Water, a popular venue today, is described as a beautiful sheet of water, which produces plentiful pink-fleshed trout, averaging two or three to the pound.

With regard to flies for brown trout, the author of the guide recommends the Zulu, the Butcher and flies with a teal wing. For sea trout he recommends standard sea trout patterns although he does say that the worm and Phantom Minnow can be deadly in both salt and fresh water.

A year after this handy little guide appeared on the market a much more detailed guide, *Anglers' Guide for the Shetlands*, was published in 1902 by John Tait & Co. of Lerwick. This guide was much more extensive and contained sections on the principal angling centres, hotels and accommodation, the close seasons, the most suitable tackle, recommended baits and flies, sea trout fishing in fresh and salt water, loch fishing, burn fishing and sea fishing. The guide consisted of 59 pages plus adverts and gives a fascinating glimpse into the state of angling in Shetland at the beginning of the twentieth century. Like the St Magnus Hotel guide, it appears that the publisher had an ulterior motive in producing this guide since John Tait & Co. had a number of retail premises at 59, 61, and 63 Commercial Street, Lerwick, which sold a range of goods ranging from groceries, alcohol and tobacco to all manner of fishing tackle and gentlemen's clothing. They took full advantage of advertising their wares in the guide.

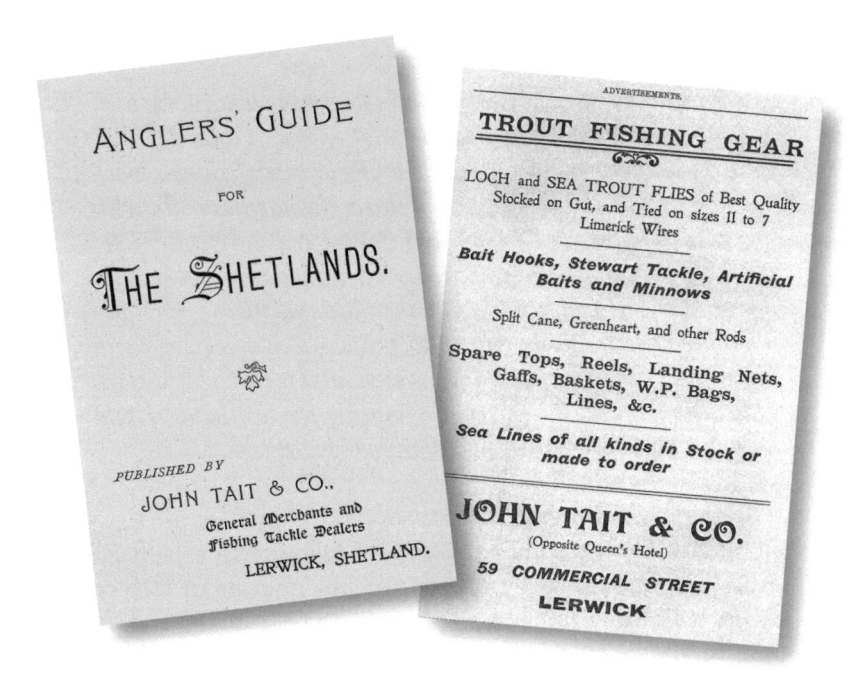

It is clear from the Introduction that, at the beginning of the twentieth century, Shetland was becoming a more popular destination for anglers and field sportsmen:

The Shetlands are annually becoming more popular as a holiday resort, and their undoubted attractions and genuine sport with rod and gun are deservedly drawing to their shores an ever increasing number of anglers and sportsmen. It is in the hope that it will prove of some use to anglers that JOHN TAIT & Co. have conceived the idea of publishing this small handbook . . . JOHN TAIT & Co. would direct the attention of anglers to their premises in Lerwick and Baltasound, where they have stocked the largest and varied assortment of tackle and gear for fresh and salt water fishing in the Shetland Isles. Their stock has been selected with considerable care, and is to a great extent specially made to suit Shetland waters, and their tackle is of the best quality and make. Anglers visiting the Shetlands should buy on the spot in order to ensure good sport.

The guide contains a detailed section on suitable tackle for use in Shetland and recommends the following rods: a 16 ft light grilse rod for heavy sea trout, a 14 ft sea trouting or loch rod, an 11 ft trouting rod and a light trolling or spinning rod. The rods should be made of greenheart fitted with phosphor bronze rings to prevent rusting. With regard to reels, simple revolving plate reels are recommended rather than models with a crank handle, which can cause loose line to coil around it and jam. The reels should be matched with the correct size of American silk line. Lists of flies for sea trout, loch flies and burn flies are included, as well as a whole host of natural and artificial baits, all of which no doubt could be obtained from John Tait & Co. The guide also recommends the use of natural flies for dapping, a method commonly employed on large Irish loughs. For this method of fishing, the guide recommends the use of a light, long rod equipped with a very light blow-line terminating in a cast of fine tapered gut:

A small hook is fixed to this, and on it is impaled a live insect. If a light breeze is blowing, so much the better. The angler stands up in the boat with his rod well up in the air, and allows the breeze to carry out the light line. The insect should alight on the water first, and it begins to struggle and flounder till it is seized by a fish.

Part Two of the guide concentrates on fishing for sea trout in fresh water and contains a great deal of useful information, some of which is still relevant to today's angler, although the actual tackle employed nowadays is vastly different from that of a century ago, especially in its materials. The guide goes into some detail on the use of natural baits for sea trout such as worm, prawn and sand eel. These methods are now generally discouraged in favour of fly fishing. With regard to flies for sea trout, the guide does give some useful advice:

> Flies with silvery bodies seem to do best, and, of course, those containing red. Combinations of yellow and black, with gold tinsel, do very well also, and flies with a claret hackle or body are equally good... Have at least one silvery bodied fly on the cast, and vary the flies as much as possible. When making up a cast of flies, always mix the colours of the flies, and do not have flies similar in colour side by side and then a contrast next. The sea trout taking to the fly in burns are generally got in the streamy part at the head of the pool, but, when in a taking mood, they will be got in the still water as well. Keep your flies moving when fishing for sea trout... Many of the lochs have a little shelving beach at the north end. Perhaps the prevailing winds have a little to do with this formation, and sea trout generally frequent this part of the loch... Sea trout take well in fresh water during rough and stormy weather, and even on the most boisterous days good baskets can be made... on a warm sunny day they feed most readily in the morning and evening, and although an odd fish or two will be got during the heat of the day, one will not make much of a basket unless at sea.

The angler fishing for sea trout in Shetland today would do well to take heed of the advice proffered in the above paragraph. The third part of the guide is devoted to fishing for sea trout in tidal or salt water, a type of fishing rarely encountered elsewhere and one that attracted many visiting anglers:

Sea trout are not very often caught in the sea in Scotland and England, but it is a matter of almost every-day occurrence in Shetland . . . Little inlets on the coast, long voes or openings after the nature of Norwegian Fjords, and places where burns enter the sea are all good places to find these fish. The tidal lochs, which are often known as 'Houlis' in Shetland, are splendid fishing grounds as a rule, and, if there is no serious obstruction at the mouth of such places, they can generally be fished at all times . . . In the sea and tidals these fish have a voracious appetite which nothing seems to affect, save a change of weather or coming storm. They seldom take well in foggy weather.

The author regards fly fishing as the most sporting method of catching these fish and recommends large flies with tinsel bodies as best in the sea. A fly known as the Terror, a three-hooked fly, dressed in imitation of a sand eel, is particularly effective. John Buchan had great sport with one of these flies on Unst in 1926. The guide advises the angler to impart some motion to the line so as to cause the fly to move through the water in a series of jerks. Again, plenty of advice is given in this section on fishing the worm and other natural baits, especially the sand-eel. As far as artificial baits are concerned, Devon and Phantom Minnows are recommended, the Phantom being best employed in weedy areas as it does not sink as deeply as a metal Devon.

The Terror

Part Four of the guide is concerned with loch fishing for trout. As the author of the guide points out, Shetland is not short of lochs and, at the time of publication (1902), many were unexplored by anglers and certainly not over-fished. However, a number of lochs had been exploited by local fishermen using nets and otter boards, the use of which had been outlawed by an Act of Parliament in 1861. The author also describes a rather ingenious method of taking trout employed by boys and young men:

The Lakes of Tingwall, painted by Thomas Woore. The small island in the foreground, connected to the shore by a causeway, is the site of Shetland's oldest parliament, the Alting. Reproduced by kind permission of Tim and Derek Heath.

*Part of a 1654 map of Orkney and Shetland
by Dutch cartographer Joan Blaeu.*

The author fishing the Loch of Voe.

Casting a fly on Tingwall loch.

The Broch of Mousa.

A beautifully marked 4lb brown trout caught by Mark Sandison.

A Sumburgh Head puffin.

Boys, and young men too, catch trout in the following manner on some of the lochs. A small toy boat is procured, and a length of line with a hook baited with worm is fixed firmly to it. The boat is set adrift across the loch with baited hook trailing after it in the water. A trout or sea trout is likely to seize it before it goes too far, and the fish endeavours to escape, but is tired out by means of the little boat. When the fish is exhausted by its struggles the wind fills the sails of the boat, and it eventually drifts ashore towing the fish behind it. This practice, it is thought, would come under the heading of set lines, and such means of taking fish, of course, are illegal.

For fly fishing the author of the guide recommends a cast equipped with the following flies: a Coch-y-Bonddu on the point, an Orange Partridge on the middle and lastly a Mallard and Claret or Grouse and Claret on the top dropper. He claims that such a cast is useful throughout the season. Other recommended casts may be fitted with a Butcher, Soldier or Red Palmer and a Green Mantle or March Brown, Silver Sedge and a Zulu. Again, the angler of today would probably not go far wrong with such casts and I have taken a number of Shetland trout on a Zulu on the top dropper.

The final part of the guide I wish to consider is that concerning burn fishing. One of the advantages of burn fishing in Shetland, as opposed to elsewhere in the country, is that there are no trees or bushes to get in the way when casting. Most of the burns, too, contain yellow (brown) trout and sea trout. Sea trout generally ascend the burns from July onwards although a number can be taken in April and May. The biggest sea trout tend to occur in September and October. The author states that the worm is the deadliest lure for these burns and recommends that it be fished on the multi-hooked Stewart tackle. On one occasion the author claims to have caught two small brown trout on the one Stewart tackle and reckons that the trout are so numerous that:

When one comes in from a day's trouting he will be a very poor hand at the game if he does not number his catch by the dozen, and that, too, after returning the smallest of the fish.

For fly-fishing on the larger burns the guide recommends the use of small flies and fine gut. Generally, two flies are better than three and less likely to scare the fish. The following list of flies is recommended: March Brown, Hare Lug, Saltoun, Professor, Priest, Red Spider, The Beetle, Coch-y-Bonddu, Blue Dun and Wickham's Fancy. A Soldier Palmer or small Claret Skipjack Beetle is recommended for sea trout. One final word or two of advice is given:

Keep as far back from the pool to be fished as possible, and thus be so far out of sight from the trout. Remember that the angler who succeeds in placing his lure before the fish without being seen by them is the one who will have the most in his basket at the end of the day.

Such sound advice is well heeded by today's angler. These two angling guides, published in 1901 and 1902 respectively, are now extremely rare but copies can be consulted in the Shetland Library and Shetland Archives. They provide a fascinating glimpse into angling in Shetland over a century ago and are well worth seeking out.

Two World Wars and two decades passed before the next important angling guide to Shetland was published - *Game Fishing - Guide to the Shetlands*. This 44-page booklet, written by James Coutts of Torlundy, Inverness-shire, was published in 1967 by the Highlands and Islands Development Board with the aim of promoting tourism in Shetland. The same author penned similar guides to fishing on Orkney and Inverness-shire.

The first part of the booklet contains general information on the Shetland Islands, the angler's quarry, and the type of tackle required. The equipment recommended is a fly rod of between 9 ½ and 11 ft long. By 1967, most fishing rods were manufactured from built cane although fibreglass rods were gradually coming on to the market. For spinning, a rod of not less than 9 ft was recommended. Concerning flies, Coutts suggests that the angler should equip himself with typical loch flies used throughout Scotland in sizes 8 to 12: Greenwell's Glory, Peter Ross, March Brown, Black Pennell, Soldier Palmer etc. He claims that his most successful fly for brown trout in Shetland is the Cinnamon and Gold. For peaty waters he advises a Woodcock and Yellow and a Dark Mackerel. For sea trout he suggests that traditional sea trout patterns will suffice: Teal, Blue and Silver, Invicta, Blue Zulu, Peter Ross, Grouse and Claret etc. His most successful sea-trout cast consists of a size 8 Dark Mackerel on the top dropper, a size 10 Cinnamon and Gold on the middle dropper and a size 10 Coachman on the point. For spinning he recommends Mepps, Vibro or Toby lures, although he claims that the majority of Shetland anglers use a strip of mackerel belly. Apparently, the mackerel belly was fished in two ways, the most common method being to attach a strip to the hooks of the treble hook on any spoon or lure. A second method involved mounting a strip of mackerel belly on the three hooks of a Stewart tackle, with a small lead shot attached to the line to provide added weight.

The rest of the booklet is given over to the lochs on the Mainland, Yell, Unst and Fetlar, with brief notes on access, fishing methods, and size of fish likely to be encountered. A number of maps, printed in yellow, show some of the main lochs mentioned in the text and black and white photographs of fishing spots and the angler's catch complement the booklet.

The author claims to have spent many hours fishing in Shetland and was captivated by its charm:

On these wonderful islands there is a peaceful freedom which does not exist in any other part of Western Europe today.

And who can disagree with that sentiment?

In 1982, the Shetland Anglers' Association produced its own guide to angling in Shetland - *A Guide to Shetland Trout Angling*. By the time of this publication, sea trout numbers in Shetland were in serious decline and, not surprisingly, this guide focuses on the splendid loch fishing for brown trout to be had on the islands. However, it does contain a list of sea trout locations on the last page. By the 1980s, Health and Safety issues were coming more to the fore and the guide contains a useful safety guide on the inside front cover warning of the dangers of wading and fishing in remote areas, particularly in the higher hill areas at the back of Ronas Hill. It advises anglers fishing these areas to carry a map and compass and to wear warm clothing, as well as informing someone of where they are going and expected time back. A general section advises visiting anglers of the species likely to be encountered, where to buy permits, together with notes on driving, accommodation and the climate.

Concerning flies, the guide suggests no more than two per cast to reduce the risk of snagging. The flies recommended are standard loch patterns in use throughout Scotland and elsewhere and it suggests carrying these in a range of sizes from 8 down to 14. It also advises on suitable tackle for spinning, and Mepps and Toby lures, often accompanied by a small strip of mackerel skin on the treble, are the favoured types.

The bulk of this booklet is concerned with the more popular lochs and around one hundred lochs are covered on the Mainland, Whalsay, Yell, Unst and Fetlar. Each loch is accompanied by a small map showing the favoured fishing areas, together with a brief description of the size of fish likely to be encountered, notes on access and hints on fishing methods. The centre-fold of the booklet contains a map showing the location of the lochs listed.

In 1998, the Shetland Anglers' Association published a very comprehensive 76-page guide, entitled *Trout Fishing in Shetland*. The booklet, printed in full colour, sold extremely well and has now become something of a collector's item. As its title implies, the booklet mainly focuses on the superlative brown trout fishing to be found in its myriad of lochs. In addition to the information in the previous guide of 1982, this updated guide gives more detailed advice on suitable tackle for Shetland, recommending a carbon fly rod of around 10 feet in length rated for a line of AFTM 6-8. A section on float tubing is a new addition and reflects the growing popularity of this style of fishing. Apparently, a few diehard Shetland anglers have used their float tubes in winds of up to 40 knots, although this is not generally recommended! Another very useful addition to the guide is a section on the trout's environment, which examines the different types of loch and their characteristics. However, one of the most useful sections, especially for the visiting angler, is the section entitled *The Trout's Menu*, which looks at the typical flies and insects in the diet of Shetland trout and recommends suitable imitations, complete with dressings. Full colour images of many of the recommended flies are a great help to the angler who dresses his own flies. About three-quarters of the guide is devoted to the most popular lochs in Shetland together with maps showing their location, fishing hot spots, advice on flies, wading, access and the size of trout likely to be encountered. Most of the information contained in the guide is still just as relevant today and it is well worth the trouble of searching out a copy of the guide on the second-hand book market.

Unst is the most northerly inhabited island in the British Isles and even though it only has a population of around 600, it is home to the Unst Angling Club. The Club was originally founded as a sea-angling club in the 1960s but, following the decline of sea trout numbers in the 1980s and 1990s, the Club decided to try to halt the decline by establishing a hatchery and restocking with native fish, reared in their natal streams. As a result of this programme catches of sea trout have improved by around 25%. As well as sea trout, Unst is also home to some excellent brown trout fishing and to aid visiting anglers the Club publishes a pamphlet - *Trout Fishing on Unst*, the proceeds from the sale of which goes towards the restocking programme. This 8-page pamphlet contains maps of the principal lochs on the island and gives advice on hot spots, wading and recommended flies. Anglers visiting the island are encouraged to join the club for a small fee, which allows the visitor to fish for the whole season.

In addition to the above guide books specifically focusing on angling in Shetland, a number of general guides on angling in Scotland feature sections on Shetland. One of the most useful is Bruce Sandison's *Trout Lochs of Scotland*, first published in 1983 and running to several editions. My copy of this handy guide is the revised and updated third edition of 1994. It is my constant companion when fishing different areas of Scotland. This guide has recently been updated to include rivers as well as lochs, and the most recent edition is entitled *Rivers and Lochs of Scotland: The Angler's Complete Guide*.

Another very useful guide is Roderick Wilkinson's *Fishing the Scottish Islands*, published in 1994. The section on angling in Shetland is extremely interesting and unusual since it takes the form of a letter. According to Wilkinson, a friend of his (named Andrew) from his younger days wrote to him asking for advice about taking a holiday on Shetland with his wife and two children. He also enquired about the possibility of some fishing whilst there. In his reply Wilkinson suggests that his friend stays in Lerwick and visits the headquarters of the Shetland Anglers' Association whilst there. He recommends a number of lochs within reasonable driving distance from Lerwick. These include: Spiggie, Loch of Clumlie, Loch of Vatsetter, Loch of Brindister, Sandy Loch and the Loch of Trebister. He also gives advice on fishing various voes for sea trout in the vicinity of Lerwick. Whether this friend was real or imagined I do not know but the letter certainly makes for interesting reading and contains a great deal of sound advice for the visiting angler.

Although the angling guides discussed above are interesting from a historical perspective, I am not sure we shall see their likes again. As I said at the beginning of this chapter, the internet is now making this type of book redundant and guide books by their very nature are nearly always dated by the time they are published. It is much easier and cheaper for angling associations to keep visitors informed via the internet than to publish a new booklet every few years. However, as an avid book collector I am a little saddened by this march of progress.

CHAPTER 5

Edward Charlton - Angler & Traveller

One of the earliest anglers to visit Shetland who has left an account of their angling exploits was Edward Charlton who sailed to these islands in 1832 on board the schooner *Magnus Troil*. Charlton was born on the 23rd of July, 1814, at Hesleyside in Northumberland. During his formative years Charlton was taught by his mother who was well versed in ancient and modern languages. He was also taught drawing by the eminent artist John Sell Cotman and he put these skills to good use in illustrating his travel journals. At the age of ten he was sent to Ushaw College near Durham where he was a diligent student but not particularly good at organised games.

In the autumn of 1831 he proceeded to Edinburgh University to study medicine and the following summer (1832) he visited Shetland for the first time.

Fortunately, Charlton kept journals of most of his travels, which he initially wrote in shorthand before writing them up in manuscript books, illustrated by his own drawings and watercolours. Unfortunately, neither the shorthand notes nor the illustrations for his visits to Shetland in 1832 and 1834 survive.

On the 7th of July, 1832 Charlton embarked on board the schooner *Magnus Troil* at Leith bound for Lerwick. He had been too late in applying for a berth but accepted the offer of his friend Mr John Henderson of Gloup on Yell, to share his narrow couch. Once they were on the open sea, however, Mr Henderson was stricken with sea-sickness and Charlton decided to keep his distance! Instead, he rigged up a make-shift bed out of various coats and coverings and slept on the end locker of the cabin. On the 11th of July, as they were nearing Sumburgh Head, two yawls full of Shetland fishermen pulled astern of the ship. Charlton's first impression of these islanders was not particularly favourable:

> *Dressed in their skin coats and breeches, with their nether limbs encased in huge boots, they rather resembled the pictures we have seen of some of the Esquimaux tribes, though having since had an opportunity of comparing these strange garments, I must confess those of Shetland to be decidedly inferior in point of manufacture.*

Later that day they entered Bressay Sound, which he described as 'the best harbour in the British dominions'.

Before the passengers could disembark in Lerwick the ship had to undergo a period in quarantine as the inhabitants of that town were terrified of an outbreak of cholera. Sadly, one of the *Magnus Troil's* passengers, a Mr Alexander Robertson, was taken ill during the voyage and Charlton, being the nearest thing to a doctor on board, was called upon to minister to him. Unfortunately, the poor man passed away and the ship was forced to spend a further ten days in quarantine by the Lerwick authorities who believed him to have been suffering from cholera. During this time a fearful storm arose in which eighteen boats were lost and over one hundred Shetland fishermen lost their lives. Eventually, after the expiry of their period of quarantine, Charlton and his fellow passengers were allowed ashore. After exploring Lerwick and its environs, Charlton boarded a boat and sailed for Cullivoe on Yell. Charlton was no mean naturalist and during his travels he made detailed observations of the bird life and acquired a number of geological specimens. As they approached Cullivoe he noted a pair of rain geese or red-throated divers and a little later saw his first shearwater petrel, a specimen of which he took home with him. After landing at Cullivoe, Charlton and Mr Henderson, his companion, made their way to Henderson's mansion at Gloup. During his stay with Mr Henderson Charlton fished a small stream running down a narrow valley into Gloup Voe:

> *A small stream steals down the narrow valley and abounds with the finest trout. I was probably the first individual who ever tried fly fishing in its waters. In an hour or so I had caught three dozen of very fair trout and one sea-trout, but the burn was at the time very low, and had I tried it after rain my success would probably have been greater. I traced the little streamlet several miles to its source up in the hills, which are I think the most dismal in Shetland.*

As well as fishing, Charlton managed to bag a few golden plover in the vicinity of Gloup. He also describes the hard life of the North Yell fishermen who rose in the early hours with a little oatmeal and water to sustain them and rowed up to forty miles out to sea to set and haul their lines. Charlton remained at Gloup until the 7th of August before he and John Henderson travelled round the northern parts of Shetland, visiting Fetlar, Unst and Northmavine. He returned to Gloup on the 18th of September and on the 22nd he fished at the head of Gloup Voe. Unfortunately, he does not record whether he caught anything on this occasion. He finally departed Shetland on the 10th of October and arrived back in his lodgings in Edinburgh on the 14th, after an absence of more than three months.

Charlton visited Shetland again during the summer of 1834 and explored the islands of Foula and Papa Stour. However, on this occasion he appears not to have fished but spent most of his time shooting and collecting geological and other natural history specimens to take back to Edinburgh.

It was to be eighteen years before he visited Shetland again.

During the intervening years he qualified as a doctor and set up in practice in Newcastle. In 1842, he married Eliza Kirsopp and the couple moved into 7 Eldon Square, a fashionable part of the city. He became a lecturer at the New Medical School in Newcastle and eventually Professor of Medicine. Charlton was very much a polymath and, as well as writing extensively on medicine, he wrote papers on local history and archaeology, ornithology, volcanology and the literature of Northern Europe.

In early July 1852 he embarked at Leith on the *SS Queen* with his travelling companion Mr George Caley. They arrived at Lerwick on Sunday, the 4th of July and wasted no time in finding accommodation at Mrs Bouwmeester's lodging house, which he describes as 'one of the best houses in the town'. There appears to have been no hotel in Lerwick at this time apart from the Temperance Hotel, which did not appeal to Charlton. Shortly after their arrival they made the short crossing to Bressay and from there to Noss. The road through Bressay had improved since Charlton's last visit and wound its way between 'two small lakes, stocked with excellent trout'. Presumably, one of these small lakes referred to is the Loch of Brough, which lies beside the present road. The author fished this loch on a couple of occasions in the summer of 2015 without success.

The following day (5th of July) Charlton called at the house of Mr Charles Duncan, whom he describes as 'one of the few good fly-fishers in Shetland'. This is an important phrase as it appears that fly fishing was not much practised in Shetland at this time. Unfortunately, Mr Duncan was not at home on this occasion.

Later that day they hired a boat at Lerwick to take them to Laxo and from there their luggage was conveyed to Voe where they boarded another boat for Hillswick. After sailing through a storm they arrived at Hillswick at half past midnight. They were hospitably received at Hillswick House by the family of Mr Gideon Anderson and given board and lodgings. Charlton very much wanted to visit this part of Shetland noted for 'its mineral treasures, and wild dark lochs teeming with trout'. The following day he was anxious to procure a pair of 'rivlins' (a type of shoe made out of untanned animal hide, with the hair outermost and moulded to the shape of the foot) to wear over his fishing stockings when walking on the moors or wading in a loch. A local shoemaker was summoned who promptly measured his feet and made him a pair out of a piece of salted cowhide.

Thus equipped, and taking their fishing rods and guns, they took a boat across Hillswick Bay to Hamna Voe. After shooting a razorbill and its young, the heavens opened and they sought shelter in an old cottage where Charlton's fishing tackle attracted much attention, presumably, the like of which never having been seen before. Charlton stayed at the cottage until mid-afternoon when he took himself off to fish Punds Water:

The rain still continued, but at about 3 p.m. I declared that I would wait no longer, and taking our rods we walked up the burn towards the lake which was distant about a mile from the house. The ascent was steep and rugged, but I found that my 'rivlins' answered their purpose well, and further experience made me walk quite easily in them. We soon neared the banks of the loch, and saw before us, embossed in dark heathery hills a fine piece of water about a mile in length by half a mile broad. There was a holm of considerable size near its centre, and on it was established the usual colony of Black-Headed Gulls. I was myself quite a novice in loch fishing, for twenty years I had never tried anything but the streams of Northumberland. It was therefore with a palpitating heart, and with all the eagerness of a young sportsman on the 12th of August, that I proceeded to tie on two of James Wilson's [author of the 'Rod and Gun', 1844 and a friend of Charlton's] *largest and most attractive loch-flies, the Greenmantle and the Grizzly-king, and marching into the loch to the edge of the deep water I commenced my labours. My first half dozen throws were unsuccessful, but at the next I felt a dead heavy pull which showed I had hooked a weighty fish. He resisted my efforts for some time to bring him*

James Wilson

ashore, but at length I got him within reach of the landing net and laid him on the grass to contemplate at leisure his beautiful proportions. He was a full short powerfully built fish of something more than a pound in weight, and exquisitely bright in colour. A few minutes after I hooked another, but in a critical plunge I injudiciously slackened the line and he escaped. Caley was not inclined to fish, but wandered off with his gun towards the south bay of the loch, where two of the Red-throated Divers were reposing upon the water. I now crossed the shallow stream that ran from the loch and continued along the banks. Almost immediately a fine fish rose and after five minutes' play was landed. He was bulkier than the other and much more powerful in his struggles, his weight would be under a pound and a half. Both these fish took the Greenmantle fly. The rain now interfered to spoil my sport, it came down in torrents and the fish gave over feeding.

Later that evening Charlton and Caley, his travelling companion, returned to Hillswick where the trout were cooked for their supper and proved to be excellent eating. 'They were deep coloured as salmon, and fully equal to that fish in flavour.'

The following day, after exploring the coastline and bagging a few oyster catchers, they returned to Hillswick and promptly went trout fishing to a loch at the head of Uriefirth (Urafirth) Voe, which, they were told, contained a fine head of trout.

A sharp walk along the new road from Hillswick to Lerwick brought us to the wished for spot. The surface of the small lake was calm and smooth as a polished mirror, and not a fish stirred. A poor ragged lad whom I had seen at Hillswick in the morning now came timidly up to me, and advised me to go further along the banks to a point where the water was deeper. About nine o'clock the trout began to rise freely, particularly around a heap of stones in the loch, said to be the remains of a brough [broch]. I did not get any large trout, but many of fair size, though they were much inferior in beauty of shape and in flavour to the Punds Water trout. It was half past ten before we left the loch, and there seemed to be even then no diminution of the daylight, though the sun had then set.

The following morning Charlton received a letter from Charles Duncan of Lerwick whom he describes as 'the most enthusiastic and the most successful fly-fisher in all Shetland'. In the letter Duncan gave him some information about the Northmavine lochs but indicated that he had not fished much in that part of the country. Around 11am they set off round the head of St Magnus Bay and made their way to fish Helga Water.

Our guide was the intelligent lad who had joined us the evening before at Uriefirth loch; he was miserably clad, even for a Shetlander, and besides suffering from scrofula he had yesterday cut his foot severely by treading on an adze. We now saw before us the whole expanse of Helga Water, it is a larger loch than Punds

> Water, but the surrounding hills are much less picturesque in their outline. After preparing our tackle we separated, and Caley took the west side of the loch, while I went along its southern banks. I soon raised and hooked three or four goodly fish and with the assistance of the boy landed them in safety.

They fished till around nine o'clock in the evening before hunger got the better of them and they returned with heavy baskets of fish to Hillswick. They enjoyed a good meal of Helga Water trout but they did not find their flesh to be as red as those from Punds Water.

As their holiday was drawing to a close Charlton and his travelling companion returned to Lerwick in a small boat manned by a crew of advancing years. As they were on their way to Lerwick, a storm arose and they were almost driven on to cliffs. Eventually they made it to Olna Firth around 2pm and, after their leaving their luggage to be conveyed by pony and cart, they decided to walk the nineteen miles to Lerwick. On the journey

Angling boats at Tingwall Loch.

Charlton stopped off at a loch at the head of Wadbister Voe where he 'tried a few throws for trout as the evening was very fine, but could only get a few rises, and the fish seemed small and scarce'. Around 9pm they decided to call on their 'brother angler', Charles Duncan, who had advised them of where to fish around Hillswick and who lived in a fine house at Gott. They were hospitably received and, as is the nature of anglers, they began discussing the merits of various lochs and flies. For supper they dined on some of the delicious Tingwall trout that Mr Duncan had captured an hour or two before in the loch. 'They were short plump fish about half a pound in weight, and exquisitely flavoured.' They stayed up long into the night over an ample supply of cigars and whisky before departing once again for Lerwick, which they reached at 3am and were amazed to find people still in the streets!

On their final day in Shetland (Monday, 12th of July), Charlton and Caley decided to walk to Tingwall and enjoy a final few hours' fishing the Loch of Tingwall. They gained permission from the local minister to use one of his boats and they were soon afloat on the loch:

The surface was perfectly smooth, as there was not the slightest breeze, and we tried all manner of tempting flies without the least success. Caley then suggested we should try the artificial Archimedian minnow [invented by a Mr Allies of Worcester and sold by Farlow's]. *I had never even seen this bait, but felt a great contempt for it, as I had been assured by old practised fishermen that it was entirely useless. However we resolved to give it a trial, and it was soon towing astern of the boat. I was looking over the side into the deep greenish water when my rod was violently shaken and it was evident that a good fish was fast upon it. I played him for a few minutes and then lifted him into the boat, and I saw that Charles Duncan had not exaggerated the excellence of the Tingwall trout. We did not get any large ones, the biggest was perhaps a trifle above a pound in weight, but there were no small ones among them.*

After partaking of lunch at a local cottage, Charlton left Caley to carry on trolling with his artificial minnow, while he himself went ashore on the east side of the loch. He tied on a Green Mantle with a Dun Professor (presumably he means the Professor, a fly invented by Professor John Wilson, the brother of James Wilson) at the tail.

> *I commenced fishing from the shore. About one o'clock I found the trout beginning to rise well, particularly in the narrow part of the loch opposite the holm near its southern end. Here I captured some fine trout, one of which Caley, when we got on board the steamboat this evening, amused himself by sketching. I have never, I think, seen handsomer trout than these, and Mr C. Duncan has often taken three or four dozen of this average size in an evening. it was plain that the sport was only now beginning, and it was equally clear that it must immediately terminate for two o'clock had come, and with a heavy heart I put up my rod, helped Caley to draw up the minister's boat, and then we turned our backs on Tingwall Loch, in all probability never to return to its banks.*

And Charlton never did return to Shetland, although he spent a number of subsequent holidays in Sutherland or Norway. His first marriage was childless and his wife Eliza died in May 1862. Two years later he married Margaret Bellasis and when Charlton himself died ten years later on the 14th of May, 1874, he left her five sons and one daughter, the youngest son still to be born!

CHAPTER 6

John Russell - The Angling Minister of Whalsay

It was the Reverend John Russell, author of *Three Years in Shetland* (1887) who wrote:

> *The only out-door amusements besides farming to a limited extent which are popularly regarded as decorous in a clergyman, and consistent with the sacred profession, are gardening and fishing.*

And John Russell was both an enthusiastic gardener and keen angler.

John Russell was born in 1829 at Duffus in Morayshire and was the son of a toll-house keeper at Elgin, also named John, and his wife Elizabeth (née Gordon). Little is known of his early life except that he was a graduate of Aberdeen University and was ordained a Church of Scotland minister. By 1851 the census records show that he was parochial schoolmaster of Rathven, Banffshire, a position he held for twenty years. He eventually became tired of teaching, not because of the work itself, but because of the environment he found himself in.

> *I had a crowded school, and the accommodation being deficient, my health suffered in consequence... Anyone who in an afternoon has entered one of the old crowded parish school-rooms can readily understand how such an atmosphere was in the highest degree injurious to health, and how a teacher in such circumstances often sighed for a change of occupation. I have heard teachers say at the end of the summer holidays, when their*

health had been recruited and their appetite had returned, after enjoying the fresh air and scenery of the country that it was with a shudder that they contemplated the idea of returning to their usual employment.

In August 1864 he married Margaret Davidson at Buckie in Banffshire, and they went on to have five children: John (b.1866), Isabelle (b.1867), Jane (b.1870), Eliza (b.1875) and Georgina (b.1876). We learn from his book that over the years he had visited Shetland a number of times and, in 1864, he sought the living of the parish of Sandsting. A notice in the *Aberdeen Journal* of 6th July, 1864 states:

> *A petition has been forwarded to the Earl of Zetland signed by upwards of 600 of the parishioners of Sandsting to present the Rev. John Russel M.A., Rathven, Banffshire, to the vacant charge.*

Unfortunately, he was unsuccessful on this occasion and in his book he mentions how difficult it was to obtain a parish living due to a large reserve of probationary ministers at that time. In Shetland, the Earl of Zetland was the sole patron of the twelve livings in the islands and until the abolition of patronage (Church Patronage (Scotland) Act 1874) it was only those who were recommended to him who had any prospect of obtaining an appointment. He was almost in despair of being appointed a parish minister when he was elected minister of the *quoad sacra* parish of Whalsay in October 1872. A *quoad sacra* parish was a parish of the Church of Scotland which is not a civil parish. Such a parish had ecclesiastical functions but no local government functions. These parishes were created as a result of the original parish becoming too populous for one church and minister to serve but the original parish remained the unit for various civil administrative purposes. Russell's appointment was announced in the *Aberdeen Journal* of Wednesday 13th November, 1872:

Presbytery of Olnafirth A meeting of this revered Court took place on the 30th of October. There was laid on the table a presentation (with relevant documents) in favour of the Rev. John Russell, presently parish schoolmaster of Rathven, Banffshire, to be minister of the endowed parish of Whalsay. The Presbytery unanimously sustained the presentation.

He clearly did not take up the appointment on Whalsay for pecuniary reasons since his stipend as a minister was little more than half his salary as a schoolmaster. Also, he was disappointed to be giving up his garden from which he derived great pleasure:

One thing in particular I grudged giving up. This was my garden. To most schoolmasters in the country, a garden is a pleasant source of recreation. Keeping bees, rearing flowers, fruit, and vegetables during spare hours and moments of leisure are a pleasant exchange for the confined and exhausting labours of a class-room.

Whalsay Parish Church and interior.

We learn that he was a very successful competitor at local exhibitions and was president of his parish horticultural society.

After arriving in Whalsay in the summer of 1873, he and his family quickly established themselves in the manse. John Russell's parish consisted of Whalsay and the Out Skerries with a church in each but, owing to the distance between them, the Out Skerries were only visited occasionally. The church at Whalsay was built on the west side of the island on a site near the shore originally chosen for the easy conveyance of building materials by sea. Near to the church were a pier and boathouse and the majority of his parishioners travelled to and from church services by boat. Attendance at church was very good since, in addition to religious reasons, it afforded people from the various districts the opportunity of meeting one another.

Although he quickly settled into the life of a parish minister on Whalsay, he was somewhat taken aback by the living conditions and attitude to hygiene he witnessed during his regular visits to his parishioners' homes. However, he was quite tactful in the way he expressed this in his book, no doubt not wishing to offend:

Candour compels me to state that in regard to domestic arrangements and culinary preparations there is yet much to learn in Shetland. The houses are constructed in such a way as that warmth is the chief thing sought after, without regard to smoke. Then, not to speak of dogs and cats, there is generally a young pig at the fireside, which has been brought into the house, until, past the delicate period of infancy, he can contend in the stye with cold and wet. The pig is quite at home. He has the freedom of the whole house, where he moves about snuffing for morsels of food. But the fireside is his favourite lounge. There he gets his meals. These consist of the remains of food left over by the family, and are often given to him in the pot in which the family dinner has been cooked.

It seems that many of his parishioners kept a heap of peat for the fire in a corner of the living room, which 'is highly favourable to the propagation of certain insects of a lively and mercurial disposition'. Not surprisingly, perhaps, he was somewhat reluctant to share in his parishioners' hospitality!

When not ministering to his flock he seems to have spent his time gardening and fishing. On leaving Rathven he took with him to Whalsay a stock of tulip and crocus bulbs. After planting at the proper time, the tulips failed to flower although his crocuses produced a brilliant display. He had some success with black and red currants, which produced a moderate crop, but his strawberries grew in abundance and had an excellent flavour. Rhubarb, too, grew prolifically and he had some success with root vegetables and lettuce and cabbage.

He regarded sea trout fishing as the 'esteemed pursuit of the skilful angler', and in his *Three Years in Shetland* (1887), he described the habits of the sea trout and the locations where they could be found. He claimed to have heard of half a hundredweight of sea trout being taken in an hour or two. Most anglers, in their lifetime, will experience a red-letter day when everything goes right and they catch a good basket of fish. John Russell's red-letter day occurred in the parish of Walls on the Shetland Mainland:

I myself, by sheer accident, once had what I consider a wonderful take. This was in the parish of Walls. There is here a stream called the Brouster, which runs a course of half a dozen miles through a chain of lochs, and terminates in something like an estuary on a small scale. This estuary is quite salt. At the east end of it is a large pool, so deep that even at low water a vessel of some size could float in it. At ebb tide it is almost cut off from the sea, leaving at one place a shallow which can be crossed over. Well, I set out one morning to fish without any fixed idea where to begin except that I would try the Brouster. The public road crosses the stream near the sea, and when I reached this place by the road, as the tide was out, I thought of taking a cast in the salt water. I had on two flies. No sooner had the line touched the water than both hooks were seized, and two sea trout were fast. One immediately broke off, and the other ran off with the line for a considerable distance, and then when I began to tighten the line the fish sprang repeatedly into the air in the liveliest manner imaginable; but as the tackle was good the fish gradually became exhausted, and I wound up the reel until coming near the side, when I was able to secure a beautiful trout of nearly three pounds weight. As this was my first capture of any magnitude, I was in a state of considerable excitement. I lost no time in making another cast, with the same success as before; in short, in little more than a couple of hours, and it seemed to me an affair of five minutes, so absorbed was I, no fewer than eleven sea trout between two and three pounds each lay on the gravel behind me. How long my success would have continued, but for an unfortunate incident, I cannot say. But it was interrupted in this way. About five or six yards from the shore a tuft of sea weed floated to the surface from the rock beneath on which it grew. The last trout which I caught was being gradually brought to land when the line got entangled with this bit of sea weed. I tried to extricate it, but to no purpose. I could not wade in, as the water was of unknown depth. I was unwilling to break the line, so I stripped off my clothes, and swimming out disengaged the line, and at the same time secured the fish, which having been exhausted before made little resistance. Dressing as hastily as I could, I resumed the fishing, but did not get a single bite again. So I prepared to leave in great spirits at the unexpected success which I had met with.

He was now faced with the difficulty of carrying his catch home. Fortunately, he bumped into a local landowner, Captain Moatt, locally known as 'Mansie Moatt'. Moatt had spent most of his life working for the Aberdeen Lime Company but had returned to Shetland and bought a piece of ground where he could live out his days. He had built a modest dwelling house by an inlet of the sea where he considered he owned the fishing rights. Moatt helped Russell to carry back his catch and invited him to help next day to net the inlet. Moatt had already tried fishing for the sea trout from a boat but to no avail. On the following day, the net, equipped with lead sinkers at the bottom and cork floats at the top, was prepared. One end was fixed to the shore and the other end was placed in the boat.

Then our friend rowed out, letting the net gradually sink into the water, and enclosing a large circuit before coming in with the other end. We now began to haul in both ends of the net, all the while in great suspense. We knew that there was no lack of fish in the water. But if the bottom was uneven, or if a rock cropped up from below, the net might be entangled or torn, and all the labour would have been expended in vain. With great delight we saw the net come in smoothly and easily. As it came nearer, the disturbance and splashing in its bight showed that it was not empty. The commotion became more violent as we made haste to haul it out of the water and on the beach. There were no fewer than twenty beautiful trout, all shining like silver, and none less than two pounds weight. We made one or two more trials, at each time with success, and then desisted, thinking that we had enough.

Moatt was ecstatic with his catch and thought he could make a good deal of money from this enterprise. Unfortunately, he was too far from a market and, although he sent his fish to Lerwick, he received very little for them since there was an abundance of fish there and it was like sending coals to Newcastle.

Sadly, the sea trout fishing on the stream at Brouster went into decline as a result of over-fishing. News of the prolific catches spread and were reported in a sporting journal. The stream was fished by both rod and net, in and out of season, and the numbers of sea trout plummeted, as Russell says:

The last time I tried angling in the place formerly so abundant, I, after considerable labour, got only one, and that by no means a heavy fish. In all parts of the islands excellent angling is to be had at the proper season. Now that communication with the south is so easy, Shetland presents a good prospect to the angler who knows where to go, and who will be at the trouble to apply to the proprietor of the land for leave to ply the gentle art. The establishment of a Fishery Board will help to prevent the extermination of trout, by rendering illegal the capture of spawning fish.

Sea trout in Shetland can grow to a large size and one of the biggest fish to be recorded, a specimen of 28lb, was reputedly caught in a net in September 1895 in Dales Voe near Lerwick by Mr Weber from the Queen's Hotel. The fish was 41½ inches long and had a girth of 25 inches and at some point had been attacked by an otter. Russell, too, records the capture of large sea trout, albeit in a net, from Sulma Water:

> *The laird told that near the island (in Sulma Water) on which the gulls breed, but in a part of the loch beside its outlet to the sea, he was in the habit of setting a hang net for sea trout. On one occasion, to his surprise, the net had disappeared. He could not account for this, and there were no poachers to be dreaded, who might have anticipated him; so he got his boat, and searched around the place where the net had been set. In a short time he discovered it rolled up and twisted round a large fish. This was a sea trout of not less, he assured me, than a stone weight (14 lb). The large size to which sea trout sometimes grow will account for the mistake which some have made of supposing that salmon are to be found in Shetland. What have been taken for salmon are only specimen sea trout; and though places are known by the name of Laxo and Laxfirth, such terms will apply to trout as well as salmon.*

Unfortunately, Russel's time on Whalsay was all too brief and a notice in the *Aberdeen Journal* (Wednesday, 10th February, 1876) records his appointment as the parish minister of Leslie in Aberdeenshire. His reasons for leaving Whalsay are given in the final chapter of *Three Years in Shetland*:

In bringing my remarks to a close, I may say that it was with no small degree of regret that I left Whalsay. My parishioners were most respectful, kind and obliging. But the seclusion of island life, the fatigue and exposure connected with boating, and the want of means of education for a young family, led me to embrace the opening presented me of obtaining a parish in what, after all, was my native country.

Following his appointment as minister of Leslie, Russell remained in the post until his death on the 2nd of May, 1895. The following extract is taken from his obituary, which appeared in the *Aberdeen Weekly Journal* on the 5th of May, 1895:

The news of the death of Rev. John Russell, parish minister of Leslie, will be learned with regret by members of the Synod of Aberdeen, and by all who had the pleasure of the rev. gentleman's acquaintance. For some considerable time Mr Russell had suffered from an internal ailment. The deceased who was a graduate of Aberdeen University, had a high ideal of the work of the ministry, and was greatly devoted to the interests of his parishioners. In the young of the congregation he took an especial interest, and many of those who were brought up under his ministry will retain kindly memories of his disinterested labours on their behalf. About five years ago the reverend gentleman introduced instrumental music into the worship of the church, an improvement in the praise which has been greatly appreciated . . .

Russell never forgot his time in Shetland and in 1887, his book *Three Years in Shetland*, based on his experiences of life in the islands, was published by Alexander Gardner of Paisley and London. The book was favourably reviewed in the *Aberdeen Weekly Journal* on the 22nd of November, 1887. In addition to fishing in Shetland, the book gives a fascinating insight into life in Whalsay over a century ago and it is well worth the effort of tracking down a copy.

CHAPTER 7

'Old Wick' on Angling

In May 1878, *The Field*, one of the leading magazines catering for field sportsmen and still going strong today, published the first in a series of six articles entitled 'Rambling and Angling Notes from Shetland'. The author of these articles wrote under the nom de plume 'Old Wick', whose real name was John Tudor. John Robert Tudor was not a native Shetlander but was born in Birkenhead on Merseyside on the 13th of October, 1839. He was the fourth son of Captain John Tudor R.N. He was educated first at Greenock and later at Shrewsbury School. He appears to have spent a number of childhood holidays at Wick, the principal town in the far north of Scotland and from which he derived his pseudonym. He loved the far north of Scotland and developed an interest in all things nautical but, instead of following in his father's footsteps and entering the Royal Navy, Tudor qualified as a lawyer.

Throughout his life Tudor seems to have been dogged by ill health and in 1875 he made his first trip to Shetland in the hope that the bracing air would benefit his condition. During the course of the next six years he returned every year. His articles in *The Field* were the first-fruits of these visits. He then had the idea of writing a longer work on the northern archipelago and went about collecting material for his magnum opus *The Orkneys and Shetland: Their Past and Present State*, published in 1883.

In his first article for *The Field*, dated the 11th of May, 1878, Tudor largely concentrates on fly fishing for sea trout in salt water, a method of fishing rarely encountered outside Orkney and Shetland. He recommends that the angler interested in the sea trout should concentrate his efforts at the mouths of the burns as they enter the salt-water voes during the months of August, September and early October. He is impressed by the sea trout's free-rising nature in salt water but warns that they are far from easy to hook:

> *In Shetland they will, however, at times rise freely; but capricious as the sea trout always are, they appear to be doubly so in salt water, and at the end of most days fly fishing for them in the sea, unless the water is coloured from heavy rainfall, the number of fish killed will bear a very small proportion to those risen and tricked. No doubt the extreme clearness of the salt water has something to do with it; and it may be that the mouths of the fish are more tender in salt than in fresh water, hooks breaking away in consequence more easily.*

He recommends that, since the area of fishable water in most voes is limited in extent, only one angler should fish at a time. He also recommends that the wading angler should wear fishing trousers rather than stockings in order to get far enough out to cast over the seaweed and bring the fish, when hooked, within reach of the landing-net. With regard to flies for sea trout he feels that it is better to fish with only one to reduce the chances of becoming hung up in the seaweed. One of the sea trout flies recommended to him had a body of dark red mohair or pig's wool, ribbed with gold twist, black-red (coch-y-bonddu) hackle under the shoulder, and a jay wing, composed of fibres from the butt of the long wing feathers. The angler (unnamed) who gave Tudor this pattern was adamant that no tail should be included in the dressing as sea trout frequently rise 'short'.

A large part of this first article concentrates on travel to Shetland and accommodation within the islands. The coming of the railway to Aberdeen in the middle of the nineteenth century made it easier for the angler from the south to visit Shetland and Tudor recommends the visiting angler to catch the overnight

Fishing a tranquil loch.

mail train from Euston or King's Cross to Aberdeen and then proceed by boat to Lerwick. An alternative route was via steamer from Granton harbour on the Firth of Forth to Lerwick. Even in the late 1870s accommodation in Lerwick and elsewhere in Shetland was extremely limited and Tudor recommends the angler to telegraph well in advance of his visit:

> *It is as well, before starting, to telegraph for rooms to the Queen's, the Zetland, or Mrs Crutwell, who keeps the temperance hotel, otherwise you may have to wander up and down the streets of Lerwick all night, which is not pleasant, especially if you have had a 'high old time' of it in the Roost of Sumburgh.*

Towards the end of this article Tudor discusses the fishing in and around the Tingwall Valley. He regards Strand Loch as the best sea-trout loch in Shetland. He fished the loch with a friend for the first time in September 1876 when he was out-fished by his friend who caught six or seven sea trout from two pounds downwards on small Francis flies. The following year on the 15th of October he caught six sea trout in the loch weighing six or seven pounds, the largest being a little over two pounds. On that particular occasion the wind blew so hard that he could barely stand in the water. A not unusual phenomenon in Shetland! A regular angler on Strand Loch was a local man, Magnus Tait whom Tudor describes as knowing 'every stone almost where a fish is to be, and knows perhaps better than any man in Shetland how to put you over a fish, and how to work the boat when it is hooked'. Unfortunately, when Tudor was fishing Laxfirth Voe that same year, he did not have Magnus Tait as his gillie:

> *I tried the voe two or three times last year (1877), but beyond small ones did nothing, though I rose and pricked several good fish, and lost a big one through my boatman (not Magnus Tait) allowing the boat to drift over the fish, who immediately availed himself of the opportunity to cut the gut against the keel.*

A not uncommon story of one that got away! However, Tudor reports on one Strand Loch fish that did not get away - one about twelve pounds - caught by a medical man from Lerwick. Sadly, he does not recount his name. He also reports an 8-pounder killed by a Mr Dunbar, of Thurso fame.

In his second article published in July 1878, Tudor concentrates on the fishing in the Walls district of Shetland and he describes in some detail his journey from Lerwick to Walls. In the course of his journey he gives a more detailed description of the Tingwall Valley:

> *About a mile from Veensgarth, on the south side, are Tingwall Loch and manse, and just beyond Tingwall Loch that of Asta. The trout in Tingwall, though they do not run large - averaging, I should fancy, a little under half a pound - are, for their size, as game fish as you can meet with.*

Further on in his journey he discusses the fishing on the Loch of Strom, which he describes as a loch of considerable size, and 'ought to abound in sea-trout during the autumn months, as the fish could run in and out with every tide, neap as well as spring'. He recommends that the angler desirous of fishing Strom stay at Airv House Inn. For the angler requiring further information on fishing this loch he suggests consulting the school-master who 'is, I believe, a great fisherman, and would no doubt give any further information'.

One of Tudor's favourite lochs in the Walls' area appears to be the Loch of Brouster, which actually comprises two lochs, the Upper and Lower Lochs of Brouster, and Tudor is presumably referring to the Lower Loch of Brouster. While fishing with a friend, whom he simply refers to by his initial 'E', he tells a story, familiar to all anglers, of one that got away:

> *E and I on the following Monday got the small coble used for the drag net, and fished and rowed alternately. We had not done much - the biggest about 1½ lb. - when on taking the rod from E, I expressed a wish to hook the father of all fishes. I had hardly spoken, when I was fast into him. His first rush as he made for one of the culverts nearly took out all my line; but luckily he changed his mind and came back, and the dance commenced round and round the lower end of the loch.*

> *The tide was falling, and the seaweed cropping up in patches here and there; so he required careful handling, as did the boat, the more as the casting-line was of tolerably fine gut. After the fish had been on half an hour, I saw the rod - a new twelve-foot spliced one - bend suspiciously under the splice, and knew*

it was a race against time. After a while, the fish began to flurry, but we had no clip or gaff, and the line by this time would no longer run through the rings; so we tried to tow him into shallow water. Whilst in deep water, the rod broke; getting hold of the top piece, I got a momentary end-on strain, and we parted, fifty-five minutes by E's watch from the time the fish was hooked. Even then, with a gaff, we could have got him, as he was regularly 'burst'. Both E and I put the fish, which was a bull trout, down at over thirty inches in length, and very thick to boot. We pulled ashore in silence, had a nip and a pipe, and then E as the Scotchman said, 'just swore at lairge'.

At Brouster his most successful fly was the Red Palmer, dressed in a variety of sizes to suit water conditions. On very bright days a Black Palmer appeared to do the trick. One of the problems facing anglers wanting to fish Brouster in the late nineteenth century was the local netsmen. Tudor complains that Brouster was regularly raked with a drag net at spring tides and several times they saw a net stretched across the mouth of the burn to prevent fish getting into the fresh-water Loch of Brouster. Apparently, the inhabitants of the area expressed concerns that netting was driving away angling tourists and, according to Tudor, resolved to do something about it:

A memorial was signed by the principal inhabitants of Walls last summer against netting, as tending to drive away visitors from the place; amongst those signing were the Established and Free Kirk ministers, and a copy was sent to me. When I came to Walls in the autumn I was told all netting would cease at the legal date, 14th of September, and that any person infringing the law would be prosecuted. On the night of the 17th of September E and I found a net stretched across the mouth of the burn, flowing from the Village Loch into Vaila Sound. We brought this case before some of the most influential of the persons who signed the memorial, with the result I had anticipated - nothing done.

Towards the end of this article Tudor relates a story concerning one of his friends who was out fishing when the fog came down and became disorientated. After hours of walking he found himself back at the same loch and had to spend the night under a peat stack. His matches or 'vesuvians', were so damp that he could not get a light. Shetland is noted for its haar or sea fog, which can descend quite quickly, and the visiting angler fishing a remote loch is well advised to take a compass and provisions with him.

Tudor's third article concerns the Dunrossness and Sumburgh areas of the mainland and the first part is largely devoted to a description of his journey from Lerwick to Boddam. He mentions the loch of Clickimin on the outskirts of Lerwick and its broch, which he describes as a 'Pictish fort', and was excavated in 1860-1861. He is less than complimentary about Sandy Loch which supplied, and still supplies, Lerwick with its water. The loch was dammed in the 1970s and its level was raised so that it is now much greater in extent than when Tudor fished it over a hundred years ago.

> *After leaving Clickimin you come to the Sandy Loch, from whence the town supply of water is drawn; it may be wholesome enough, but put me in mind of the senna tea of my youthful days. There are trout in this loch, and of fair size, if I may judge from some I saw which had been caught there.*

From Sandy Loch he made his way to Easter Quarff where a small burn empties itself into the sea in a small rocky basin, some hundred and fifty yards broad by sixty to eighty deep. He fished there with a friend whom he names as 'H'.

> *H (who had great sport here in former years) and I fished it twice last year, but with little success - H killing, our first day, one about 3 lb., and losing another about the same size in a small creek to the south of the basin, from 'yacking' it into him too hard, while I got one of barely a pound.*

Between Quarff and Cunningsburgh he refers to the Loch of Fladdabister, which, he says, contains fair brown trout although the wading appears to be dangerous:

> *The bottom is said to be of the 'bubble-and-squeak' order - that is, you see the air bubbles rushing up before you, and are lucky if you get off with a narrow squeak.*

Surprisingly, Tudor remarks that, although he had seen it from the road, he had never actually visited the Broch of Mousa, one of the most iconic sites in the whole of Shetland. From here he proceeded to Channerwick and recommends the angler to fish the burn between the road and voe head. He reports that he had fished this burn one July and caught a fair number of brown trout although he claims he was too early for the sea trout.

His fourth article, published in September 1878, focuses on the area around Boddam and he complains bitterly of the lack of accommodation and of beer and spirits for the visiting angler. Apparently, in the 1870s, there was no place south of Lerwick where the tourist could obtain alcohol and he advises the visitor to take his creature comforts with him! Fortunately, this situation was rectified when the Spiggie Hotel opened around 1880 and offered accommodation for visiting anglers. The best and the most productive loch in this area is Spiggie and, not surprisingly, Tudor fished it:

> *It is a biggish loch, about a mile and a half long, by perhaps half a mile broad at the widest part; has a shelly, sandy bottom and produces as fine, if not finer, trout than the loch of Watten in Caithness. Like all well-fed fish, they are very 'dour' to rise at times; but if you can only hit on the day when they mean business the basket would probably satisfy even Mr Adams himself. The first day I fished it this year, on June 3, I had a biting northerly wind, and for hours I fished on, hardly moving a fin; then I had half an hour of rise, and then they knocked off work, and I had to do so as well. In the half-hour I got twelve, which,*

Spiggie Loch.

with two I had caught shortly after commencing, weighed 8 lb. 12oz., biggest 1¼ lb.

*The next day I got too late on the water, as the rising period was over, and I only got two - 1lb. 10oz. The next day I was again late on, and only got seven - 3lb. 14oz. I tried again on the 7*th*; but a bright sun and easterly wind prevented the fish showing at all, and I only got small 'finnock'. It was bitterly cold the first three nights, and not a fair test of the loch; the third night they were rolling over in shoals like porpoises, and I had ocular proof of their number. The twenty-three I got averaged nearly 10 oz. apiece, and cut like salmon.*

He goes on to report that he saw a 4½lb fish that had been killed on a night line and that the locals employed otter boards on the loch to catch bait for their long lines. He was appalled that trout should be used as bait to catch cod and saithe, which 'to a properly constituted Waltonian mind seems nothing short of sacrilege'. He adds that if the fish in Spiggie were protected there would be no finer loch in Shetland.

Tudor then records that an old friend of his, whom he simply refers to as P, had great sport on Spiggie one July evening, catching over forty trout averaging twelve ounces each. The fish were all taken on fly close to the shore without the angler even wetting his feet!

In his penultimate article Tudor concentrates on the fishing in the Northmavine area, which he describes as the 'largest, wildest and most beautiful parish in Shetland'. The area can be reached by road or by sea. If the visiting angler prefers the latter mode of transport, the *Earl of Zetland* steamer departs from Lerwick every Thursday morning bound for Northmavine and beyond. He goes on to describe the journey by road, pointing out some of the lochs along the way. He mentions the loch of Girlsta, which is the only loch in Shetland to contain char although it appears that Tudor made no attempt to catch them.

According to Tudor, roads in Shetland were a relatively recent phenomenon. Before the great potato famine of 1846-1848, the only road in existence was the one between Lerwick and Scalloway. Most of the roads in Tudor's time were built during the famine years to provide employment for the starving population.

He fished a number of lochs in the Northmavine area and was a little disappointed with the sport on the loch of Burraland. He was told that it contained fair brown trout but he only managed to catch thirteen small fish of about five to the pound. However, he believes that after a spate it would be a good loch for sea trout. He is more complimentary about Punds Water, so-called from the sheepfold, or 'pund' built on a small peninsula jutting out into the loch on the south-western side. Apparently, this was a favourite loch of Professor William Aytoun, a Scottish lawyer and poet who was appointed Sheriff of Orkney and Shetland in 1852. He was married to Jane Emily Wilson, the daughter of the famous angler and writer Professor John Wilson (Christopher North). He describes the water in Punds Water as being exquisitely clear and showing every stone in the rocky bottom. He fished the loch on a number of occasions as his records show:

The trout, which are a dark tortoiseshell-marked fish are like all well-fed fish in clear water, very shy at rising, though when they do rise they rarely do so 'short'. June 26. Bright sun, wind southerly . . . I got five fish, which I did not weigh, but were up to the average. June 28. A broiling sun, fish not rising till evening, when wind died away completely; three, 2 lb. 4 oz., losing a very good fish from reel jamming. July 3. Dark cloudy day, cold northerly wind; ten 7lb. 4 oz., losing five large fish from the hold of the very small flies giving way. July 5. Heavy thundery day, with wind all round the compass in slight flaws; six 3 lb. 12 oz. July 16. Dark, showery, and wind westerly, a 'beau ideal' of a fishing day you would have said. I whipped away for four hours, rose two fish and caught none. I found the quill dun kill all on bright days, and the red badger (gold tip, scarlet body, and coch-y-bonddu hackle) did best on July 3. There is a small holm on the loch, in which the rain goose (red-throated diver) builds, and the young ones were at times swimming about the loch, glistening in the sunlight; and you might do a worse 'moon' than sitting down by the side of Punds Water, when the fish are not on the rise, and watching the gulls and wild ducks, who occupy the holm in joint tenancy with the rain geese, and listening to the weird note of the golden plover and snipe.

Red-throated diver.

Another loch in the area which Tudor comments on is Eela Water. Like Punds Water, he describes it a beautiful clear loch with a red stony or gravelly bottom. Large baskets of trout can be taken in this loch although they are smaller than those of Punds Water, averaging about four ounces. Tudor observes that in his day this area of Shetland had very little accommodation for visiting anglers. John Anderson of Hillswick had been in the habit of accommodating visitors to the district but they had become such an intolerable nuisance that he was forced to put an advert in the *Shetland Times* stating that he no longer had any accommodation available. Fortunately, the situation improved in 1900 with the building of the St Magnus Hotel at Hillswick, an establishment that is still going strong today.

The final article in the series is largely concerned with sea fishing and Tudor gives a detailed account of the methods of long-lining for ling, tusk and cod and the methods used for preserving and curing them.

Although John Tudor visited Shetland for health reasons between 1875 and 1881, it appears not to have helped and by 1882 his health had seriously deteriorated. He seems to have been suffering from *locomotor ataxia*, a condition that made it difficult for him to control his bodily movements, although his mental faculties were unimpaired. He claimed that it was sleeping in a damp bed that had exacerbated his condition although he does not say whether that damp bed was in Shetland! He died at St Leonards-on-sea on the 11th of November, 1890, aged just fifty-one. Fortunately, his book and his angling articles for *The Field* give us a fascinating glimpse into life and sport in Shetland in the latter part of the nineteenth century and serve as a fitting tribute to his memory.

CHAPTER 8

Mr Gaskell's Fishing Excursion

The following article appeared in The Angler *magazine and is dated the 25th of November, 1893. The article was originally read before the Wellington Angling Society, Nottingham. The account gives a fascinating insight into the social conditions prevailing at the time.*

Much may be said in favour of the fisherman of conservative habits - for the sportsman who for a lifetime frequents the same old haunts season after season. The odds are always in favour of the angler who knows his water. He knows the position and nature of each swim; what water, whether high or low, suits it best; the time of year most favourable for a good bag; and the class of fish to be found in any locality. Hence he talks of the 'barbel', 'chub', or 'dace swim', or the 'bream hole', the most likely place to pick up a big pike, and whether to spin or live-bait. There is no beating about the bush with such an angler. From the moment he leaves his own door-step, he knows what he is about - he is simply 'on the job', and seldom returns with an empty basket.

At the water-side, if an angler is not sociable he is a cur; and yet what an amount of curiosity does his precarious recreation incite! What passer-by can restrain the same? "What sport, sir?" is the oft-repeated query. How interestedly and cheerily this question is always put. But what a variety in kind and style of answers. We often hear of human character being delineated in a person's style of handwriting. Whether that is so I can't say - I only know that some of the cleverest men of the present day are horrid writers - but the answer given to our question of 'What sport, sir?' is a most delicate indicator of the kind of angler and the style of character he is; what class of society he belongs to; whether educated or not; the kind of temper he possesses; and, above all, whether he is honest and truthful! But to our subject.

The man who confines himself to his old familiar pitch year after year, is like 'the quality of mercy twice blest' - not only does he reap advantages, but he also confers pleasure on others. By his frequent appearance on the banks of any stream, he becomes an important figure in the pleasing landscape, which is never complete when he is absent. So note the look of welcome, the cheery 'How do you do?' as he makes his first appearance, as seasons come round. And how each day's bag is enquired into by the friendly natives. If a big catch rewards a day's skill their hearty rejoicing and congratulations are heard at the 'village inn', where such things are carefully noted and scrupulously preserved from the tongue of exaggeration. If, on the other hand, the day has been a blank, what a thousand and one excuses are advanced in extenuation of the disaster, with other expressions of sympathy of a more practical nature. I am speaking to those who can endorse the sketch I have roughly drawn. For over twenty years such was my experience in Sir John Harpur Crewe's water at Sawley. Since the death of this worthy baronet time has worked many changes, and this lovely renowned stretch of private fishing has now become a club water. It is not to be expected in the ordinary run of things, that when an old angler has been turned off his nest, that he will easily settle down again or transfer his old habits to a new abode. And so it has come about that for the last few years, your otherwise staid and regular president has become somewhat of a roamer, and gone far afield for his sport. As it was understood that my contribution was to be rather brief, I will give you a sketch of my last year's trip to the Shetlands, and leave this year's 'Tour among the Broads' for another occasion.

The Shetland excursion was as un-meditated as it was enjoyable. My summer vacation commenced on July 21st, and on the evening of that day I was crossing 'The Bridges', when I brushed against Mr. W. H., an esteemed and honoured member of this society, who informed me that he and a mutual friend, Mr. F., were off to the Shetlands on the Saturday on a fishing excursion, and would I go with them. As I could not make arrangements so speedily, I promised to follow on the Monday.

Accordingly, with bag and baggage, I left the Midland Station here by the 'Flying Scotchman' at midnight, arriving at Edinburgh about seven a.m. on Tuesday morning. After breakfast I spent the time I had to spare in making a hasty survey of this noble town, but time will neither allow me to dilate upon its attractions, nor yet upon what I saw of that early morning's impressions of the last stage of the railway journey known as the Waverley route. A few minutes' run brought me to Leith, Edinburgh's port. At a quarter past two p.m. I went on board one of the Orkney and Shetland Steam Navigation Company's boats. These are small coasters, splendidly fitted up with every comfort and convenience for passengers - bath, electric light, &c. As I enjoy the sea, the voyage was a magnificent treat. The scenery leading out of the Firth of Forth and away past the Bell Rock is fine in the extreme. The boat kept well within sight of the land, affording her passengers an opportunity of judging of the general contour of the mainland and of the irregularities of the shore. Aberdeen was reached about midnight. We left about eleven a.m. next morning, and as the herring fleet had made a 'good shot' during the night, hundreds of the craft were in a hurried motion, some to port to give up their silvery burdens, others hastening back to the fishing grounds for another haul before the shoal could get away. Towards night our boat no longer hugged the shore, but made across the open sea towards the Orkneys. Here it was that for the first time sea-sickness paid the ship a visit, but I am glad to say it was of short duration. On entering Kirkwall harbour about eleven o'clock, the channel suddenly became foggy, and what wonder that the smart little craft ran aground. Fortunately we landed on a shingly beach, or we might have fared worse. After waiting an hour or so, with the assistance of the rising tide and reversed engines, we got off, and came to anchor off Kirkwall soon after one o'clock. All the passengers were so excited by the late episode that sleep was out of the question, and as the moon was now shining brightly, the exploration of Kirkwall was suggested. This was a most enjoyable change, and put all in good spirits. By four a.m. (Wednesday morning) all had turned in, and breakfast at eight produced a very poor muster. By a quarter past eight the vessel was under way for her destination. Again the morning was glorious, and the sea as calm as ever. Lerwick, the capital of the Shetlands, was gained about half-past twelve. I may here remark that I travelled by a Cook's tourist ticket, as did my brother anglers who preceded me, the whole cost of third-class rail and first-class cabin on boat being a little over £4.

Lerwick is a small but a well-built port, containing two or three good hotels, where all the luxuries of modern comfort may be enjoyed - and for the tourist who does not care to rough it, here is his home. There is plenty of fishing to be had around the town, but not of the best.

By two o'clock I was making a twenty-six mile drive in a westerly towards Walls, a small port. This drive afforded an excellent opportunity of noting the various features of the island, the most striking of which are the mountains, which are high, steep, and covered with stunted heather and mosses. A profusion of grey boulder lends a general tameness to the landscape. Numerous lochs connect the descending burns, and, except when swelled by heavy rains, the rivers are too shallow to allow of the passage of fish to the higher spawning grounds. The cultivation of the soil is confined to patches in these valleys. The higher and more exposed areas are the morasses and peat bogs, which supply the only fuel obtainable. The crofter system of farming prevails throughout the land. The island is in the hands of but few owners, and I was told in one case the agent was the gentleman, and the landlord swelled his rent-roll by keeping a shop. When a native is in form for starting life as a crofter he makes his selection of an open fertile patch, and the agent accepts his tenancy on a nominal payment of say £2 a year. He builds his own

Lerwick Harbour today - complete with replica Viking longboat!

cottage out of the bountiful supply of stone ready at hand - a one-roomed, one storied affair, some twenty feet by fifteen, a thatched roof well bound down against wind and storm, an open hearth with or without chimney, and two small windows and a door complete the mansion. The sleeping accommodation consists of a kind of shelving built in the wall. Adjoining are the outbuildings for the cattle. Around the cottage are the irregular cultivated patches. The native corn mill is a feature of every crofter colony. It is built over the neighbouring burn, and is so small as to excite a stranger's curiosity as to what it can be. I examined several, to do which one has to crawl on hands and knees through the doorway, and peer in the darkness to make out the primitive machinery.

There are no trees or hedgerows, low rough walls marking the scant boundaries. Each crofter has certain grazing rights on the commons in proportion to the amount of rent he pays. This also regulates his 'peat-cutting' rights. A summer visitor will scarcely have set foot on the land before he makes acquaintance with peat either from a nasal sense, as burning peat gives out a very 'woody' stench, or from seeing troops of women with their loaded creels wending their way homewards. Cows and sheep are exceedingly small in size and are usually tethered when grazing. Nearly all the work on the land is done by women. They till the soil, sow the seed, reap the harvest, and tend the cattle. I was told it is not an uncommon sight to see a fisherman on landing give his better half all his traps to carry home, while he walks by her side with his hands in his pockets and his pipe in his mouth. Nevertheless the Shetlandereress is a great relief to the general sombreness of the landscape. You meet her at all ends and turns - on the highway, the sheep tract, the moss, the mountain top, and with shawl as head dress, short garments, naked feet, creel on back, and knitting in hand, she forms a picture worthy of an artist's admiration. Some few I met wore sandals made of undressed cowhide. The female population outnumbers the male in the proportion of two to one, and yet for laughter and merriment a group of Shetland girls cannot be surpassed. The natives appear to be of Danish origin, and repudiate most strongly any Scotch or Orcadian descent. They are not a tall race but lithe and nimble, and while young very good-looking. The men spend most of their time fishing, either at home on the voes or with the herring fleets. The island is so intersected with arms of the sea, that no portion of the interior is more than three miles from the 'briny'. Herring and haddock are the chief harvest, and the drying and salting shed finds room for a certain amount of female labour. The facilities for obtaining drink are very limited. Tea is the usual beverage all round and its excessive use is said to account for the extreme sallowness of middle age and onwards. They are a thrifty, warm-hearted, and loyal people, and can boast of being, perhaps the only part of Her Majesty's dominions devoid of paupers.

The roads are few, very winding, but good and well looked after by the various County Councils of the island. They were constructed a few years ago by the natives in the employ of the Government, as a means of tiding over the failure of a fishing harvest. Outside the highways travelling is difficult, as most of the remote places can only be approached by sheep tracks, and as one mountain is so like another no tourist should ever venture out without chart and compass or a guide. Our juvenile knowledge of this outlying island is somewhat mixed up with ponies, and my sketch would not be complete without a notice of this lovely, saucy apology for the noble horse. They are, indeed, a pretty sight in their native hills. They go in flocks, and range the hills at large, scampering hither and thither like the wind. They have their owners, however, are periodically collected for sale, and will fetch as much as £10 each, while a cow will go for £3 10s., and the price of a sheep may range from two shillings and sixpence to ten shillings. Inland birds are rare, the commonest being the lark, starling, and raven.

I reached the village of Walls about six in the evening, and found my two friends absent on a sea fishing excursion. On looking round, the hamlet seemed to consist of about forty houses, a post-office, and three or four shops, all of fairly modern build, and scattered round the head of Vaila Sound. There is no hotel, but several houses can give very good accommodation. We stayed at Farratwat House, and were most comfortable as far as it was possible to make us so; of course we had to forego many of the luxuries of town life, but pleasant surroundings, good sport, and bracing air, more than made amends. Walls is a very good centre for fishing. Some two hundred lochs abounding with brown trout are within walking distance. Our average takes per day would be from fifteen to thirty brace of good-sized fish. A few of the lochs have boats on them, but, generally, the different sheets of water are devoid of boats. This is no great drawback, as deep water can be found on one or more sides of the lake close to shore, and as there are no fringing trees, casts are nowhere difficult. Wading is dangerous. Bottom fishing is next to impossible on account of weeds. In fact it was our experience that the bait we took was practically useless, so we confined ourselves to the fly - and it may be stated here for the encouragement of the amateur fly-fisherman., that if he only possesses sufficient skill to land a fly on the water, his chances of a heavy basket are almost equal to those of the expert. An 11 ft. or 12 ft. greenheart is the best for the lochs, but on the voes, where sea trout abound running up to 7lb. or 8lb., a two-handed 14 - 18 ft. is required. Boats and men can be had on all the voes. The sport is most enjoyable, as the fish are every bit equal to salmon for game. We were out two or three days and got about twenty brace, some of which we brought home. They are an excellent fish for the table. It is necessary to obtain the permission of about two gentlemen for loch-fishing - Mr. Grierson, of Lerwick, and Mr. Scott, of Melville - which is never denied. Fishing on the voes is all free. Those who would like to combine shooting with fishing should go in September, as the close season ends with August. The voes abound with all manner of fowl, from the black cormorant to every description of duck. Seals and herring whales add variety to these charming nooks of the sea. Inland are wild duck, plover, and snipe. There are no grouse or partridges, but a few rabbits. The weather in summer is enjoyable. The air is too humid ever to be very clear in the day, but the ozone makes up for it in giving appetite and sleep. In the middle of summer there is no real night, as the district borders the land of the midnight sun. The expense of such a holiday as we took is well covered by £1 a day including everything, so that one might say three weeks for £20, double journey included.

CHAPTER 9

Sir Edward Grey on Shetland

Sir Edward Grey is, perhaps, best remembered today for his ominous remark to the editor of the *Westminster Gazette* on 3rd August 1914 at the outbreak of the First World War, 'The lamps are going out all over Europe; we shall not see them lit again in our life-time'. The following day the British Cabinet voted to declare war. Grey hated war with a passion and, as Britain's longest-serving Foreign Secretary (1905-1916), he felt that he had failed by not preventing it. According to G. M. Trevelyan, the distinguished historian and biographer of Sir Edward Grey, 'No pacifist realized more clearly than he the irreparable damage to civilization that must ensue from war under modern conditions . . . It was all against the grain to him, sheer waste, contrary to the slow peace and growth of nature that was his soul's life.'

War and politics aside, what is less well-known about Sir Edward Grey, especially to non-anglers, is that he was a very keen angler and naturalist who wrote one of the most delightful books on angling ever written, simply entitled *Fly Fishing* (1899). An enlarged edition containing two additional chapters was published in 1930 and has rarely been out of print ever since. Grey was also a keen bird-watcher whose book, *The Charm of Birds,* was published in 1927 and is a volume much loved by ornithologists. Towards the end of the nineteenth and beginning of the twentieth century Sir Edward Grey and his wife, Lady Grey, visited Shetland on a number of occasions where he fished for sea trout and, no doubt, closely observed the diverse bird life.

Sir Edward Grey at Fallodon.

Sir Edward Grey was the eldest of the seven children of Colonel George Henry Grey and Harriet Jane Pearson. His grandfather Sir George Grey, Second Baronet of Fallodon was a prominent Liberal politician. Edward Grey was born in London on the 25th of April, 1862, the only one of his six brothers and sisters not to be born at the family seat of Fallodon in Northumbria. However, Fallodon was his home from childhood to his death and his ashes lay buried in its garden. At the age of nine he was sent to prep school near Northallerton and two years later he was sent to a larger and better school, Temple Grove, East Sheen, which he attended from 1873 to 1876. During his second year, on the 11th of December, 1874, his father passed away and he came under the influence of his grandfather Sir George Grey who acted as surrogate father to his seven grandchildren.

It was during his childhood years in Northumbria that he developed his love of fishing, as he himself relates in *Fly Fishing* (1899):

> *I remember very well being seized with a desire to fish. I was about seven years old, and was riding on a Shetland pony by the side of a very small burn. A mill was working higher up the stream, and the water was full of life and agitation, caused by the opening of the sluice of the mill pond above. I had seen small trout caught in the burn before, but now, for the first time and suddenly, came an overpowering desire to fish, which gave no rest till some very primitive tackle was given me. With this and some worms, many afternoons were spent in vain.*

However, it was not long before he became proficient in catching small burn trout ranging from four to six ounces. Eventually, he graduated to using multi-hooked Stewart or Pennell tackle and managed to catch a fresh run sea trout of 3lb from a local burn which flowed into the sea.

In 1876, aged fourteen, Grey was sent to Winchester and it was there that he learnt to fish the dry fly for the wary Itchen brown trout. When he arrived at Winchester in September 1876 there was only about a fortnight left before the close of the trout fishing season and Grey did not wet a line in its waters until the following spring:

> *So on the opening day of the season, at the beginning of March, I hurried as soon as possible into the water meadows. Surely no one ever fished the Itchen with greater anticipation and with less chance of success. I must have been a strange uncomfortable figure, in a large white straw hat, a black coat, trousers and thin ungreased boots, splashing in the meadow (which was under water at the time), and stumbling in haste into the un-familiar maze of runnels and water cuts. The real obstacle was that I knew nothing, and had heard nothing of the dry fly, and was setting to work with a whippy double-handed rod of some thirteen feet in length, and three flies, probably a March Brown, a Coch-y-bondhu and a Greenwell's Glory, which I generally used in those days.*

His first clumsy attempts proved fruitless but, eventually, after observing local anglers at work, he had his first success and caught a reasonable sized trout of a little over a pound - the only one he caught during the whole of that first season! The following season he managed thirteen trout, in 1879 thirty-two, and in his final year at Winchester he managed seventy-six.

In the autumn of 1880 Grey went up to Balliol College, Oxford to read Literae Humaniores (Classics). He proved to be an indolent student and only achieved a Second in Honour Moderations. In 1882 his grandfather died and Grey inherited a baronet's title, the Fallodon estate of around 2,000 acres, and a private income. On returning to Oxford he switched from Classics to Jurisprudence but became even less inclined to academic study, although he did excel at real tennis and became university champion. In January 1884 he was sent down for 'incorrigible idleness' but was allowed to return to sit his exams and achieved Third Class honours.

Following his time at Oxford, he entered official life in London and was elected Liberal M.P. for Berwick-upon-Tweed in November 1885, thus becoming, aged twenty-three, the youngest M.P. in the House of Commons. Later that year he married Dorothy Widdrington. Grey retained his seat in the 1892 election and was made Under-Secretary of State for Foreign Affairs by Gladstone.

During this period of his life he continued to fish and a note in the *Edinburgh Evening News* of 1st September, 1896 stated that Sir Edward and Lady Grey were then in Shetland and a similar snippet in the *Shetland Times* of 4th March, 1899 stated that he had spent the last two summers at Lunna House, which he had leased for the fishing. The *Shetland Times* of 1st September, 1900 announced 'Sir Edward Grey will visit Shetland next week, and spend a week at Lunna House with St Clair Stobart Esq., who has again leased Lunna House for the autumn'.

During his holidays in Shetland Grey spent his time fishing for sea trout and in his book *Fly Fishing* he devoted a large part of his chapter on sea trout fishing to his experiences on Shetland.

Lunna House on Shetland.

Lunna House, where he stayed, is situated in the north-east of mainland Shetland near Vidlin and was built on the site of a medieval 'Haa' (Manor House), which in turn was built on the site of a Viking longhouse. The house was originally built around 1660 but was extended in the eighteenth century and again between 1893 and 1910 when the final wing was added. During the Second World War the house was requisitioned by the Special Operations Executive and became the original headquarters of 'The Shetland Bus' Norwegian Resistance Movement before relocating to Scalloway. Grey describes the area thus:

> *It was on a property of some 12,000 acres remote from all hotels, and so indented by small and large voes that the actual coast line was about thirty miles, all wild and rocky. There were innumerable lochs, but the overflow of most of them fell into the sea over some precipice, which no fish could ascend, and the sea trout lochs were practically only two in number. Two burns flowed from these lochs to the sea, and joined each other about a mile from their common mouth.*

It appears that in Grey's day very little angling for sea trout was carried out in the area and he was delighted by the prospect of exploring the possibilities of both salt and fresh water. His first sight of the burn was a little disappointing. It was very low and had so little water that it seemed as if no fish would be able to ascend it. However, ascend it they did and eagerly took the fly and, as a result, he landed a number of fish up to two pounds' weight. When a spate came he found a number of fresh-run fish in its pools willing to rise to the fly in all heights of water.

He found the loch fishing less satisfactory and was very wary about wading in the peaty water:

After wading a few steps into the water, one's feet sank into the soft bottom, masses of bubbles came up with a wallowing sound, and one had an impression of standing upon a yielding surface, which would collapse suddenly and let one down into an abyss. There was no firm ground in the lochs whatever, but we became used to the alarming feel of the soft peat and to the bubbles, and in time lost our fear, though we observed a certain caution to the end.

He also found the lochs became thick with tiny particles after a night of wind or rain, which made the fish disinclined to rise.

He much preferred fishing for sea trout in the voes in salt water. One voe, in particular, looked promising and local crofters reported seeing fish jumping. One day Grey walked over to try his luck:

I seldom spent a more wretched and hopeless morning. There was no sign of sea trout, and to be wading amongst seaweed, throwing small flies in common salt water with a split cane rod, seemed perfectly foolish and mad . . . Discomfort was added to hopelessness, for my mackintosh had been forgotten, and some miles of rough peat hags and bogs were between me and the house: the morning had been fine, but about ten o'clock a series of cold, pitiless storms began, which lashed the voe with wind and heavy rain. This would not have been intolerable, if it had not been for the long waders, without which the deep water of the voe could not be reached; but to stand in heavy rain with waders nearly up to the arm-pits, and without an overcoat, is to turn oneself into a receptacle for collecting fresh water.

I feel sure that many Shetland anglers must have experienced similar conditions! Eventually, after flogging the water for hours in vain, he decided to return to the house but, as he was leaving, he heard a splash and saw where a fish had jumped - the first fish he had seen all day. He went straight to the spot and almost immediately caught a sea trout and in the few remaining hours landed sixteen pounds' weight of fish on the fly. The largest fish of the day was just under three pounds but he lost two good fish in the seaweed and saw some much larger.

With regard to flies, Grey had reached the conclusion that most anglers carry around too many fancy flies and he believed in using a few patterns of proven merit and persisting with them. For sea trout he relied on four patterns dressed in a range of sizes: Soldier Palmer, Woodcock and Yellow, a Black and Orange Spider and a Black and Red Hackle fly (see illustration on page 223). His rod of preference was a ten foot six model made of split cane by Hardy of Alnwick.

Following his visits to Shetland between 1896 and 1900, Grey became increasingly involved in international affairs, especially after his appointment as Foreign Secretary in 1905. During the early years of the First World War he was heavily involved in negotiations with foreign powers but in 1916 he resigned from the House of Commons and accepted a peerage as Viscount Grey of Fallodon. In 1919 he was appointed Ambassador to the United States, a post he held until 1920. During this busy period, however, he still found time for fishing and most weekends during the trout fishing season he would escape from London down to the cottage he had built on the Itchen at Itchen Abbas in Hampshire. When time allowed he continued to visit Scotland and fish for salmon on Highland rivers, especially the Cassley which was his favourite.

Sadly, towards the end of the war his eyesight began to deteriorate and by 1918 he was unable to see a small fly floating on the water. When the 1919 season came around he could no longer see fish rising and, as a result, he was forced to give up dry fly fishing. He continued to fish for salmon and to fish the wet fly for trout but eventually he had to give up fishing altogether. Ironically, considering his academic record at Oxford, he was elected Chancellor of the University in 1928, a position he held until his death on the 7th of September, 1933.

Grey was thirty-six and in his prime when he penned the first ten chapters of his book *Fly Fishing*, which was published in 1899. The last two chapters were added over thirty years later, by which time he was blind, and included in the second edition published in 1930. It is impossible to read his final chapter 'Retrospect' without a tinge of sadness. His book is well worth seeking out and not just for its Shetland content.

CHAPTER 10

Fishing with the Doctor in Shetland

As well as Sir Edward Grey, another distinguished angler who fished in Shetland during the last decade of the nineteenth century was Doctor James Brunton Blaikie, who left an account of his angling and shooting exploits in these remote islands in his charming book *I Go A-Fishing*, first published in 1928. The author was born in 1873 on a farm in the Scottish Borders and, like his near contemporary John Buchan, served his angling apprenticeship fishing the worm on the feeder streams of the Tweed:

> *Before I could use a fly rod, however, I had many delightful days fishing with the worm. I remember my father taking a small cousin and me to a little river some miles away. It had been heavy with rain the day before, and the river was big and brown. Our rods were innocent of reels and we used a single bait hook with a couple of sinkers. We spent the entire day at one pool. The river ran with a strong rush under the bushes opposite, and, at our side there was a grassy bank and a slow stream.*
>
> *I had hardly dropped in my worm when there was a jerk of a bite. I waited and then heaved the trout on the bank. And so it went on for hours.*
>
> *When we had - most reluctantly - to stop, we had got seventy-two trout weighing about 10lb.*

You cannot help but wonder whether such a prolific basket of trout would be taken from a similar river and in similar circumstances today? I doubt it somehow. As well as fishing the worm,

Brunton Blaikie soon became skilled in the art of 'gumping', or tickling trout, as it is more commonly known. Indeed, the present author was no mean practitioner of this devious art in his younger days, but, alas, not in Shetland! On one momentous occasion, when 'gumping' trout on a local burn, the Young Blaikie got more than he bargained for:

> *Another time, when 'gumping', I put my hand down a submerged rat hole. I was violently bitten and sprang to my feet, dragging from the hole a large eel, hanging on to my middle finger, which it had swallowed and bitten almost to the bone. The eel wriggled quickly back into the burn, but I finally caught it. It weighed 2lb - the largest fish I ever got out of the burns at home.*

After qualifying as a doctor at the University of Edinburgh, Brunton Blaikie moved to London where he appears to have specialised in paediatrics and worked at Great Ormond Street Hospital. During his medical career he contributed a number of articles on paediatrics to *The Lancet*, one of the world's oldest medical journals.

Like many anglers, I suspect, his love of fishing helped him to overcome the stresses and strains of a demanding career and a career dealing with sick children and their anxious parents must have been extremely difficult at times. The following quote is taken from the book's Preface:

> *All my life I have been fond of fishing. The prospect of being in possibly beautiful and certainly peaceful surroundings with a rod in my hand has helped to keep me cheerful when the clouds of anxiety and the weight of responsibility and worry have darkened the horizon and pressed on my spirits.*

Brunton Blaikie worked hard and played hard and, following on from his early attempts at catching trout on the Tweed's feeder streams, he fished extensively for salmon, trout and sea

Dr Brunton Blaikie (left) with his angling companion and a fine catch of trout.

trout throughout Scotland and abroad. In Scotland his angling expeditions took him from the waters of the Tweed to the Western Isles and Shetland and abroad he fished in Norway and Sweden.

With regard to fishing in Shetland he tells us in his book that some thirty years ago (the 1890s) he went up to Walls for three successive years. He was impressed with how little it cost:

> *The fishing was free, we had most comfortable rooms, a bathroom, four-course dinner, excellent breakfast, and our bill - with no extras - for food and accommodation was 25s. a week each!*

During his time on Shetland he managed to catch brown trout up to 2lb 14oz in weight and sea trout to nearly 4lb. He particularly enjoyed fishing the voes for sea-trout and, on one occasion, his angling companion, whom he does not name, hooked something he hadn't bargained for:

> *We had finished fishing for the day, and were sitting outside the house after an excellent dinner, smoking our pipes. The light was fading, when we saw a large sea-trout jump in the voe. We had never fished in this particular voe and were unaware of any sea-trout being in it, so we at once got our rods and waded out - we scorned waders - and began to fish. After about ten minutes without a rise, I tired of it and stopped. As I was wading ashore my friend's flies fouled a piece of seaweed and by jerking his rod, so that the reel screamed, he tried to make me think he had hooked a fish. As he did so there was a great splash, and his line began to slowly sail out. From the size of the splash we concluded he must have hooked a very big sea-trout, and yet it would not take out any line, but contented itself by swimming round and round and occasionally splashing. By this time it was too dark to see the fish, but I eventually got my net under it. I well remember our intense disappointment when we found it was a plaice weighing 2lb.*

On another occasion Brunton Blaikie, while fishing another voe, had the unusual distinction of catching three different species of fish on the same cast. A sea trout of around 1lb took the tail fly, a haddock of about ¼ lb took the fly on the middle dropper while an immature lythe of about two ounces took the fly on the top dropper!

Most anglers, myself included, at some time or other have experienced a scenario where one angler catches most of the fish while another angler fishing in close proximity and using the same tactics catches nothing. Such an occasion occurred when Brunton Blaikie was fishing a Shetland voe from a boat:

> *One day - we were a party of four - we were in two boats on the voe. It was a cloudless afternoon and hardly a ripple stirred the surface of the water. To fish seemed hopeless and we sat smoking and dozing in our boats. Presently I saw a sea-trout jump some 300 yards away, at a place where there was no burn, and where we never fished. We rowed down and anchored our boat by dropping over the side a large stone fastened to a rope. We at once began rising and hooking trout. When the men in the other boat saw this they came and anchored close to us, but although we continued to catch fish they could get nothing. I see from my notes that we actually got twenty good sea-trout whilst they got only two.*

A day or two later, when the tide was out, he rowed down the voe to see if he could find an explanation for this occurrence. He discovered that he and his boat-fishing companion had anchored over a narrow strip of sand, while the other boat had anchored over a tall forest of seaweed. The sea trout had all collected on the sandy strip.

On one occasion, towards the end of September, Brunton Blaikie and a number of companions decided to do a spot of shooting for snipe and wild duck. Two young local lads, equipped with a rope to which tin cans containing pebbles were attached, acted as beaters. After bagging a number of snipe, Brunton Blaikie winged a bird which flew off into a bog. He went off in hot pursuit to retrieve it and suddenly went right through the surface of the bog up to his middle. The two young beaters found this highly amusing:

But to me it was no laughing matter. I know of no more uncomfortable sensation than to feel yourself slowly sinking into unplumbed depths of mud, whilst the bright green of the treacherous surface sways up and down. As far as I was able I lay back, the while I took the cartridges from my gun. Then one of my friends grasped the barrels whilst I hung on to the stock. At first it seemed as if he, too, would sink through. But I felt I was no longer sinking, and, finally a couple of natives grasped my friend and amongst them hauled me to safety.

Brunton Blaikie was fortunate but his experience does highlight the danger of straying into unfamiliar territory. The angler who goes off the beaten track in Shetland in search of a remote loch needs to take extra care and provide himself with a good map, compass and extra provisions, as well as informing someone of where he is going and the time he is likely to be back.

As well as fishing this remote archipelago, Brunton Blaikie frequently fished nearer to his home in London. He was an expert with the dry fly and he fished a number of southern chalkstreams, including the Bourne with his friend Harry Plunket Greene. The Piddle in Dorset was one of his favourite streams. He passed away in February 1937, aged sixty-four. However, he has left behind a delightful book recounting his angling experiences in both Shetland and elsewhere.

CHAPTER 11

Sir George Aston on Shetland

Sir George Grey Aston was a distinguished Royal Marine officer who rose to the rank of Brigadier-General and served briefly in the First World War. During his lifetime he wrote a number of books on military matters as well as a couple of books on angling, *Mostly About Trout*, published in 1921 and *Letters to Young Flyfishers*, published in 1926.

Sir George Aston came from a military background. He was born in Cape Colony in Southern Africa on the 2nd of December, 1861, the youngest son of Lieutenant-Colonel Henry Aston, Indian Army (retired). His mother, Katherine, was the daughter of the Rev. Abraham Faure of the Cape of Good Hope. After education at Westminster School and the Royal Naval College, Greenwich, he joined the Royal Marine Artillery in 1879. His first posting was to the Mediterranean Fleet and he saw active service ashore in the Sudan in 1884. He then served with the Admiralty in foreign intelligence before passing Staff College, Camberley in 1891. After a period as intelligence officer (1892-1895) again with the Mediterranean Fleet, he was appointed Professor of Fortifications at the Royal Naval College (1896-1899). It was during this period of his life that Aston ventured up to Shetland to fish for sea trout.

We learn from his book, *Mostly About Trout* (1921), that he had been fascinated by fish since his early childhood. One of his earliest recollections is of a long sea-voyage and spending a day at anchor on St Helena in the South Atlantic, where he made his first clumsy and unusual attempt at catching fish:

> *It was a baking-hot day, the sun blistering the pitch caulking between the deck-planks; but lying on those warm planks, I could see the calm sea through the hawse-pipe and jelly-fish innumerable floating in the clear water. No one could get me away from that hawse-pipe. I had secured a reel of cotton and a bent pin, baited with gingerbread biscuit, warmed in a hot little palm and softened by the sea air. Nothing would persuade me that the morsels would not be as succulent to the taste of a jelly-fish as they were to my own: I cherished that illusion during the whole time we were at anchor.*

I have read hundreds of accounts of anglers' first attempts at catching fish, including some involving a cotton reel and bent pin, but none with gingerbread as bait and jelly-fish as the quarry! Fortunately, a later attempt in a rock-pool in South Devon proved more satisfactory and he managed to catch 'an evil and bloated-looking little fish' on a leathery morsel of limpet. At the age of thirteen he graduated to fly fishing and managed to catch his first trout. He was spending the summer holidays with an uncle in Glamorganshire whom he describes as 'a fine old sportsman'. After taking casting lessons from the gardener's boy who seems to have been a skilled poacher, his uncle lent him a ten-foot greenheart fly rod made by Farlow and accompanied him to the river Ewenny:

> *I can see myself now, desperately proud of a huge fishing-basket strapped over my shoulder and containing a packet of sandwiches, a slice of cake, an old leather flask fitted with a cup and filled with weak sherry and water, and, greatest joy of all, an old fly-book, with parchment pages and covers of Russia leather, smelling deliciously.*

I cannot imagine many young anglers nowadays being sent out to fish with a flask full of sherry, no matter how weak. How times change! With his uncle's help he managed to attach three flies to a gut cast which he had remembered to soak before setting out.

His reel was an ancient multiplier furnished with an old-fashioned plaited silk and hair line. With the wind in his favour, he managed to put a reasonable line out on the water and then:

> But there is no language to describe the thrill of it. Something had hold of one of the flies under the water, and that something was giving wriggling tugs. The rod throbbed deliciously to the very butt; through the butt and through my wrist and arm those throbbings passed through nerve and brain, seemingly to my very soul. Two or three seconds in doubt what to do, and then the memory of a word recalled from a book on fly-fishing, the word 'strike' - a word that has cost many young fishers many fish and much expensive tackle. I 'struck', and far behind me on the long grass fringing the mill-pool lay, struggling, a four-ounce trout. There had never been such a trout. Its head was small, its body of a fatness adorable, gleaming like copper above and like gold below. Its spots were scarlet, of the scarlet of poppies, rimmed with white and set off with other spots of black. It was my very own.

I can well remember catching my very first trout on fly but I don't think I could have described its beauty so eloquently. That first trout had taken a fly dressed with a yellowish-green body and soft grey hackle. That same day the trout were on the feed and Aston went on to catch six and a half pounds' weight of sturdy little trout from four to six ounces, with one fish weighing between ten and twelve ounces. On one occasion he had two fish on at the same time. In over fifty years of fly fishing he claimed never to have known a day like it.

After such a wonderful beginning it is not surprising that Aston became a life-long devotee of fly fishing and he soon graduated to fly fishing for sea trout and salmon. He believed there was something special about the play of a sea trout, once hooked, that you get in no other form of fishing with the fly. His first experience of sea trout fishing was on a loch on the west coast of Scotland, where he fished from a boat:

> *At first I found casting from a boat with a long rod rather awkward, but soon got into it, and landed, or rather 'boated', thirteen sea trout, averaging two pounds. It was one of those days, like my first with brown trout, when they attached themselves without any skill on my part, and, obviously purely through luck, I caught several more than my highly skilled host.*

However, he was not particularly impressed by his first encounter with sea trout since he was using a long rod of 13 or 14 feet and 'there really seemed to be no reason why a fish should ever be lost when once hooked on such tackle'.

He was much more impressed with the sea trout in the salt water of a Shetland voe, which were in the full vigour of their life. He visited Shetland in the long, hot summer of 1898 and was glad of a break from a demanding work schedule. He boarded a ship on the Thames bound for Aberdeen and from there he changed to a smaller vessel bound for the Orkneys and Shetland. He was accompanied on his visit by the man who was to become the first Commander-in-Chief of our sea forces in the First World War, who appears to have been a novice fly fisher. Aston had been lured to Shetland by a hotel advertisement holding out hopes of an average of thirty pounds' weight of sea trout in a day, taken on the fly, in lochs within range of the hotel. Although Aston does not mention the hotel by name it may well have been the Clousta Hotel at Bixter (see advert opposite), which opened in August 1895 and burnt down in October 1907. It seems that the hotel owner may have stretched the truth a little since the total weight taken by 'the most fortunate fisher at that hotel in five weeks was about fifty pounds'. Some of these fish, it transpires, were not captured on fly but by trailing a spinning-bait in the voes.

At Lerwick the 'simmer dim' made an impression on him as he found he could read a letter in his hotel room at 11.30pm. The following day Aston and his companion were driven the twenty miles by post-cart to their hotel, where they were placed on the fishing roster. It appears that one of the guests at the hotel

> # CLOUSTA HOTEL
> ## BIXTER, SHETLAND
>
> CHARMINGLY Situated at the Head of the beautiful land-locked Voe of Clousta. Shooting over 20,000 acres ; also, Seal Shooting on the coast in the immediate vicinity. Fishing for Brown Trout and Sea Trout in 18 lochs ; 20 to 30 lbs. Brown Trout, and 25 to 35 lbs. of Sea Trout for Day's Fishing.
>
> ### GOOD BOATING, BATHING, & SEA FISHING
>
> *ROUTE*—ABERDEEN to LERWICK or WALLS, thence drive. Arrangements have been made with Messrs. GANSON BROTHERS, Coach Hirers and Livery Stables (near Lerwick), to run a Coach to Clousta in connection with the Mail Steamers arriving in Lerwick, by which Visitors will be taken to the Hotel at a charge of 5s. each, exclusive of luggage.
>
> Telegraph and Post Office, 4 miles
>
> TERMS :—£3 per week for Fishers, except during August, September, and October, when the charge will be £3 : 6s. 10s. per day, except during August, September, and October, when charge will be 11s.
> Non-Fishers £2 : 15s. per week, or 8s. 6d. per day.
> Shooting and Fishing Free under those charges. Boats on all the good lochs at 3s. per week.
>
> **SPECIAL TERMS WILL BE MADE FOR FAMILIES**
>
> Visitors for this Hotel coming to Lerwick are recommended to the Grand Hotel there, the Manager of which will give them all further particulars in connection with this Hotel they may desire.
>
> For further Particulars apply to J. C. GRIERSON, Solicitor, Lerwick, Secretary to the Proprietors.

was a lady skilled in the art of fly dressing, whose flies (Teal and Red, Teal and Magenta, Grouse and Orange, and Zulu) were in great demand. After engaging the services of a gillie, they commenced fishing on one of the voes. Aston at this point gives the reader an important piece of advice:

> *It is essential, when fly-fishing in salt water, to use eyed flies. A little spot of brown rust forms just where the gut touches the hook, and very soon the fly drops off, if exposed to the least strain; with eyed hooks you can get over the resultant danger of a break by re-tying the fly to the gut, cutting off half an inch thereof every time you do it, which should be at least every quarter of an hour.*

Fortunately, the sea trout angler of today no longer has such problems!

After fishing for several hours without result, they suddenly saw a boil on the surface, close to some rocks and brown seaweed. The gillie turned towards the boat towards the spot and put Aston over the fish. The next thing he knew his reel was screeching and its handle was spinning:

That first rush, tearing line off the reel was terrific. It was comforting to know that there was plenty of 'backing' on the reel, strongly spliced to the end of the silk casting-line, and soon the backing began to show. The fish seemed to be making for the open sea at the mouth of the voe, several miles distant. Then came disaster. I held the rod-butt a little too close to my body. The handle of the reel, still spinning madly, just touched my waistcoat. It felt like only a little flick, but with a big sea trout still in the momentum of his first rush and a long and heavy line towed behind, keeping the fine gut as taut as a violin string, it was enough. I reeled in sadly, put a fresh point and fly on the cast, and sat for some moments silent, in blank despair, not daring to glance towards the gillie.

I suspect that most anglers reading that account of a lost fish will have similar stories to tell of the one that got away and will empathise with the writer's feeling of despair. Fortunately, events made a turn for the better and Aston spotted another boil well out in the little bay. Again, the gillie put the angler on the spot and Aston gives a wonderful account of the fight:

By inconceivable good luck I got that sea trout on the very first cast; he took the dropper fly, deep down in the water, as I was reeling slowly in before gathering up the slack more rapidly with my hand in readiness for another cast. Then came a most glorious tussle, to the accompaniment of a constantly screaming reel. A steady wind-in with fingers lightly touching the handle, very lightly, ready to let go instantly and so save a break, when the check began to screech again with the next mad rush - and there were many, two of them ending in a leap out of the water. That is always a moment of moments. I read once that whether on such occasions you ought to lower the point of your rod to ease the strain or not depended on whether the fish jumped head away from you or head towards you. There was no rule about what to do if he jumped across the line of direction between rod and fish. All I know is that I always lower the rod, instinctively, if a fish jumps, and I never remember having lost one thereby, so these were the tactics pursued with that Shetland trout.

When the mad rushes were over, there came a heavy strain on the fine gut, the fish playing very deep in water. Then came short rushes, the spray spouting in a sort of V on the surface where the line cut its way through the sea. Then a steady but severe strain, the rod bending to it. The gillie backed me slowly to the fish just at the right pace to enable me to reel in the line, and soon we could see the fish astern of us, swimming upright and apparently not the least incommoded by the full power of the rod. I shall never forget the view of his broad, greyish back, or the feeling of helplessness, and of wonder whether I should ever get him into the boat or whether the usual spot of rust was rotting through the fine gut-point. A quarter of an hour had passed away, seeming like a week. I will cut short the remainder of the tale, only adding that, in the end, the fish swam past the boat still upright and apparently still full of fight; the gillie hastily shipped his oar, and scooped him out just as I shouted to prevent him from attempting so mad a venture. He was a short fish, broad and very deep, and he weighed just over 4½lb.

Although he caught a number of other sea trout during his sojourn in Shetland, this encounter was by far his most memorable and left a deep impression on him, as this account written twenty-three years later demonstrates. He also had the satisfaction of seeing his fish displayed on a plate in the hall of the hotel that evening when all the other angling guests had blanked. On several days he caught more sea trout and, on one occasion, he took eight in half an hour, but none could match the 4½-pounder. The fish was actually taken on a rather non-descript fly, which had a body made of dull silver twist and a short, soft, smoky-grey hackle. Sadly, Sir George Aston never returned to Shetland, although he continued to fish for trout on the chalk streams, for salmon in Scotland and grayling in Wales. He also fished abroad for trout in South Africa and Albania.

During the South African War (1899-1902), Aston served in logistics and as an intelligence officer, although ill health forced him to return home in 1900. Following a period as an instructor at the Staff College (1904-1907), Aston was again posted to South Africa, this time with the rank of brigadier-general (1908-1912). In 1909, he married Dorothy Ellen Wilson, daughter of Vice-Admiral William Wilson, and they had three sons and two daughters. At the start of the First World War he served on the Admiralty war staff before being dispatched with a brigade of Royal Marines to Ostend to create a diversion to cover Belgian movements. Sadly, his health deteriorated and in 1917 he retired from military service. During the last twenty years of his life he turned his attention to military journalism and wrote a number of books on military themes, as well as his two books on fishing. He died on the 2nd of December, 1938, aged seventy-seven.

CHAPTER 12

Trout Fishing in Shetland by 'Black-Beetle'

This article on trout fishing in Shetland appeared in the Fishing Gazette *of 12th July, 1902. The article was written under the nom de plume of 'Black-Beetle'. Unfortunately, in spite of extensive research, I have been unable to find the real identity of Black-Beetle.*

From the description given in some old books, one is apt to form a wrong idea of what the Shetland Islands are really like. When the name occurs, the imaginary picture crops up in the mind of a group of barren isles and rocks, tenanted by a few hardy ponies, sheep, and sea-fowl, with a fisher's hut here and there. These, together with stormy seas, rocks split by storms, and honeycombed by caves, are all to be found along with the advantages to be had. The sunnier side of the picture is seldom taken notice of. To see Lerwick in the fishing season with all its stir and bustle would be a surprise to many coming for the first time. Passenger steamers coming into the roadstead have to proceed very cautiously owing to the number of fishing craft from all parts of the kingdom. Smacks, luggers, trawlers, steam netters, Dutch luggers, and one or two small gunboats, to protect the fishing, all block the way in the roadstead.

On shore, common herring fishers and gutters from everywhere are met. Great numbers of Dutchmen are to be seen swaggering along in stylish-looking knickerbockers about a yard wide. They usually wear sabots, which make a regular clatter on the stone pavements of the narrow streets. Lerwick is the first port that steamers call at when taking the east side of the islands, and one has often to make a stay of a day or two to get the local steamer to the other parts, unless they hire a trap. Hotel accommodation is to be had here to suit all classes, and private parties cater for those who wish to make a short stay. Nothing is to be had to entice the angler to stay long here, although there are one or two good lochs within driving distance, and whiting, flounders, and haddock are still to be found in small quantities. Trawling within the limit has destroyed the chances of getting anything like decent sea-fishing in the Shetlands, unless one is content with coalfish or saithe.

The islands of Mainland, Yell, Unst and Fetlar are the four largest of the group, and in all these good loch and sea-trout fishing is to be had. All the islands contain a large number of lochs and a few fishable burns. Many of these lochs are tidal, and nearly all are connected with the sea by small burns. The sea itself in the many voes, as the large inlets are called, holds sea-trout nearly all the year round. In it I have caught sea-trout from March until October, and thereby had a splendid chance of seeing them in all their stages, as well as having a splendid opportunity of observing their habits and what they fed on in salt water.

To give the angler some idea of their food, I may state that the principal items found in them were sand-eels, shrimps, and sand-hoppers, small shellfish, various marine worms, and the fry of herrings, haddock, and coalfish. This is practically the same as what any sea-fish would eat, and I found that the place where the fish were caught had an influence on the kind of food in their stomachs. Sand-eels and shrimps were generally found in those taken in sandy places, between the rocks and weed, and these two different kinds of creatures were seemingly the principal food all the season, as these were found in the trout on more occasions than anything else. My best fish were also taken on artificial sand-eels about three inches long, and on shrimps of from one to one and a half inches in length.

The sea-trout of Shetland are magnificent in point of size and quality, while their sporting propensities exceed those of salmon of equal weight. This year I saw a specimen of 12lb netted in a voe, and many others of 6lb and 7lb apiece. These heavy fish are very seldom taken by rod and line, however, but the angler cannot complain when he gets fish of 4lb and 5lb. Two-pounders are common, and there is generally a quantity of finnock, herling, or whitlings as well. These latter (the young of the sea-trout) are generally included along with and mentioned as sea-trout in the angling reports here - not with any intention to delude, but through ignorance, as the natives know them by no other name than sea-trout. These fish are to be found in salt water at all times between March and October and perhaps longer, as I only mention this time as being when I have caught them myself. Sea-trout are very seldom taken in the sea to my knowledge unless in the Orkneys, Shetlands, and some parts of the Hebrides. They rise to the fly with freedom and eagerness in the sea and seem to have a voracious appetite at all times. A common and perhaps the lure to which the majority of sea-trout succumb is the common earth-worm. This kills well in fresh-water, and is moreover almost a 'sure thing' in the sea. The method of fishing it in salt-water differs from the general way employed in fresh-water. A light grilse rod of fifteen feet is the best for sea-trouting in this style. Well scoured and toughened earth-worms of four to six inches long are best, and these should be put on a Stewart tackle made of reliable gut and No 8 rustless sneck hooks. Anything smaller in the way of hooks will cause grief and disappointment as the fish have often to be 'held' to prevent them from making into the immense clumps of sea-weed found all round the coasts. Anyone attempting to hold a three or four-pounder with a smaller hook than that named would have small chances of success, and equally small chances if they allowed the fish to get among the weeds. One kind termed 'Lucky Lines' by the Shetlanders are a particular nuisance. These are long, trailing, round stemmed weeds often ten and twelve feet in length. When the tide is up all is well, but as soon as it ebbs the heads appear, then more and more of the weed floats on the surface to annoy the angler. Grilse and light salmon casts may be used, even in bright weather, as the trout are not particularly gut shy. Finer tackle is better, but it cannot be used with safety on account of the weeds. The worm should be cast out and wrought slowly through the water like a salmon fly. No shot or sinkers of any kind should be used, as the trout take the lure best when used near the surface and when some motion is given to it.

Mr. E. M. Tod's method of spinning the worm answers admirably, and I have had good baskets by using this plan. An 'Archer Spinner' with the usual hooks taken off and a Stewart tackle substituted, makes a good tackle for this style of fishing. Sea-trout must mistake this bait for a sand-eel or some other lively marine creature. They will also take the worm off the bottom, but it answers best when kept floating about or moving not far from the surface. Deadly as this style is, as good sport, if not better, may be obtained by using a small imitation of the sand-eel. Most of the imitation sand-eels used are too stiff and hard in the water, and have no more individual movement about them than what it would be possible to impart to a poker. This is a drawback to the killing properties of these artificials, and when these baits are selected care should be taken to see that they are, to a certain extent, pliable and not too stiff. These are usually fished alone, or they can be fixed to the point of a cast and fished in conjunction with one or more flies. Natural sand-eels are the best when they are to be obtained. Shetland fishermen know the value of this bait for all kinds of sea-fish, and at times are able to procure them for anglers. Sand-eels can be fished on a Stewart tackle, an Archer Spinner, or on special tackles made for the purpose. Small shrimps are also good baits, and either natural or artificial may be used. The type of cast I prefer for sea-trout fishing in the sea is made up thus: I fix on an artificial sand-eel to the point, then an artificial shrimp, and lastly a Soldier Palmer. All the usual lures used in the north of Scotland for sea-trout do well, particularly the demons or terrors.

No angler coming to Shetland should fail to bring a dozen or two of these. Have them made in a variety of sizes, dressed with very light badger hackles. The usual patterns sold have the silver laid on too sparingly. A foundation should first be made of white floss, and the silver should be wrapped on over this. These are really an imitation of the sand-eel, and when properly made are very deadly. Dandies, Tubes and Silver Devons kill well, as do small salmon flies dressed on irons about the size of No 6 Limericks.

Many anglers coming up to Shetland will think this large for sea-trout, but they will find a fly of this size answers better than one smaller. The best flies are those with silver-tinselled bodies, such as the Silver Doctor and Silver Grey. Jock Scott, Popham, and Blue Charm will take fish also. All flies brought here should be dressed with untarnishable tinsels. Salt spray and peat fumes are common in Shetland, and these tarnish and corrode certain metals very soon. Flies and other silvered baits should be carefully wrapped in tissue or silk paper, and kept in an air-tight case, if possible. The usual type of sea-trout flies will kill, but the following have all been proved: Soldier, or Red Palmer, Red and Teal, Butcher, Peacock, or Alexandra, Jungle Cock, Orange Bumble, Green Mantle, and Teal and Green. The teal-winged flies named should be dressed with broad silver tinsel. Devon Minnows and Phantoms from 1½ inches to 2½ inches are very good. The Phantoms are better than Devons in weedy places, as they do not sink so deeply as the metal baits. Waders or fishing trousers are almost a necessity unless one intends fishing by boat. It is no doubt superfluous to warn sensible persons wading in strange waters to do so with extreme caution as there are so many ways by which one may be deceived by the depth. In many parts of Shetland the shingle and stones are very slippery and slope into deep water where strong currents run. One with observant eyes can see this danger, but in certain lochs, and by the side of some burns where the ground is boggy, there are mud-holes more treacherous than quicksand. These places are often dangerous to experienced bog-trotters, so that the angler should proceed with caution and wade where he is able to see stones and gravel only. A small telescopic gaff is much to be preferred to a landing net where the larger fish are found. The small ones of a pound or so can be played out and cautiously drawn on shore, or lifted into the boat by the rod, and anything heavier can easily be gaffed by a practised hand. If a net is preferred, let it be of the size used for landing grilse or pike as the ordinary trouting nets are not sufficiently large.

Tidal lochs, voes, or estuaries, and sandy or gravelly beaches are where the sea-trout are usually found when not in freshwater. If burns enter these the chances are better, but I have caught sea-trout over a mile away from the mouth of a burn. These fish enter the burns and fresh-water lochs generally about the beginning of July, and continue to run until well on in November. There is also a run of finnock or whitling in the spring. The spring fish run from ¼lb to ¾lb, but are often got 1½lb in weight. They are very sportive and free takers, remaining bright and silver for a much longer period than those that come in the summer and autumn. The majority of burns in Shetland are very small, but some of them widen out into really good pools for fly fishing. A rod of ten and a half feet is long enough to fish them. There is nothing in the manner of trees and bushes to impede the casting of a beginner here. The yellow trout caught in the burns are for the most part small, evil-looking fellows of a very decided brunette type. These persist in hanging on to flies or anything in the way of bait that is put into the stream, and sea-trout fry are equally bad for this. If the angler wants good yellow trout he will find them in the lochs. The most of these contain splendid trout of good quality. In many favoured localities these loch trout cut almost as pink as sea-trout, and are caught of heavy weight frequently.

The usual natural Duns and Spinners are scarce here, but then there are great numbers of large sedges, daddy-long-legs, cochy-bonddus, and other insects. The best artificials to use for the lochs are Coch-y-bonddu, Red Tag, Zulu, Soldier Palmer, Butcher, March Brown, Green Mantle, Red and Green Teals, Orange Partridge, and Claret and Grouse or Claret and Mallard. Loch flies should be dressed slightly smaller than those for sea-trout, and No 11 Limericks should do for the majority of the lochs in Shetland. Large moths are also taken by trout at night,

> **The Scalloway Hotel**
> Under New Management — SCALLOWAY, SHETLAND — Thoroughly Renovated
>
> For Tourists and Commercial Gentlemen. Nearest Hotel to Steamboat Pier, overlooking beautiful Harbour.
>
> **Grand Sea Trips:** A comfortable Yacht can be hired, on moderate terms, by the day or week, to visit the finest scenery in Shetland; Steamer St. Nicholas from Aberdeen via Stromness calls every Tuesday, and goes along West Side, returning on Wednesday, passing grand Scenery
>
> Waggonette to Lerwick (7 miles) every Day in Summer— 1s. each way
>
> *Visitors are recommended to Wire for Bedrooms, and are assured of every comfort*
>
> C. LENNIE, Proprietor.

especially in the early autumn, and splendid sport may be had during the greater part of the night in midsummer. Light is never really absent when the sky is clear, and one can read small print at midnight. At this time magnificent sunsets are not uncommon, and when the sun sets among the many islands and sounds some pretty effects are seen.

Sea fishing of a kind can be had here at almost any time, but the best time for trout, in my opinion, is June. Sea-trout begin to gather in the voes, and netting operations have scarcely begun, so that the rod gets a chance. Sometimes these fish will not take anything, and when this is the case the angler can safely depend on having bad weather, as sea-trout are easily influenced by a coming change. Many of the inland lochs contain boats. These are of the kind known as Norway skiffs, and which float in very shallow water. This is necessary, as most of the Shetland lochs are shallow, allowing one to wade in for forty or fifty yards in some places. Boats are plentiful on the coast, as nearly every crofter possesses a four oared boat, and this, as well as the services of the crofter himself, may be hired for much less than elsewhere. He is generally an experienced oarsman, but his notions of trouting with rod and line are usually very hazy, being accustomed to netting instead. Private lodgings are to be had at nearly all the calling places of the steamers, and hotel accommodation is to be had at Lerwick, Clousta, Hillswick, Spiggie, and one or two other places. From what acquaintances say, the private lodgings, in many instances, are to be preferred to some of the hotels, as their charges are not exactly in proportion to the treatment guests and their belongings receive. Lodgings should be arranged for beforehand, and these are easily got by an advertisement in the *Shetland News* or *Times*, both of which papers are published in Lerwick. If the poor angler has to fall back on the comforts of a Shetland croft, he may spend his time, especially at night, in catching something else than trout, and a tin of Keating's powder or a shot-gun would then come in handy. If good lodgings and suitable weather are to be had, the angler should both fish and fare well, although angling is a lottery at all times. Shetland is no exception to this rule, but the chances of obtaining good sport are decidedly high when compared with many other places. An angler that often comes here declares that the average take he gets on a small loch in Yell is better than to be got on Loch Leven. Fishing it one evening for about one and a half hours, I got eight trout, weighing 7lb. Guns should also be brought as well as rods, as shooting is generally to be procured. Seals, porpoises, duck, rabbits, curlew, snipe, and plovers are the usual game, and if the angler is fond of the gun, an enjoyable holiday can be spent here. Cartridges loaded with No 1 shot are the best for all round shooting in Shetland, and nothing smaller is much good for sea ducks. Of course this is too large for plovers and snipe, as No 6 or 7 shot is large enough for them. If a fowling-piece only is taken, a few cartridges loaded with ball can be brought for seals and porpoises. Swan shot will kill both of these if they are as near as thirty yards. If a native gillie is engaged, keep him at his work, as many of these are not very enterprising and lazy to the last degree. They look innocent and simple when brought to task, but can easily give the most heathenish Chinese points for duplicity and cuteness.

CHAPTER 13

Fishing with the Professor on Unst

Unst is the most northerly inhabited isle in the Shetland archipelago and is noted for the excellence of its trout and sea trout fishing. Although sea trout numbers have declined during the last thirty years or so, the Unst Angling Club has commenced a programme of restocking with these sporting fish. During the early decades of the twentieth century Unst was a popular destination for visiting anglers in search of first-rate sport amidst the peace and quiet of the island's stunning scenery. Among them was Duncan Fraser, author of *Angling Sketches From a Wayside Inn*, published in 1911, whose book contains a detailed account of his fishing on Unst in the company of a man whom he refers to as the 'Professor'.

Duncan Fraser was a resident of Edinburgh who had the distinction of becoming the first President of the Edinburgh Saturday Angling Club, which arranged fishing outings for its members in and around Edinburgh and the Borders. Unfortunately, Fraser does not tell us when he visited Unst but he was tired of the 'congested state of the free rivers in the south' and wanted to fish for trout and sea trout in the island's quiet and uncrowded waters. After setting sail from Edinburgh, Fraser and the Professor arrived in

Landing from a Shetland loch.

Lerwick at 6am and had to wait three hours before making the ten hour voyage to Unst. During the journey Fraser was impressed by the magnificent coastal scenery and wildlife to be seen from the deck of their steamer. He was particularly taken by the cormorants as they dived into the sea and reappeared twenty seconds later and forty yards away with a sillock in their mouth. After arriving at Baltasound, Fraser and the Professor took up residence at the Queen's Hotel, thankful of a rest after travelling for forty hours.

Their arrival on Unst caused a certain amount of curiosity among the native Shetlanders who were obviously not used to seeing many fly fishermen on the island:

The native Shetlander looks upon the mild enthusiast who crosses the sea to fish for trout as an individual to be tolerated and humoured, it may be, but not to be taken seriously. His tackle and appurtenances are of a piece with the character they assign him. We remember half-a-dozen small boys drawing their frail boat ashore a little above the spot where we were fishing, and after they had looked on for a few minutes the leader gave expression to their thoughts by asking in a somewhat superior tone: "And that's what you fush wi'?" We felt extremely apologetic, but before we got time to explain we happened to strike a good fish and safely land him, whereupon the boys squatted round to have a look at our fly-book. To the question of how they fished they were not very responsive, one of them remarking: "Oh, we fush another wey" - which doubtless is true, if not very lucid. From 'information received', a long pole, with line and worm attached, and worked on the surface of the water as in minnow fishing, is one 'wey'; but set lines and hang nets serve the purpose better, besides requiring less exertion.

Not surprisingly, since it is the largest and one of the most productive lochs on Unst, Fraser and the Professor spent a lot of time fishing the Loch of Cliff, which they preferred to wade rather than fish from a boat. They generally fished for about six hours daily and seldom caught less than thirty nice trout in a day. On their best day they caught forty trout and two sea trout of around a pound each. They were particularly impressed by the peace and tranquillity of their surroundings, far removed from the bustling streets of Edinburgh:

> *In a new country every day is a new experience, brimful of incident and creative of memories. Thus, wading slowly in and out of the bays that give character to the shores of Cliff, we were ofttimes oppressed by the great loneliness of the place. Save for the fitful screaming of a flock of seagulls that hovered over the north end of the loch, there were few sounds to break the stillness. Human beings you saw at rare intervals, and these, from shyness or politeness - probably a mixture of both - gave you a wide berth.*

Such peace and tranquillity is hard to find in today's world and is one of the reasons why Shetland is still such a magnet for the contemplative angler who is less concerned with the size of fish he catches than with the environment in which he catches them.

With regard to flies for fishing on Cliff, they employed a limited variety dressed on small hooks. Their most productive patterns were the Zulu, Coch-y-Bonddu and Governor. Although some anglers on the island fished with bigger flies, Fraser and the Professor found that their small flies out-fished them by two to one.

Loch Watley (Watlee) proved to be another favourite venue during their stay on Unst and they were particularly impressed by its location:

> *Loch Watley had a strong attraction for us, because of its surroundings. Lying in a deep valley on the right, as you wend your way along the cart track between Baltasound and Uyeasound, at first sight it has all the appearance of a Highland loch. This arises from the hills on either side being covered with short heather, plentifully interspersed with crimson heath and wild harebell... Watley was even lonelier than Cliff, for there were*

no boats on it, nor did you hear the far-off sound of the waves breaking against the rocks of Burra Firth. Yet the hush brought a delightful sense of rest and increased power of fancy which idealised common things, and quickened your optimism. It was like fishing in a dream-land . . . Here we could fish alone, and could fish, or sing, or dream as the fancy took us, conscious that no one would be startled save the ponies and peewits.

In such idyllic surroundings they found that the Watley trout rose freely and a basket of two to three dozen fish of between six and twelve ounces was often the result at the end of a day's fishing.

After sampling the delights of Watley, Fraser and the Professor moved on to Bentley (from his description of this loch near Blue Mull Sound, I suspect he is referring to the Loch of Belmont), which they fished only once, owing to its distance from their hotel. However, the occasion proved to be a memorable one and in addition to several fine trout they caught a beautiful fish of almost two pounds in weight. According to Fraser this was the largest 'yellow' (brown) trout they caught during their stay, although they did hook a larger one on Cliff one afternoon:

This latter rose almost at our feet as we were drawing in the line for another cast, and, as trout that hook themselves always do, he made such a frantic fuss about it that it was impossible to bring any strain to bear upon him. Taking advantage of this, he gave two or three porpoise-like wallops, and we were left lamenting.

Two weeks after returning home they received a letter informing them that an 8lb yellow trout had been taken near to the spot where they had hooked their large fish. Such is the lot of fishermen. The fishing is always better before you arrive or after you have left!

One evening, after returning to their hotel after a successful day's fishing for brown trout, they were shown a sight guaranteed to make the heart of any angler race faster:

One evening when we returned with a fellow angler to our hotel, after a pretty successful day with the brown trout, the landlord beckoned to us to come and look in at the door of an outhouse, where truly our eyes were almost dazzled by the display set before us. Lying on a rough slab were eight sea trout, the smallest weighing about two pounds, while the largest touched seven pounds. An Unst acquaintance of the landlord had been fishing from a boat on Burra Firth that day, and this was his catch.

It should come as no surprise that on the following day Fraser and the Professor set off to fish Burra Firth, a distance of six miles from their hotel. Fraser states that it is an interesting walk, but preferably not to be undertaken in waders! They commenced fishing at the spot where the burn from the loch joins the sea. Sea trout were jumping in a tantalising fashion and they started off by fishing a phantom minnow. After casting in vain for over half an hour and only hooking one or two sillock, which were smaller than the actual lure, they decided to fish the fly and tied on a sea trout fly, composed of mallard wing, green wool body ribbed with gold twist complete with brown hackle and red tip. This proved to be the winning formula and in less than two hours nine sea trout were lying in a cosy nest of seaweed on the beach. After putting the fish into their creel, they began fishing up the burn towards the Loch of Cliff.

As they fished up the burn they managed to catch a number of yellow trout and nine finnock (small sea trout). They became a little complacent and missed a fine fish when a voice suddenly exclaimed, "Ah! you've lost that one!" They were somewhat startled and, on looking behind them, they spotted a police officer sitting on top of a sandbank watching them. It transpired that the officer had cycled all the way from Uyeasound to call on a croft in the direction of Flugga. They eventually discovered that two weeks prior to their visit to Burra Firth, a French sloop had been spotted not far from the shore, making mysterious signals. A fishing boat put out from the shore and, on reaching the

French sloop, the two crews exchanged goods. Following the exchange, the French ship put out to sea while the fishing boat returned at speed to the shore. Unfortunately for the crew of the fishing boat they were spotted by a 'spy' with a telescope, who made haste to the Customs House at Baltasound. The policeman was on his way to a local croft to leave a summons for the fishermen to appear at Lerwick on a charge of smuggling. A few days later, after a hard day's fishing at the north end of the Loch of Cliff, Fraser and the Professor were given a lift back in a boat to the south end of the loch. The boatman was unusually talkative but on being asked, "How did the smuggled brandy taste the other day?" he became unusually quiet. Eventually, he answered: "Ah, it was poor stuff; it was brunt."

One hopes that the French cognac on offer that evening in the anglers' hotel in Baltasound was of a better quality and was not 'brunt'. Although Fraser very much enjoyed his fishing holiday on Unst, he was less enamoured of the long sea voyage to and from the island and vowed never to return until the Moray Firth was bridged!

CHAPTER 14

A Sea Trout Courtesy of a Seal

In 1901, a short guide to fishing in the vicinity of the St Magnus Hotel was written and published by C. J. H. Cassels, author of several books on Shetland. A number of years later, in August 1910, the *Scottish Field* carried an article written by Mr Cassels - 'How I Killed a Shetland Sea Trout'. The story of that capture is given below.

It was all on account of a seal. But I anticipate. We had been fishing Spiggie Voe, a beautiful little sea inlet in the south of the Shetland Isles, which is a favourite haunt of sea trout, having connection by means of a short burn with the Loch of Spiggie. Near the mouth of this rivulet the fish could be seen on almost any day during the season 'playing themselves', as a gillie would say, but they were often averse to taking any lure.

And here for the sake of those anglers who are unacquainted with the angling methods adopted on 'the old rock', I may explain that the best sport with *salmo trutta* is frequently obtained in pure salt water. There he is fished for in the voes, especially near the entrance of fresh water, by anglers 'in the know', with fly, minnow, worm, sand eel, etc. When the last-named lure cannot be had, sometimes the silvery part of the belly of a herring is used for trolling instead, and makes an excellent substitute.

To hark back to my story, upon the day in question, a good fishing one, it had come to my knowledge that a number of fine sea trout had been caught in Spiggie Bay. It had further been made known to me that these fish were taken on set lines by the natives. They are terrible poachers, the Shetlanders, where sea trout are concerned. Brown trout they do not trouble themselves much about, except occasionally to procure them for bait when herrings are scarce.

Well, though there were no boats lying in the bay for the use of anglers, there were several in the voe. My gillie and I accordingly, having launched one, rowed the whole length of the latter, round the promontory that faces the little eider-duck haunted island of Colsay, and alongside the beautiful rocky coast of the mainland, a distance in all of about a mile, till eventually we made the bay. After thoroughly searching the water there with different flies for about two hours, and drawing blank, I was just about to change my lure for a minnow, and try a little further from the land, when a seal projected his bullet-like head out of the sea quite near to where I was fishing, and, having taken a short inquisitive look round, disappeared. Thus I was obliged to leave the bay, as of course it would have been useless to fish on after one of the 'phoca' tribe had been angling there.

Nolens volens, therefore, we set out on the return journey, and having got back to our starting place I found the wind was blowing nicely off the land, and decided to try a cast or two on the chances of avoiding the indignity of going ashore with a 'clean' boat. I put on what is known as a 'Demon' or 'Worm-fly'. This lure is made up of three hooks arranged like those on a Stewart tackle. Over these are dressed two black hackles with white fringes extending to more than the length of the hooks. The enticement is a favourite one on tidal and salt waters.

At the third cast, and within only a few yards of the shore, a heavy fish came up 'head and tail', and appeared to have jumped right across the cast and missed the fly. I struck, and found I was into him.

He took out between thirty and forty yards of line, and performed a fine salutatory feat thereafter. Then he pursued his way a little further seawards. Subsequently I persuaded him to turn towards the boat. But before he was nearly alongside he gave me a beautiful 'encore', with rather less gusto, of the aforesaid pretty performance. Reeling in a second time, I at last steered him, now considerably less speedy in his movements, to within about a rod's length of the boat. Then I suddenly remembered that, owing to a mistake, I had only a suspiciously small landing net aboard for the negotiation of so heavy a fish. I thought I would try him, head first, nevertheless, and that, failing success I would wade ashore and play him lifeless if possible. Meanwhile I kept him circling round and round within a small area of water.

Fortunately at this juncture an angling acquaintance arrived on the scene, and at once taking in the situation threw me his net. Now changing the rod into my left hand and taking the net in the right (Shetland gillies can seldom be trusted to net a good fish), I slipped it under him, and he was brought to boat, a beautifully symmetrical specimen 5¼lbs in weight, caught on the aforementioned Demon fly, and having afforded me 15 minutes' exciting sport.

Had I not left Spiggie Bay for Spiggie Voe when I did I should in all probability never have seen this fish. Therefore, as said at the onset, I look upon the capture of one of my best sea trout as due to the presence of a seal. A paradox indeed! Not many anglers, I fancy, can have had a similar experience!

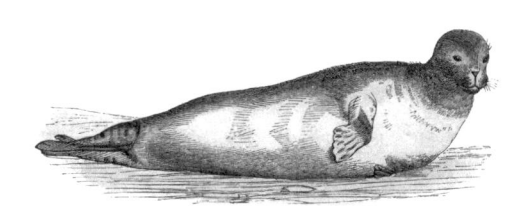

CHAPTER 15

Heather Moss in Shetland

In this article, which appeared in the Fishing Gazette *on the 18th of April, 1925, the author (writing under the pseudonym 'Heather Moss') describes his experience of fishing in the Shetlands during a holiday with his brother in 1912 and a year later with a friend. Presumably the author kept a detailed diary of the two holidays and he provides us with a fascinating insight into angling and life in Shetland in the second decade of the twentieth century.*

Through the good offices of a Shetlander I knew, my brother and I, in July 1912, made arrangements to fish in the Shetland Islands. In addition to giving us information, this gentleman fixed us up with accommodation in a crofter's cottage for the latter part of my visit.

My holiday was for a month, but as my brother could not manage more than three weeks I went first and he joined me later.

Booking a passage on the *St. Magnus*, I joined her at Aberdeen, and after a pleasant journey landed at Lerwick. From there the small coasting steamer *Earl of Zetland* took me to Baltasound, where the first part of my holiday was to be spent. On the way up she called at various small places and landed or embarked passengers, horses, cattle, etc., into and from smaller lighters. She kept close to the shore, and navigated her way in and out amongst numerous islands. What struck me most was the absence of trees and shrubs, caused, I suppose, by the proximity of the sea and the almost constant strong winds. I understand there is only one small plantation on the whole of the islands, and this is near Lerwick, being composed of trees only a few feet in height.

A room had been reserved for me at the Queen's Hotel, Baltasound, which is quite a small hotel, but very comfortable.

Baltasound at one time, like a good many villages in the Shetlands, was a prosperous little place, with keel boats for herring fishing sailing out of it, but now, since the introduction of steam, these are laid up. Practically the only herring fishing is done from Lerwick, where, when I passed through, there were as many as 1,000 boats operating, including, besides British, French, Dutch, Germans, and Russians, and probably other nationalities. The inhabitants, except at Lerwick, now mostly live on the produce of their crofts, and do a little fishing from small boats. They catch quantities of piltock (juvenile coalfish) by rowing close to the shore and fishing with bamboo canes angled out from the stern. To the end of the canes they have a short length of line tied; to this a hook is attached, on which a few short strands of catgut are fixed, making a sort of fly. The fish are split open and dried outside, to be eaten in the winter.

Next day I went to fish a small loch about two miles from the hotel, the landlord having obtained the services of a man as boatman for me. A strong wind was blowing down the loch, causing quite considerable waves. After putting my rod together, an 11 ft. 3 in. Hardy split cane, I attached a cast made up of March Brown dropper and Zulu tail fly, both No. 1 size.

Pulling the boat with some difficulty to the head of the loch, which was about half a mile long, we drifted down, and I caught only one trout of ¼ lb. The best place turned out to be a shallow near the end, towards which the wind was blowing, and there I caught most of the fish. There were no sea trout here, and the trout ran small, averaging about four to the 1 lb., but were nicely marked and good fighters for their size. On counting them I found I had 34. They rose at my flies all day, but very seldom came up at anything on the water. I spent another day there and landed 30. There was nothing heavier than ½ lb. in the lot.

Meanwhile the landlord of the hotel had made arrangements for me to fish in Burra Firth. This, at the most northerly part of the British Islands, is an arm of the sea, shaped somewhat like a wedge, with precipitous and hilly shores on the sides, and a fine, steeply-shelving beach at the end, at one corner of which a small

Essentials for the modern angler on Shetland.

burn runs in from Loch Cliff about half a mile away. There is a sanctuary here for the great skua gull, which was in danger of becoming extinct.

To reach Burra Firth from Baltasound it is necessary to walk over the hill which is a distance of about three miles. There is no road and no real path. On the right are high cliffs falling precipitously to the sea.

On arrival there I found my boatman waiting. For a time I tried fishing with sea-trout flies and lures, casting over the sea trout I could see jumping or breaking the surface. There were plenty of them, mostly along the sandy beach, where they came after the sand eels. The morning went in this way, and I only had one pluck at my flies, but failed to connect.

After lunch I tried spinning with artificial minnows and sand eels, but only hooked one small fish of ¼lb. It was my first experience of fishing for sea trout in the sea, and the methods I had so far used did not seem very successful. I asked the boatman if he would try to get me a supply of live sand eels, but he was never able to get any during my stay. I feel certain that great sport could be had with these.

I had brought with me a good supply of worms (ordinary gardenia) for emergencies, and as I was at the end of my resources, determined to try them. Tying on a Stewart tackle and baiting it with a good-sized worm, I fixed one or two small Simplex leads on the cast. Letting out about twenty yards of line and rowing slowly along, very shortly there came the tug, tug, of a fish, and, on striking, I was into a sea trout. He was a lively fellow, and, immediately on feeling the hook, jumped clean out of the water, and proceeded to fight as only sea trout can. After a minute or two he was landed and lay in the boat gleaming silver, with sea lice on him, straight from the sea. That day I had seven, weighing 6 lb. Not a very grand day, perhaps, but I was satisfied, though disappointed with the method of their capture.

The day after I again fished the Firth, confining myself to worm, and had a basket of seventeen, the largest 2½lb. I also walked up the burn flowing into it, and tried it with fly, but with no success, the water at the time being very low and clear.

There were a good many cormorants about, and one could get quite close to them, as they were gorged and sitting on rocks jutting out of the water. They eat so much fish they find it difficult to rise to fly. A seal used to follow the boat at a distance, being attracted by the sound of the human voice. He swam, only showing his head above the surface, and at a distance was hard to detect. This was not an asset from a fishing point of view; but the worst nuisance was a school of porpoises, which every now and then came close to the boat, and even occasionally right alongside, when they would come to the surface, grunt and dive under. They were, of course, after the sea trout. I was told that a gentleman fishing there had got so engaged at this that he had purposely foul-hooked one on a fly rod, and had lost the whole of his line.

Just before I started to go back to the hotel that night a fog came down. The boatman wanted to see me safely on my way, but I persuaded him I could manage alone. After walking over an hour I found myself back where I had started. There were no houses round about that I could see, so there was nothing for it but to go on again and try and find what path there was. After wandering about for another two hours, I eventually saw a light shining, and lost no time in getting to it. It came from a cottage, and on my knocking a man came to the door, half-dressed. He had evidently been in bed, as it was now 11 p.m. He said if I would wait a minute he would get a lantern and see me to the top of the hill, from where I could not miss my way to the hotel. He did so, and when I got near the hotel I saw several men with lamps. The landlord was with them, and told me that he had got frightened at my being so late, and had organised a search party to look for me, as he was afraid I might fall over the cliffs.

Next day I went to fish Loch Cliff, which is about 3 miles long, though not much more than a half-mile broad. The wind was, as usual, very strong and it was difficult to keep the boat steady. It was rather early for sea trout here, and I did not catch any. Fishing with two flies on my cast, and I very seldom use more, I landed 17 trout, none of them weighing more than a good ½lb., though a fair proportion were around that weight. Fishing near the middle of the loch, I rose a fish, and saw his head and shoulders as he came at the fly. Its weight must have been at least 4lb., but I missed him clean. The boatman said there were some very heavy trout in the water.

Cliff is a very nice loch to fish, shallowing off nicely near the shore, and with some good looking bays. Near the south end there was a lot of marsh grass growing out into shallow water, and this seemed as if it might be an ideal place with a rise on. I saw only a very occasional fish move all day, and there was an entire absence of fly on the water. Any loch fly appeared to answer the purpose, but most of the trout were caught on Greenwell's Glory and Hofland's Fancy.

That night I was sitting with the landlord in a sort of verandah outside the front door of the hotel, having a drink and yarning. He knew I was a lawyer, and said, "I'll tell you a story about one of your profession, and you'll see they may be very smart, but they don't always come off with the cash." It was as follows:

In the old days there was a Border riever called Rab Robson, and he was caught stealing sheep. He was taken to Edinburgh to be tried. When he got there he engaged a lawyer, and the arrangement was that if Rab got off he paid £50. He was told what he must do; and when the case came on was asked to plead, but all that could be got out of him was "Ta-ra-ra, ta-ra-ra, ta-ra-diddle-di-do." This was apparently enough, and he was declared insane. According to the landlord, by the law of Scotland this released him. The next night he gave a dinner to his friends, including the lawyer, to celebrate his acquittal. After they had finished this gentleman thought it a good time to ask for his fee as agreed, but all the answer he got was "Ta-ra-ra, ta-ra-ra, ta-ra-diddle-di-do."

The landlord sang the 'ta-ra-ra' part, accompanying himself on a mandolin. In the morning the only other guest at the hotel asked me if I had heard singing during the night, as he thought he had heard someone singing one of the old Shetland sagas.

One morning, on the incoming tide, I fished for an hour or so in the voe at Baltasound, taking off my shoes and stockings, wading in a little, and using sea trout flies. Noticing the tail of a fish sticking out of the water between two lots of seaweed, amongst which it was evidently nosing, I cast over him, and he rose at once. Striking, I hooked him, and had some difficulty in keeping him out of the weed, as he was a strong fish. Eventually netting him, he turned the scale at 1¾lb. Later on the same day I tried Burra Firth with worm and secured ten sea trout weighing 12¾lb.

July is rather early for sea trout fishing in the Shetlands, August, September and October being the best months, particularly the last two. Not only are the sea trout then more numerous, but they run much heavier, and after a fresh are to be found in the lochs which are connected with the sea and there are many.

The time had now come for me to join my brother in North Roe, which is the most northerly part of the main island. The first part of my journey was made by pony trap, the harness held together with string, over a precarious and hilly road to the west side of Unst, the island on which Baltasound is situated. On the way we passed a number of Shetland ponies running wild. This island is their principal breeding place. Reaching the coast I was sailed over to North Roe in a small fishing boat. The seas round here are treacherous, the tide currents being very strong between the numerous small islands, but the Shetlanders are able to manage their small craft in almost all weathers.

On landing at North Roe I met my brother, also the crofter, with whom my friend had arranged we should stay. He took us along a footpath to his home, some one and a half miles away, carrying most of our luggage on his back. They carry big loads this way, tying up the package and leaving loops at each end to go over the shoulders.

The house was a good deal better than the usual crofter's cottage, and was of two storeys. We had a sitting-room and a bedroom to ourselves. The former had the only firegrate in the house, all the food being cooked on a peat fire in the middle of the kitchen floor. The result was that all joints, etc., had to be boiled, and there was no bread, only bannocks and oatcakes, which were made every morning on the hot floor after the embers had been raked out.

Before leaving home we had bought a large scale ordnance map of the district. After consulting it next morning, we determined to try the voe, which lay over the hill, behind the cottage. This was only about half a mile away. A small burn, some two miles long, flowed into its head. There was the usual rocky shore, except where the burn flowed in, where it was shingly. There were a fair number of sea trout moving in it, but we were only able to rise one on a silvery lure. He was landed, 1 lb. weight. After spending some time here we walked up the burn to its source, casting a fly into the best-looking pools, but only caught small trout of 5 or 6 in. long and dark in colour. These were, of course, returned to the water. At the top of the stream there was a small loch, only a few hundred yards long, and from seventy to one hundred yards across, mostly very shallow and full of a sort of marsh grass. There was nothing to be got here, so we retraced our footsteps.

That evening we walked down to the harbour at North Roe and saw a man fishing off the wooden jetty, with flies, for sea trout. He had caught nothing, but said that sometimes when the tide was right he had quite good sport, but mostly a little later in the year.

The country west of where we were is very rough, covered with heather, and slopes away to Ronas Hill, the highest in the islands. On the north there are precipitous cliffs, at the base of which numerous seals may be seen sunning themselves. The whole of the way over to Ronas Hill is dotted with lochs, all of them containing trout, but none, except the small one already mentioned, from which the burn flows, ever have any sea trout in them, as there does not appear to be any outfall except over the cliffs.

The next few days were spent prospecting these lochs, fishing sometimes with waders on, and a good many trout were landed up to 1¼ lb., on Loch Leven sized flies. Eventually we got as far as Sandy Water, some five miles away at the foot of Ronas Hill. Here there were splendid trout, and much the best trout fishing we had had. The fish ran up close on 2lb., and fought like sea trout. They were more than pink-fleshed, almost red, and great eating. Fishing from the shore we did not get many, 14 between us being our best day. Walking some five miles, even carrying waders, is, however, no joke, especially when every now and again one has to jump over boggy ditches, and make detours of the various lochs. Added to this there is not much to guide one, and until within a few hundred yards the loch is hidden from view in a fold of ground. Sandy Water has no outlet except over the cliffs into the sea, where the waterfall must be a wonderful sight in spate.

Some 10 days had now gone, and we had only killed one sea trout here, having given up fishing in the sea for them, though we had tried with worm from a boat in the voe, but had had no success. We were hoping for a spate to fish the burn and small loch at the top. This came suddenly one morning as we were on our way to fish. It rained for some two hours, so we hurried back and got out worms and then made for the burn mouth. There was a small flood coming down when we commenced throwing up-stream and allowing the worm to travel out below us on a short line, repeating this whenever it had reached the end of its tether. We had evidently just arrived on the beginning of a run, and immediately commenced catching fish. We kept close together, fishing pool and pool about. Before we had been at it long my brother lost a small fish, leaving the Stewart tackle in his mouth. I was below, and some five minutes after hooked and landed the same fish with the tackle still in its jaws, a small one of ¼lb. This shows how they were taking. Finding that the stream was every minute running in, and no fresh fish coming from the voe, we followed the run up-stream, catching fish till our bags began to be heavy on our shoulders. Not being able to do any more in the burn we changed our tackle for flies and tried the small loch at its top. As I mentioned before, the water was shallow, and, seeing a big dorsal fin sticking out of the water, my brother said: "I'll have a chuck over him and see if he'll take it." Sure enough he did, the first time, and when we got him in, which was not easy, into the rough grass sticking up all over, he weighed 3lb., the best fish of the day. Our combined basket was 43 sea trout, weighing practically the same number of pounds.

Next day we tried the burn again, but only caught one or two small ones, evidently left behind when the flush went down. In the loch, however, there was better sport, and we had 17 between us on fly, but none so large as the three-pounder.

With only one day left, the loch was again fished, but proved very disappointing, there being no wind, and the water much shallower than it had been. We only caught five sea trout, and mostly small.

We gave all the fish we did not eat to the crofter, and he split them and hung them up inside for the winter. On settling up with his wife, she asked us one shilling a day each, which included food and everything, and the utmost we could get her to take was two shillings, and then she said she was robbing us. We lived on the fat of the land, mutton, chicken, and plenty of fresh eggs and milk, and good home-made butter. Almost everything came from their own croft.

When I got back I was so delighted with the holiday that I determined, if possible, to return the following year. My brother was unable to go, but I arranged for a friend to accompany me.

We intended this time to camp out at North Roe, and for this purpose bought an old army bell tent, and were loaned two folding camp beds. Provisions, etc., we also took with us.

July was the only month we could both get away, so in the middle of that month we safely arrived at Lerwick, and, to save time, hired a car there to take us and our effects the thirty odd miles north to our destination. The road was very bad in places, with nasty hairpin turns.

On the way up, a whaling station was passed. There are three of these on the main island. They are all run by Norwegians. As we came to this one the whaler was just coming in, and we could see a whale towing alongside. When a whale is sighted it is the skipper's job to do the harpooning. At a favourable moment he shoots the harpoon from a gun in the bows of the boat into it. When it is dead it is pumped full of air and is secured by a line from the boat around the flukes. It thus floats alongside.

We obtained permission and went into the station. The whole structure was composed of a long, wide platform running down to the sea, on to which the whale is pulled. On each side are the various buildings for boiling down the blubber for oil, for crushing the bones for manure, and for making the remainder into an ingredient for cattle cake. At the end farthest from the sea is a huge saw used for cutting the whale's head off. Everything is run by machinery and nothing is wasted. The whale we saw was a finner, the common whale, and was ninety feet long. They told us that it would be all disposed of in about two hours. That week they had caught, as near as I can remember, somewhere about 20 whales. The day was perfect, and we got some good photos of the whole operation.

Arriving at North Roe, we got out all our luggage, and, as it was still fairly early, determined to go on our two selves, with the tent and pole, and carrying our fishing tackle, to Sandy Water, where we intended to camp. Our host of last year, with his womenfolk, were to carry the remainder of the baggage over later that day and meet us there.

We carried the tent slung between us on its pole, in great style for a mile or so, but eventually it began to be heavier and heavier, and after a time we thought we had lost our way. We were now tired, and dusk was coming on, and we decided to pitch the tent. We did so, and then I thought I would go to the top of the ridge in front of us and see if I could make out where we were. On getting there I saw we were close to the loch, and could make out the figures of the carriers waiting for us. The tent came down in quick style; we carried it over and had it pitched and everything stowed in no time. We had not reckoned, however, on the soft, peaty soil, and, as it came on to blow during the night, a surprise awaited us in the morning. Lying in bed, just awake, we could not make out what had happened for some time. The tent seemed to be getting smaller and smaller. A bright moment came when we noticed that the pole was sinking deeper and deeper into the ground. We nailed two pieces of wood at right angles across it and stopped it sinking, but, all the time we were there we left it as it was, being more comfortable that way.

I forgot to mention that during the summer we had bought an old dinghy at Lerwick for £3, and had it taken across to Sandy Water from North Roe. It was carried across, but must have been hard work, though we were hardly charged anything for it.

Fishing from the boat, we caught a good many beautiful trout, similar to those caught the year before, but were rather disappointed, as we had hoped to get some larger ones from it.

It was a very dry time, and the loch had fallen evidently, for at the north end there was a small strip of water separated by a few feet of ground from the main body. My friend was fishing here one day and caught several good trout of more than 1 lb. weight.

I joined him, and we caught over 20 fish here in a very short time. They were in good condition, but would come at anything in the way of a fly.

Fishing one evening in a loch not more than a mile away, I noticed some good fish rising near the shore of a long, narrow part. Creeping along, I saw they were taking a moth which came off the heather. The rise did not last very long, but while it was on I got seven good fish up to 1 ¾ lb. with a heather moth. On returning to the tent I found my friend asleep, but when he saw the fish he woke up quickly enough. This was a place we had previously not done much in. Later on we went there again, and a little higher up there was a small, round boggy piece of water, with grass sticking up in it all over, and the trout were simply boiling there. They were small, between ¼ lb. and ½ lb., but we had as many as we could carry in a very short time, till it got dark.

Every day we were visited by our crofter friend, who brought over milk, eggs, etc., for us. Close to, there was a white sea-eagle, which lived in the cliffs. There had originally been a pair, but one had disappeared - died or been shot, perhaps. They had nested on these cliffs for some years, I believe. We saw it fly over once or twice.

During the holiday there was no rain, and consequently no sea-trout fishing, but, as I mentioned earlier, July, is not the best time for this, September and October being far and away better. In some parts, where the tide flows over into lagoon-like places, and in the voes, there is fairly good sea-trout fishing early on, but the largest fish are caught in the back end.

So ended two holidays in the Shetlands, and if the war had not come I had intended to go farther north to the Faroe Islands or to Iceland. I have, however, not been able to do so, but have had to content myself with fishing at home.

It is questionable whether we had any right to be fishing where we were, but all the time we were camped we never saw a soul except the man who brought us our provisions.

CHAPTER 16

An Old Etonian on Unst

During the early decades of the twentieth century Unst, the most northerly inhabited isle in Great Britain, seemed to be a relatively popular destination for anglers in search of its trout and sea trout. More recently (2016) the island has once again come to prominence following the broadcasting of *Island Parish*, a BBC TV series filmed on Unst.

George Brennand, author of *Halcyon*, first published in 1947 and with a limited edition published in 1968, visited the island at some time during the 1920s or early 1930s. It is impossible to pinpoint the exact date of his visit but he mentions going snipe shooting with 'the present Member of Parliament for those parts'. He also states that the MP had recently returned home to Unst from the Sudan. Unfortunately, he does not name him but the most likely candidate is Sir Robert William Hamilton, Liberal MP for Orkney and Shetland from 1922 to 1935 who had been a Chief Justice in East Africa. Brennand made the long trek up to Unst from Aberdeen with two delightful and bearded uncles of a close friend of his, whom he referred to as the 'Twin Brethren'. These two brothers had apparently spent much of their childhood in Shetland and were experienced anglers for the island's loch and sea trout. During the course of the voyage from Lerwick, the captain of the *Earl of Zetland* supplied him (as he did John Buchan's son) with a piltock wand, a bamboo rod armed with a length of string and feathered treble hook. As the ship stopped at various islands *en route* to Unst, Brennand was instructed to lower the feathered hook over the side where it was eagerly snatched by one of the ubiquitous piltock that frequented the shores. The captain was apparently an expert at this style of fishing and kept the ship supplied with fresh piltocks.

George Guinness Brennand, was born in 1897 at Birch, near Rochdale into a well-to-do family. His mother was a member of the famous Guinness family, hence his middle name, and his father was involved in the textile manufacturing industry. At the age of four, his family moved to Baldersby Hall, near Thirsk in North Yorkshire. Some of his earliest memories are of fishing from a pier on Lake Windermere and catching ten perch that were hauled out on a cheap rod. All the while, his nurse held on to the belt of his coat to stop him from falling in. She could not, however, stop him from becoming an angler, and from that day onwards, he fished at every available opportunity. He was an all-round angler who retained a love for perch, which he regarded as one of the most beautiful fish that swim. The best perch he ever landed was a magnificent-looking specimen of two and a half pounds, which he caught near his home on the Swale while trolling for pike with a Wagtail spinner. The first trout he ever caught came from the little river Dove in Farndale in Yorkshire. One hot day, he let his worm float down the stream and into a deep hole under a clump of over-hanging bushes. Almost at once his worm was snatched and he found himself attached to his first trout - a fish of four ounces. During the next few days he caught a number of other trout on worm and a half-pounder, which he caught on a live bluebottle that he had impaled on his hook and lowered on to the surface of a deep pool - and so the fly fisherman was born.

While a pupil at Eton College in Berkshire, Brennand became

interested in fishing for the dace that swam in the nearby Thames. After bathing in Cuckoo Weir, it was the custom of the boys to feed a certain shoal of dace with crumbs and small pieces of hard-boiled egg. Some of the dace grew to a large size and a dace of three-quarters of a pound is a sizeable specimen. During his second year at Eton he made himself a rough fishing outfit out of a thin willow branch, a length of cotton and a bent pin. With such primitive tackle, he managed to catch the largest fish in the shoal, which, after a close inspection, was returned safely to the water.

When he arrived on Unst Brennand had high expectations of the fishing from his previous reading and expected the trout and sea trout to be queuing up to snatch his flies. After a couple of days, when reality struck, he had to revise his ideas.

On arrival at Baltasound and settling in to his accommodation, he was eager to go fishing and, after dinner and in spite of the protests of his hostess, he ventured out to fish the voe, thinking that the evening was the best time to fish for sea trout. As night started to fall, his anxious fellow guests found him up to his armpits amidst waves and floating seaweed, trying feverishly to catch his first Shetland sea trout. Within a day or two he became acclimatised and regularly tramped the six-mile round-trip to fish the Loch of Cliff. Although sea trout do get into this loch, he never caught more than one or two in a day. However, Brennand and the Twin Brethren caught large quantities of brown trout from the loch on a Blue Zulu. The resultant catch was distributed among local crofters and tenant farmers.

Another favourite venue was the voe at Burra Firth, where he was able to wade out over a quarter of a mile on the sandy bottom. The pale green water of the voe was gin clear and he was able to see the sea trout, which appeared like brown streaks over the sandy bottom. On his first day at Burra Firth, he walked the nine miles from Baltasound with a fellow guest at a rapid pace. On arrival, his companion proceeded to strip off, don a pair of bathing trunks, and plunge into the icy water to cool off. Brennand, needless to say, did not follow suit. Instead, he put on his waders, walked along the top of the beach and spotted two large shoals of sea trout. Within three minutes he had hooked and lost a good sea trout, estimated to be about a pound and a half. After this brief moment of excitement, he tied on a fresh fly, a Cardinal, which he regarded as one of the best flies in Shetland and proceeded to net two good fish in quick succession and lose a third. Shortly afterwards the shoal moved off and he never saw another fish for several hours. He then tried the burn, which runs into Burra Firth from the Loch of Cliff, without touching a fish. Later that afternoon, on returning to the voe, he caught another two or three sea trout but missed quite a few fish that followed the fly but refused to take hold. The Twin Brethren appeared not to have had that problem as they explained to him that they had regularly been catching sea trout in Shetland for thirty years or more.

Frustrated by his attempts at hooking sea trout on the fly, Brennand resorted to worm, much to the disgust of the Twin Brethren who considered the method unsporting. Unfortunately, Unst is not noted for its abundance of lobworms and, after digging up a damp patch in his hostess' garden, he only managed to unearth a number of small worms. Undeterred, he rowed up to the head of Baltasound Voe where he spotted a number of sea trout jumping among the weeds in shallow water. His tackle was simple and consisted of a 12-foot rod, equipped with a reel and line, to which was attached a hook holding several worms. As soon as he cast over a jumping sea trout, his worm was instantly taken, and he soon found himself attached to a lively sea trout of just under three pounds in weight, far exceeding his best fish caught on fly - a fish of two pounds. He went on to catch two more fine sea trout, one of two pounds and another of nearly three.

On returning to his accommodation, his sea trout were duly admired and eaten but he could not help noticing a distinct chill in the air due to the fish being caught on worm. In deference to the Twin Brethren, he did not persist with the worm and resorted back to fly fishing. Apart from the Loch of Cliff, he fished a number of the other lochs on the island and, although he caught numbers of brown trout, he did not catch any noteworthy specimens. Twice he made the long nine mile trek to the south of the island to a 'wild and inhospitable loch called Snarra Voe in which there are reputed to be good trout'. On both occasions he failed to rise a fish and never even saw one. As well as fishing, Brennand enjoyed other field sports, especially shooting and he considered the snipe shooting on Unst to be better than the fishing.

Brennand hoped to return to Unst one day but it appears that he never did. He was, however, a keen angler throughout his life and one of his favourite haunts was the Shiel River in Ardnamurchan. He also enjoyed fishing the Tweed and even trained a few steeplechase horses, which ran at the Kelso Hunt meeting. In addition to Scotland, Brennand fished in Ceylon and the Antipodes.

Brennand appears to have followed in his father's footsteps and made his living as a textile manufacturer. He died at Cape Town on the 7th of November, 1983, at the grand old age of eighty-six.

CHAPTER 17

The Buchans in Shetland

In the summer of 2015 my wife and I ventured up to Shetland to spend a fortnight's holiday in these remote and beautiful islands. We had briefly visited Shetland the previous year and had been so entranced by the spectacular scenery, the wildlife, the archaeology, and the friendliness of the people that we wanted to return for a longer period and explore some of the more remote islands in the archipelago. After leaving Lancashire we drove up to the Scottish Borders where we spent the night in a very comfortable hotel. The following morning we drove up to Aberdeen and, after spending some time exploring the granite city, we embarked on the overnight ferry to Lerwick. Fortunately, the crossing (this time!) was relatively calm and we arrived refreshed in Lerwick at 7.30am the following morning. Our base for the fortnight was a comfortable apartment in Lerwick, the capital of Shetland. During our visit, apart from fishing and exploring the rich archaeological heritage, I particularly wanted to visit the island of Unst and follow in the footsteps of John Buchan, who visited the island in August, 1926. Unst is Britain's most northerly island with a population of around 700, most of whom earn their living from crofting and fishing, although Unst is also home to Britain's most northerly brewery, the Valhalla Brewery at Haroldswick.

Our journey from Lerwick to Unst took over two hours and involved two ferry crossings. From Lerwick we drove up to Toft and boarded the ro-ro ferry to Ulsta on Yell. After driving across Yell to Gutcher we boarded another ferry for the short ten minute crossing to Belmont on Unst. When John Buchan visited Unst

The Rev. Charles Dick (left) with John Buchan, his wife and son Johnnie on Unst, August 1926. Courtesy of Shetland Museum & Archives.

in the summer of 1926 with his wife and eldest son, Johnnie, the journey to Unst was undertaken by ship *The Earl of Zetland*, which regularly sailed from Lerwick to the more northerly isles and was an important lifeline for these remote communities. According to Susan Buchan, when they boarded the *Earl* at Lerwick, their son Johnnie was lent by the captain a long bamboo rod adorned at intervals with old toothbrushes and told to fish. With this outfit he whiled away the time in catching some unwary piltocks (juvenile coalfish). When I read this account by Susan I was puzzled by the reference to toothbrushes and, as a result, I contacted Dr Ian Tait, curator of the Shetland Museum, who solved the mystery. In the early years of the twentieth century, simple bamboo rods were extremely popular and were sold at most of the rural shops in Shetland. People made their own fishing rods from them, invariably fishing for piltocks with them from the shore and from boats. If the fish were in a taking mood they could be caught on bare hooks, often made from bent pins, which enabled the fish to be flicked off. Otherwise the fish were caught on simple flies similar to mackerel feathers which were attached to a line tied to the end of the rod. The material most prized by the Shetlanders for making these flies was the bleached fibres from the tail of a dogfish. Dogfish were commonly caught off the Shetland coast and a few tails were brought ashore, tied in canvas, and sunk in the sea for a time, and left there until the white gristly filaments were left. These had a glossy sheen in the water and proved very attractive to small fish when tied on a hook. To all intents and purposes these flies looked like the bristles on toothbrush heads, hence Susan's remark.

The Buchans' host on Unst was John Buchan's lifelong friend, the Reverend Charles Dick who was the minister of the church at Uyeasound. It is, perhaps, not surprising that John Buchan and Charles Dick were such close friends since both were born in the same year (1875), both were sons of the manse, both were educated at Hutcheson's Grammar School and both studied at Glasgow University. Both men enjoyed walking and fishing and both edited editions of Izaak Walton's *Compleat Angler*, Charles

Dick in 1895 for Walter Scott Ltd and John Buchan in 1901 for Methuen. According to Anna Buchan, Charles often spent his holidays with the Buchans at Broughton and on one occasion he and John cycled to Penicuik to call on S. R. Crockett, the novelist. In the summer of 1893, following their first year at Glasgow University, they explored the Scottish Borders together on bicycle or on foot. They would often take their fishing rods with them and fish the Leithen or Manor waters or the headwaters of the Clyde. Charles Dick, however, followed in his father's footsteps and became a Church of Scotland minister. Prior to his induction at Uyeasound church in 1924, Charles Dick had worked as a missionary in the West Indies.

Most of what we know of John Buchan's time on Unst comes from his son Johnnie who included a chapter on Shetland in *Always a Countryman* (second edition, 1971) and from his wife Susie in *John Buchan by his wife and Friends* (1947). During their time on Unst the Buchans stayed at the manse at Uyeasound where they had use of a T model Ford during their stay. According to Johnnie, the manse was ideally situated for their fishing expeditions. Nearby was a small loch, with a burn connecting it to the sea, containing brown and sea trout. Sea trout could also be caught in the sea when the tide was right. The brown trout that they caught from the loch rarely exceeded half a pound in weight but they had a silvery hue as if they slipped down into the burn into brackish water. Charles Dick was an expert flyfisher who at that time only used two flies of the same pattern but dressed in different sizes. John Buchan and his son, however, preferred to ring the changes and experimented with the colour and type of fly. As a result, they out-fished their host. Their most successful fly appears to have been a three-hooked sea-trout lure with a long Eton blue wing, silver body and red tail. With this fly they pricked far more fish than they actually landed and a sea trout of two pounds was their best fish, caught at the burn mouth. According to Susie Buchan, Johnnie also spent a lot of his time clad in waders and fishing in the shallows off the shore for piltocks (coalfish) and flounders.

Muckle Flugga lighthouse.

Uyeasound Church.

The Buchans and their host fished a number of lochs on Unst and on one occasion John Buchan and his son only managed one fish between them - a brown trout of just under half a pound. They left the fish lying on the grass with their rod cases and tackle bags while they fished around the loch. As they were returning to pick up their gear, they spotted a gull, flying with extreme difficulty, carrying a fish. They stood fascinated as the gull slowly mounted away. When they reached their rod cases they realised that the gull was flying away with their one and only fish!

On another occasion Johnnie learnt a salutary lesson. He accompanied his father and his host to a distant voe where the Reverend Dick had previously caught some good sea trout. On setting up his fishing tackle he realised he had forgotten that most vital piece of an angler's equipment - his reel. Fortunately, the Reverend Dick knew of a minister who lived nearby who might be able to help. The minister very kindly lent Johnnie an old brass reel that had seen better days, complete with a frail-looking line. Not to be deterred, young Johnnie cast into the waters of the voe and soon found himself attached to a very large sea trout. The fish dashed out to sea and promptly snapped his line. His father estimated the fish to be over seven pounds in weight! Johnnie was devastated and ever since that day he never set off on a fishing expedition without repeating a short incantation, "Rod, reel, flies, casts, and net," and patting each item to assure himself that they were really there.

Apart from fishing, the Buchans spent some time exploring the island and visited Muckle Flugga, the northernmost lighthouse in the British Isles. They also visited Baltasound where the 'ribs of derelict ships rotted on the tide line, and there was a so strangely strong Scandinavian flavour'.

Susie Buchan appears to have been somewhat less enamoured of Unst than her husband and son. She found the weather rather taxing:

The weather alters every quarter of an hour and the greeting of one islander to another consists of one word, 'Showery'. The wind blows incessantly and often with great fury, and the cloud effects are lovely as they move rapidly in all sorts of fantastic shapes across the sky.

On one occasion Charles Dick took them out to tea with two charming and immaculately dressed ladies. Johnnie had been fishing and she had been out in a boat and both of them presented a rather bedraggled appearance. She felt a 'crushing sense of inferiority' about her own and Johnnie's clothes and wondered what her hostesses would think of them. She need not have worried since they were received hospitably and had a wonderful tea of home-made scones and strawberry jam!

Ostensibly, John Buchan had been invited to Unst by his old friend to formally re-open Uyeasound Church, which had been repaired and redecorated. His visit did not go unnoticed by the press as the following extract from the *Aberdeen Journal* of Thursday 26th August, 1926 demonstrates:

Uyeasound and the Manse.

Uyeasound Church, Shetland, which has been repaired and decorated, was reopened on Sunday, when the minister (the Rev. C. H. Dick, B.D.) conducted the service, and the congregation was addressed by Colonel John Buchan, who congratulated them on possessing so seemly and suitable a place of worship. It reminded him, he said, in its four-square solidity of a lighthouse - a parallel most apt to a Christian church. They lived in an age of great mechanical progress, but science, for all its power, did not touch the greater matters of human life. It did not make easier the conquest of self or the struggle of the soul with sin. In such an age the Church was in danger of being drawn from her true purpose into meritorious, but irrelevant, activities, and the chief need was for insistence upon the intense spirituality of the Gospel of Christ...

The Buchans' return journey to Aberdeen was not as calm as their outward journey and they ran into heavy seas. Both Johnnie and his mother succumbed to sea-sickness, which was not helped by an over-zealous ship's steward who kept asking if they would like to partake of sheep's head! John Buchan was completely unaffected by the weather, but Susie and Johnnie were mightily relieved to set foot on *terra firma* at Aberdeen.

My wife and I visited Unst for just the day but, during that time, we managed to see several of the places the Buchans had frequented including Uyeasound, Baltasound and Saxa Vord, from where we were able to see the famous Muckle Flugga Lighthouse, perched on a rocky outcrop in the distance. On our return to Lerwick I visited the splendid Shetland Museum and Archive where I was shown a wonderful photograph of the Buchans and Charles Dick attired in their fishing gear. Johnnie looks extremely proud and confident decked out in his waders and fishing hat.

Charles Dick was minister of Uyeasound Church from 1924 to 1927, before being transferred to Cunningsburgh Church near Lerwick in 1927. Such was the success of their Shetland fishing expedition that John Buchan and his eldest son ventured

Cunningsburgh Church near Lerwick.

even further afield in the summer of 1932 - to the Faroes. They enjoyed some excellent sport with the sea trout, which averaged over three pounds. On their return journey, four miles from Sumburgh Head, they transferred from their Danish ship bound for Copenhagen to a fishing boat which took them into Lerwick. They were met by a delegation of port officials who informed them that their Danish ship, by dropping them as passengers for Lerwick outside territorial waters, was liable for various dues. Buchan, who was by now an MP and a former lawyer, stated that this was a matter for the Port of Lerwick authority and the Danish Steamship Company to resolve and did not concern him. Apparently, the case dragged on for a number of years but Buchan himself heard no more about the matter. The following evening John and his son boarded a vessel bound for Aberdeen but, no doubt, during this fleeting visit he met up with his old friend Charles Dick.

A year later, when John Buchan was appointed as King George V's High Commissioner to the General Assembly of the Church of Scotland, he appointed the Reverend Charles Dick as his chaplain. In 1936, Charles Dick also visited his friend, now Lord Tweedsmuir, in Canada and was asked to preach at St Andrew's Church, Ottawa, where Tweedsmuir was an elder. Charles Dick outlived his old friend by twelve years and died in Shetland on the 20th of March, 1952. Today, the Reverend Dick is perhaps best known for his *Highways & Byways of Galloway and Carrick*, first published by Macmillan in 1916 and reprinted as recently as 2002. It is a book that has stood the test of time and is still a useful guide to that beautiful area of Scotland.

CHAPTER 18

John Leslie - An Angling Member of Parliament

*Let those now fish
Who never fished before,
And those that fish,
Fish all the more.*

Former Prime Minister Tony Blair is, perhaps, the most well-known Member of Parliament for the Sedgefield constituency in County Durham. He served as its MP from 1983 to 2007, when he resigned his seat following his resignation as Prime Minister. As far as I am aware, Tony Blair is not an angler but one of his predecessors as the Labour MP for Sedgefield certainly was. John Robert Leslie (MP for Sedgefield from 1935 to 1950) was a native of Shetland who was born in Lerwick on the 3rd of November, 1873. In a series of articles written for the *New Shetlander* magazine during 1949-1950, he recalled his early days in Shetland and how he became an angler. Like many other natives of Lerwick he attended the Anderson Institute but left school at the age of fourteen to assist in his father's (also called John Leslie) grocery business.

As well as being an angler Leslie was also a keen sportsman and captained the Our Boys Athletic Club rugby team. On one occasion, he recalled an historic victory over the senior team by a try - three points. The sea is in the blood of most Shetlanders and it is not surprising that he soon became fascinated by boats and enjoyed participating in the Lerwick regattas. Young men enjoyed testing their skills against the crews of the Revenue cutters and he recalled crewing for a Ness yoal (a clinker-built boat) owned by a local shoemaker in which they won first prize in the rowing race. On another occasion, however, he was less successful. He was part of a crew rowing a Fair Isle yoal which leaked badly and, before the course was completed, their clothes were floating about in the boat. Needless to say, they did not win a prize on that occasion!

Leslie and his brother also had a very lucky escape one day when they truanted from school and took off in a dinghy at Twageos. Within a short time, the boat capsized and, since neither he nor his brother could swim, they had to be rescued by the local Quarry flit boat. Another escapade nearly ended in disaster when he and his brother were caught in a fog off Bressay Lighthouse. They rowed for hours until a break in the fog enabled them to row back home - at 3 o'clock in the morning! Stealing neeps and firing catapults at rats in local pig styes also proved to be attractive diversions to the Lerwick youngsters.

In his articles Leslie recalled several of the local characters in and around Lerwick including: Jeems Williamson the fiddler who entertained the locals at the Market Cross with his Shetland Reels, John Work, a local boatman who ferried passengers ashore from the mail steamer anchored in the Bay and Robbie Snuddie, a local pilot who guided ships in and out of the harbour.

Like thousands of Shetlanders before and since, Leslie left Shetland in November 1892 in search of a better life in Edinburgh. He soon found employment in a grocery store but conditions were harsh. Hours were long and wages were low. There was no weekly half holiday, only a night off once a fortnight at 5 o'clock.

It was while he was working as a grocer's assistant in Edinburgh that the political side of his nature started to come to the fore. He played a major part in the founding of the Shop Assistants' Union (later USDAW) in Scotland and quickly ascended its ranks. In 1904, he was appointed Union Organiser to cover the whole of Scotland, Ireland and England, as far south as Yorkshire. Being an accomplished athlete, he was instrumental in forming the Edinburgh Grocers' Athletic Club, which proved an excellent conduit for recruiting new union members. Every year the club held a sports competition and Leslie was frequently on the list of prize winners.

In 1912, he was invited to become editor of the Union's official organ *The Shop Assistant*, which entailed his moving to London and working in Fleet Street. That same year, John, the first of his five children (three sons and two daughters) was born. It wasn't long before he became involved in a dispute with the local council when several council employees were dismissed and trade union membership banned. He fought hard on the side of their cause, which resulted in their eventual reinstatement and the right to join their union. Shortly afterwards, he himself was elected to the local council where he sat for twelve years and became Chairman of the Housing Committee.

From 1925 to 1935 he served as General Secretary to the Shop Assistants' Union and steered it through some of the worst days of unemployment and hardship. In 1935, he stood as the Labour Party Parliamentary candidate for Sedgefield in County Durham and won with a majority of 1771. It was a tremendous victory for Leslie to win in a constituency that had previously been held by the Conservative Party. Such was his popularity that, by 1945, he had increased his majority to over 11,000. He remained as the Member of Parliament for Sedgefield for fifteen years before retiring from office in 1950.

His time as an MP, however, was not without controversy and in 1938, when discussing the Hire Purchase Act, he made anti-Semitic accusations over the apparent involvement of Jews in extortionate hire purchase. Throughout his parliamentary career he always gave his backing to any action that might benefit Shetland and on at least one occasion he spoke against the party line when a piece of legislation appeared to be detrimental to Shetland. He also pursued many personal cases involving Shetlanders who came to regard him as highly as their local MP.

You can take the boy out of Shetland but you cannot take Shetland out of the boy and throughout his life Leslie took an annual holiday in his native isles. During these annual visits to

Shetland he went off in pursuit of the wily trout and sea trout to be found in its lochs. Although he was no stranger to fly fishing, Leslie had a penchant for spinning for trout and even compiled an article, 'Spinning for Trout', in the *New Shetlander* (No. 27, Voar edition, 1951) on the subject.

From his article, we learn a great deal about Leslie the angler. Like many an angler before him, he started fishing with a wooden rod about six feet in length to the top of which was fastened a piece of string equipped with a hook. With such primitive tackle and with worms as bait, he managed to catch a few small trout. Eventually, his grandfather presented him with a proper rod, reel and line and his angling career took off.

His preferred method of angling was spinning although he quickly came to realise that there was a lot more to the art of spinning than simply a chuck it and chance it approach, and, in his article, he provided the tyro with some sound advice. He advised the beginner not to buy an expensive spinning rod to start with but to cut down an old greenheart rod to around seven or eight feet. However, he recommended the purchase of a fixed-spool reel of a good make and, in Leslie's day, one of the best fixed-spool reels on the market was the Hardy Altex, which was available in a range of sizes. When fishing for brown trout he recommended the use of the recently introduced 'nylon' line with a breaking strain of four pounds and for sea trout a breaking strain of six pounds. He found 'nylon' line much better for casting in a wind (and there is plenty of that in Shetland!) and it did not require drying after every outing. For a trace, he preferred a three or four-foot length of the same 'nylon' line, which he attached to the main line by means of a size 9 or 10 swivel. He had experimented with larger swivels but found that trout sometimes would go for the swivel rather than the minnow.

He used a variety of artificial spinning baits but his favourites were a blue and silver Devon minnow with treble hooks at the tail and a Quill minnow with treble hooks at the tail and sides. This latter bait he found particularly useful when spinning for sea trout towards the end of the season. In the early part of the season

Archer flight

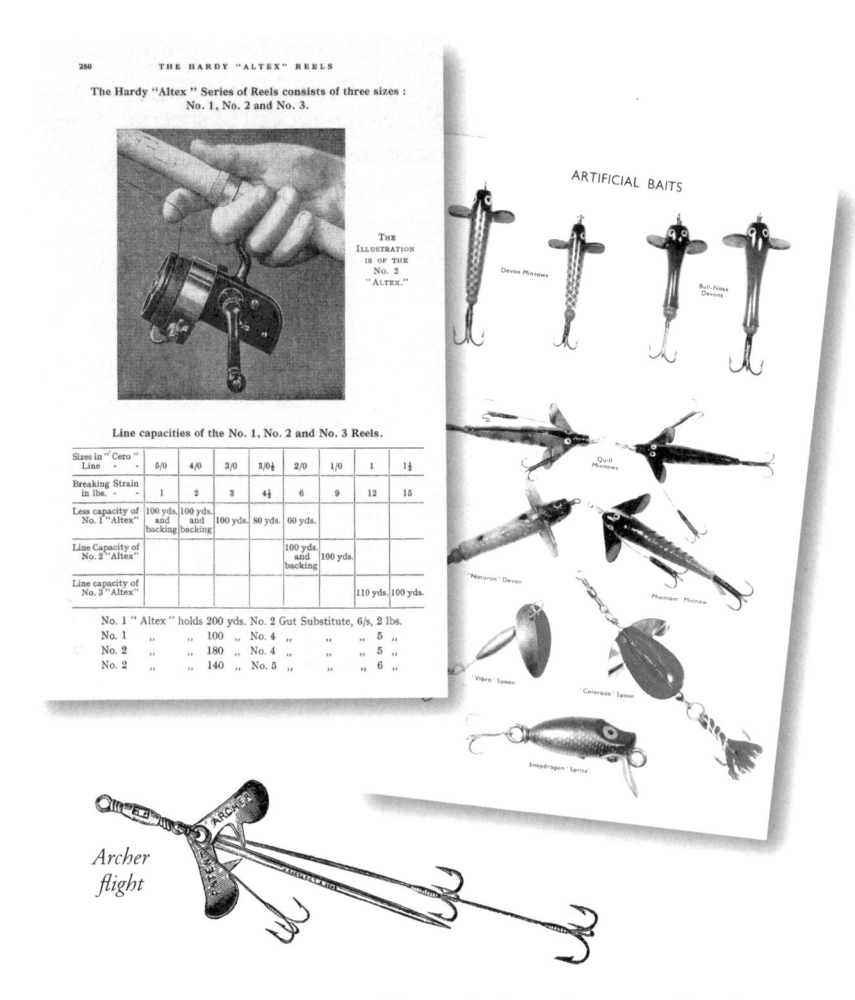

he found the Vibro spinner in blue and silver, silver or gold to be most effective. For brown trout his preference was for a one inch model and for sea trout the larger one and a half inch model.

His favourite spinner, however, was the natural preserved minnow mounted on an Archer flight. He caught trout on this minnow when all artificials failed, especially in the early part of the season. Like most anglers he was quick to learn from his mishaps. When he first started spinning he frequently got his line into a bird's nest or his baits snagged in weed or stones resulting in many losses. He soon came to realise that the weight of his minnow or artificial spinner was crucial to success. When spinning in shallow water three to four feet deep he found a lighter minnow to be more effective while in deeper water a heavier minnow could be used.

Leslie also discovered that it was not necessary to cast long distances and found that he had more control if he hooked a trout at a short distance. On more than one occasion he hooked a trout at the very start of his spin just as the minnow came to rest in the water and before he had time to start reeling in. The fish must have been near the minnow when it was sinking and took it on the drop. At other times, he witnessed both brown and sea trout follow his minnow and seize it just as he was about to take it out of the water.

As seasoned lure anglers know, spinning can be a frustrating business, as Leslie himself found out. Once, when spinning on the sands at Levenwick, he saw several sea trout of around two pounds and above follow his minnow. If he began to retrieve faster, the trout came faster, if slower the trout did the same, but they would not take and, when the minnow came out of the water, they turned and went slowly away.

On one occasion while spinning he landed, within half an hour, ten brown trout averaging three quarters of a pound each. His biggest trout caught whilst spinning was a specimen of three and a half pounds. In March 1950, when spinning at the head of Laxfirth Voe he hooked a nice sea trout which ran out ninety yards of line, then took a turn and headed straight towards him. He backed up the bank and reeled in his line as fast as he could but, unfortunately, the line became entangled in some seaweed and the hook pulled out. He estimated the fish to have been at least five pounds. Still, all anglers have tales of the one that got away and Leslie was clearly no exception!

Leslie was sufficiently experienced to realise that trout have days when they will not look at a minnow but may rise to the fly and other days when they will take a minnow but not a fly.

As a result, he did not completely eschew fly fishing and would fish the fly when conditions were favourable. He found the following flies to be the most effective patterns on the waters he fished: Greenwell's Glory, March Brown, Butcher, Peter Ross, Teal and Red, Dunkeld, Red Spinner, Silver Cardinal, Soldier Palmer, Coachman, Black Spider, Zulu, and Red and Blue Terrors. Most of these flies can still be found in the fly boxes of today's anglers on Shetland and are just as effective as they were in Leslie's time. One of his best baskets of brown trout on the fly was taken in less than an hour one night in 1949. At the top of Loch Strand he caught nine brown trout, several of which were over a pound in weight.

Although Leslie claimed not to be an expert angler, he was clearly no novice and during the 1950 season (February to October) we learn that he landed 123 trout, both brown and sea trout, with a combined weight of 109lb. These fish were caught in fifty-two outings, many of which were less than one hour.

Loch Strand

However, he also recalled that a fly fisherman from Edinburgh fishing Loch Tingwall caught almost half Leslie's total for the season in just ten days of fishing.

Shetland is truly an angler's paradise with literally hundreds of lochs at the angler's disposal. Amongst Leslie's favourites were: Loch Trebister, Loch Girlsta, which he claimed contains trout of up to seven pounds, Loch Spiggie, Lochs Asta and Tingwall and Loch Strand. Leslie was a great advocate of the work done by the Shetland Anglers' Association and encouraged his readers to join.

Sadly, John Leslie passed away suddenly on the 12th of January, 1955 at his home in Muswell Hill, London at the age of eighty-one. His wife predeceased him and of his five children, two sons and two daughters survived him. Such was the high regard in which he was held in Shetland that a street in Lerwick was named after him.

John Leslie MP, at Jarlshof. Courtesy of Shetland Museum & Archives.

CHAPTER 19

Negley Farson on Shetland

Hugh Falkus (1917-1996) was one of the most influential game anglers of his generation and his two seminal books *Sea Trout Fishing* (1962) and *Salmon Fishing* (1984) are still in print today. In June 1940, Falkus' Spitfire was shot down over France and he spent the rest of the war in various German prison camps. During his time in the prison camps he helped in the construction of a number of escape tunnels before being transferred to the infamous Stalag Luft III, built on a site specifically chosen to make escape by tunnelling extremely difficult. During a period of solitary confinement, a kindly guard smuggled into his cell a copy of Negley Farson's *Going Fishing* (1942), a masterpiece of twentieth century angling literature, combining travel and adventure with a love of angling. For a couple of months it was Falkus' only reading material. He read and re-read the book several times and came to regard it as the best angling book ever written and such is the enduring popularity of this book that it has been in print almost continuously since it was first published in 1942.

It is, perhaps, not surprising that Hugh Falkus found Farson's book so compelling since both men were passionate anglers, both led adventurous and even charmed lives, and both were very fond of whisky. James Negley Farson was born on the 14th of May, 1890 in Plainfield, New Jersey. He was raised by his grandfather, the Civil War General and ex-Pennsylvania Congressman James Negley, who had fallen on hard times and was constantly fighting his creditors from the door. Even though his grandfather had financial worries, he was still able to retain three black servants, one of whom, Abner, taught the young Farson how to trap rabbits and muskrats, whose pelts they sold for 25 cents each. At the age of eleven, Farson was shot in the leg by a friend whose gun went off accidentally while they were hunting partridges. An oozy red stream of blood trickled through a hole in his boot but eventually he managed to crawl on his hands and knees for help before ending up in hospital. This was the first of several unfortunate escapades involving his legs that happened to him during his lifetime.

It was a friend, Dave Stewart, who first ignited Farson's lifelong passion for angling. After catching a 12lb carp on canned corn in a pond beside a local swamp, the young Farson rode home ecstatically with the fish tied to his handle-bars. Sadly, his grandfather was none too impressed and the fish ended up on the brush pile! From carp he tried his hand at lure fishing for smallmouth bass before progressing to the delicate art of fishing for them with live frogs. From bass he graduated to surf-casting along the Atlantic coast of New Jersey for bay trout, flounders and king-fish. Equipped with a two-handed lancewood rod he and his friends cast out their four ounce leads hundreds of feet out to beyond where the waves began. On one occasion, a German friend of his hooked a 25lb channel bass, which led him a merry dance up and down the beach before Farson pounced on it in the waves and stuck his arm through its gills. Even though the rough gills cut his hand, he refused to let go and carried it triumphantly into the dunes.

Following his grandfather's death, his grandmother was awarded a pension and Farson was sent to Andover Academy, one of the finest prep schools in America, from which he was eventually expelled. From there he went to live with his father in a small town in Pennsylvania and attended the local high school where he excelled at athletics and won the interscholastic championships in the shot put. Eventually, he proceeded to the University of Pennsylvania where he read civil engineering and represented the university at rowing.

After a spell in business in New York, Farson set sail for England at the outbreak of the First World War in 1914 and worked for an engineering firm in Manchester. Before he had been in England one week he fell in love with the 'simplicity and substantiality of British life'. It was in Manchester that he learned how to drink and he developed a taste for whisky and soda. Sadly, he became too fond of drink and in his later years he became an alcoholic and is even reputed, on one occasion, to have out-drunk Ernest Hemingway.

Farson's stay in Manchester was relatively brief and he moved on to Russia where he spent several years as an agent for an Anglo-American export business trying to secure war orders from a corrupt Tsarist Government. During the summer of 1915, in the absence of a Russian motor-cycle 'expert' who had been engaged as a demonstrator, Farson was forced to give a display of one of his company's motor-cycles. Unfortunately, he had never ridden a motor-cycle before and ended up going clear over a shallow ditch and through a board fence. He badly damaged his legs resulting in a violent streptococci infection. It was over a year before he was able to walk again without crutches. His company, however, won the order for motor-cycles! When the Russian Revolution broke out two years later Farson was in Petrograd (St. Petersburg) and witnessed the events. Later that year he returned to England and joined the Royal Flying Corps and was sent out to Egypt. One morning, while trying to impress his comrades on the ground, he sent his plane into a spin and crashed. He shattered his left tibia and broke some bones in his right foot. That crash, at one time or another during the next twenty years, resulted in him spending a cumulative total of three years in bed.

In 1919, he married Enid Eveleen (Eve) Stoker, a niece of Bram Stoker and author of *Dracula* (1897), in Killarney in Ireland. After a spell selling motor trucks in Chicago and two years living by a lake in Victoria Island, British Columbia, Farson was appointed foreign correspondent for the *Chicago Daily News* in 1924. That same year he and his wife sailed their 26 foot Norfolk yacht, *Flame*, from Rotterdam to the Black Sea. In his mother-in-law's house in South Kensington, London, on the 8th of January, 1927, Farson's son, Daniel Negley Farson was born. Farson himself was laid up in the house following an operation on his leg in Stockholm. In the spring of that year, with his leg still in plaster, Farson left his wife and new-born son for the first time and ventured up to Shetland. While recovering from his operation he had read a book about whaling and he wanted to write about the Norwegian whaling boats that were then working out of Shetland. A vivid account of this first visit is given in his autobiography, *The Way of a Transgressor* (1935).

At Olna Firth, he embarked, with some difficulty, on the *Skeena*, a whaling ship manned by eleven Norwegians, one of whom, Olsen, was the 'dean of Norwegian gunners' and had killed 2,600 whales. Their hunting-ground was a patch of the Atlantic off Shetland 200 miles long by 50 miles wide. The hunt was proving fruitless until the last day when they were due to return to port. Suddenly, the look-out man spotted two fin-whales forty yards to windward and Olsen sprang into action. At less than forty yards one of the whales rose and Olsen fired the harpoon gun. The 6-inch whale-line whizzed out and the whale made its first run like any trout or salmon. He took out nearly a quarter of a mile of six-inch Manilla rope as he charged along the surface only to reveal that he had been shot just behind the back fin. None of his vital organs had been touched and he was still fresh and fighting. Eventually, the harpoon pulled out to reveal a mass of tendons clinging to its barbs. The hunt continued and, as the sun was setting, the whale was shot again. This time the shot proved deadly and, after a two hour struggle, the whale was brought alongside.

It is impossible to read Farson's account of this gargantuan struggle without feeling a great deal of sympathy for such a magnificent creature - 'A strange head emerged from the waves, as if for a last look at the sky, and, across other waves a delicate tail curled out, massive, yet beautiful as a butterfly's wing.'

While waiting at Lerwick to go on his whaling expedition, Farson observed the numerous British, Dutch and Scandinavian herring boats tied up in the harbour and the Scottish herring girls, clad in rubber boots and with bandages around their fingers, gutting the fish and packing them into barrels. By the time Farson was in Shetland the herring boom was on its last legs and many of the boats' crews were barely making enough money to keep them alive. Nevertheless, Farson wanted to experience the life of a herring fisherman and he embarked on a fishing trip on board the *Kitchener*. The boat headed for the Skerries where they shot their two miles of nets. As the nets were hauled in, Farson was aghast at their emptiness. All the crew's hard work resulted in a meagre four crans (baskets) of herring.

In his autobiography Farson wrote, 'See the Shetlands once, and they will haunt you for ever'. And haunt him they did, with the result that he returned three years later, this time with his wife and young son in tow. Prior to this second visit in 1930, he had been reporting on the troubles in India where he had interviewed Gandhi and witnessed his arrest.

During this second visit his aim was to relax and for him the best way to do this was by fishing. Most of what we know of this visit comes from his much-acclaimed *Going Fishing* (1942). He was impressed by Shetland and thought that nowhere else in the world could match it for its grandeur. He was particularly impressed with its dramatic coastline with its numerous cliffs, stacks and arches. He was less taken by the scenery inland with its lack of trees, black peat bogs and lonely moors. Although it may seem perverse, he enjoyed fishing in the north of Scotland and Shetland more than in British Columbia and felt that the sea trout caught in the voes and the brown trout caught in windy lochs 'will provide you with memories with which you can invigorate yourself for the rest of your life'.

He fished for brown trout on a number of windswept lochs and on one occasion, while philosophising about the dourness of life in Shetland, his fly was suddenly seized by a hard-fighting trout. The fish put up a tremendous battle and he could feel its every move telegraphed through his taut line and delicate split cane rod. He was amazed to find that, when he eventually landed the beautifully spotted brown trout, it weighed less than a pound. It led him to conclude that he would rather catch a dozen 14-inch Shetland trout than one lazy 4-pounder. He considered the hard-fighting Shetland trout to be the athletes of the brown trout world. One of his most memorable catches of brown trout was taken on Eela Water between four o'clock in the afternoon and eight o'clock in the evening. He caught thirty fish weighing a total of 9¼lb and he regarded it as one of the finest day's fishing he had ever had. As well as Eela Water he cast a line on the Loch of Girlsta, famed in Norse mythology as the loch where Geirhildr, the daughter of Flokki (discoverer of Iceland) was drowned, and the Loch of Clousta.

Loch fishing in Shetland was very different from the type of fishing he had experienced in British Columbia and, in *Going Fishing*, he advised the angler not to strike loch trout but to let them do the striking. He also regarded dull days to be good for fishing but vile days, when the wind is blowing and rain squalls are passing over, to be even better. It was on a day such as this that he had his memorable catch on Eela Water.

During his visit to Shetland he managed to make his way up to Unst where he stayed in a grand house with Sir Robert Hamilton (1867-1944), MP for Orkney and Shetland, whom he regarded as one of the best sea-trout fishermen he had ever met. Clad in his deer-stalker cap, Sir Robert would set out every morning after breakfast and return every evening with at least one 3 or 4 lb sea trout, which he had caught among the seaweed-laced rocks of the salt water.

Like most good angling books, *Going Fishing*, contains a story of the one that got away. Back on the Shetland Mainland, Farson was offered a day's fishing by the local laird on Laxo burn, famed for its large sea trout. The day was gin clear, with no breeze, and little hope of catching a big fish - or so he thought. He put on an ordinary loch cast and started fishing his way up the burn towards the loch above. He picked up a couple of small sea trout along the way before coming to a pool where he spotted a good fish. His wife was sat nearby in the sun reading a detective story. Suddenly, as he was idly casting with one hand and trying to eat a sandwich with the other, there was a whoosh and a huge sea trout leapt clear of the water at the foot of the pool. He quickly cast his flies over the fish and on the second cast the fish took. There then followed an epic struggle. Contrary to Farson's expectations, the fish did not rush downstream but instead made a dash towards the bank where he could have netted him quickly. Instead, 'like a fool', he stepped back from the bank and gave him a longer line. The fish decided not to run to the pool below but went to the bottom of the pool where it sulked for the next hour or so. Every time Farson tried to work him to the surface and the dropper appeared, the fish bore irresistibly down again. By this time a crowd of locals had started to appear, including the driver of the local bread van, who asked him why he didn't pull the fish up. As Farson explained to him that this was impossible on a frayed 3X cast, the driver went off shaking his head. Two young men appeared and leaned over the bridge to watch the spectacle, followed by an old woman with a creel of peat on her back. Eventually, in despair, Farson threw in some small stones to try and move the fish, but to no avail. The laird's factor came along and advised him to pull the fish up. Following this suggestion, Farson took the line in his left hand below the first guide ring, held it firmly, and bent the rod. The fish refused to move and the line parted! After a fight of two hours and forty minutes with a fish estimated to be at least 8lb in weight, Farson sought consolation in a bottle of whisky. The memory of that encounter lived with him for the rest of his life.

After his time in Shetland, Farson returned to England where he was given the coveted post of London correspondent for the *Chicago Daily News*. After a number of years in this role, he resigned from the paper, and set off with his wife and eight-year-old son to drive across Europe. The second instalment of his autobiography, *A Mirror for Narcissus* (1957) picks up the threads of *The Way of a Transgressor*, and tells the story of his later years, years dominated by his increasing dependency on alcohol. Finally, after settling down in Devon in a house by the sea with his ever stalwart wife Eve, he died of a heart attack on the 13th of December, 1960. Thus ended the life of a truly remarkable man.

CHAPTER 20

The Petersons

During my early teenage years I seem to remember that one summer a group of friends and I thought it a good idea to build a raft for use on our local mill lodge. We managed to obtain half a dozen old oil drums from the local garage and some scrap timber that was lying around in the back of my friend's garden. Thus equipped, we set about making our craft. With some old rope we managed to lash the timber boards on to the top of the oil drums to form some sort of platform. Duly impressed with our handiwork, we carried the fragile-looking craft to the edge of the lodge. Somehow we managed to scramble on to the unstable craft and, using a piece of old timber as an oar, we launched ourselves on to the lodge. I would like to say that the raft was a great success and gave us endless hours of pleasure as we drifted around the lodge. Unfortunately, I cannot. The wretched craft was extremely unstable and after sailing out for about twenty yards it overturned and we ended up with a soaking and a certain amount of damaged pride. We never bothered with another raft after that and contented ourselves with fishing the lodge instead!

While I was carrying out research for this book I came across a series of wonderful photographs in the Shetland photographic archive taken by John Peterson. Six of the photographs, taken in 1932, portrayed a smartly dressed angler, complete with wicker fishing creel, fishing a loch, thought to be Clingswater near Clousta, from a floating chair. The caption on the archive's website referred to the sedentary angler as Professor J. Peterson. Intrigued, I decided to find out a little more.

The floating chair, which doesn't look particularly stable, appears to be something of a Heath Robinson contraption. The floats, on to which a scaffolding superstructure has been attached to accommodate a seat, look to be made out of large metal jerry cans or something similar, and a wooden oar has been attached to the side rail by a length of stout string. Presumably, the oar was used to propel the angling professor to his desired location on the loch and a conveniently placed landing-net was also strapped to the side, ready for use on hooking a fish. Apparently Professor Peterson was a keen angler and regular visitor to the islands in the 1930s. His unusual craft was kept ready for him at the water's edge so that he could go afloat as soon as possible on arrival. Unfortunately, I have been unable to track down any records of the professor's success or otherwise while fishing from his floating chair. The photographs in the archive show him fly-fishing on a relatively calm day but, as Shetland is no stranger to wind, you cannot help wondering how his contraption might fare in a rough wave and it appears that, despite its ingenious design, the professor's chair did eventually sink without trace.

The fishing professor in the photograph was Professor James McInness Peterson who was born in the Schoolhouse at Gruting in Shetland on the 22nd of February, 1899. He was the third of seven children born to John Scott Peterson (1863-1932) and Christina Ann McInness (1873-1960). His parents, who were both schoolteachers at Gruting School, were married on the 1st of August, 1895. It appears that his father taught the older pupils at the school while his mother taught the younger ones. At the turn of the century when James was born the school had a population of around eighty pupils, which had dropped to around thirty at the outbreak of the First World War. After education at his parents' school, James went on to the Anderson Institute in Lerwick and Aberdeen University. He subsequently became a lecturer in Physiology at Aberdeen University before being appointed Emeritus Professor of Physiology at University College, Cardiff in 1947. He remained at Cardiff for twenty

*Professor Peterson fishing from his floating chair.
Courtesy of Shetland Museum & Archives.*

years before retiring to Shropshire where he died at the ripe old age of ninety-seven on the 8th of June, 1996. A funeral service was held for him at St Mary's Church, Cleobury Mortimer on the 18th of June and a memorial service was also held for him on Shetland.

His elder brother John (1895-1972), more commonly known as Jack, was a noted poet who served in the Seaforth Highlanders during the First World War and was wounded twice. Some of his most powerful poetry concerned the war and was published in two volumes, *Roads and Ditches* (1920) and *Streets and Starlight* (1923). After the war he became a Customs and Excise officer, returning to Shetland after spending some time in the south. As well as writing, Jack was a very keen photographer and in 1948 he published an evocative volume of black and white photographs, *Shetland, A Photographer's Notebook*, which contains a section devoted to trout fishing. This section has a photograph of a wonderful catch of sea trout and an atmospheric photograph of an angler fishing for sea trout in the sea (shown below). We know that Jack himself fished for sea trout and in the accompanying text to his photographs he bemoaned the decline in sea trout numbers in the twenty years prior to his book being published in 1948. Clearly the decline in the sea trout population was a gradual process and in 1964 Jack published a couple of articles in *The New Shetlander* magazine (Numbers 68 and 69) in which

A fine catch of sea trout (top) and sea trout fishing in the open sea.
Photographs by John Peterson from Shetland, A Photographer's Notebook *(1948).*
Courtesy of Shetland Museum & Archives.

he examined the causes of the decline (see Chapter One). His articles were clearly based on an extensive knowledge of the sea trout and sea trout fishing over a long period of years and he recalled listening to the recurrent splashing of sea trout in Shetland voes on autumn nights fifty years previously and of seeing them leaping at any hour of the day.

Unfortunately, neither Jack, nor his brother James, appears to have left behind any record of their fishing experiences. However, their younger sibling Magnus Fraser Peterson, wrote a fascinating article for *Shetland Life* magazine (September 1984, No. 47) in which he recalled the family's early days and embryonic fishing careers at Gruting. He was inspired to write the article following the announcement that Gruting School, where both his parents had taught from the early 1890s until 1928, was to close down. It appears that pupils attended the school from as far afield as Hoganess, a journey of three miles over exposed moorland with two burns to cross. The children made the journey twice a day, both summer and winter, and Magnus recalled that they were the best attenders who always arrived at school early.

As well as learning basic subjects such as reading, writing and arithmetic, the children were taught other more practical skills, which might benefit them in their future lives. During the dinner break, the children were given instruction in handling small boats, a ready supply of which lay on the beach fifty yards from the school. In addition, the children were encouraged to make their own rafts and this is, perhaps, where Professor Peterson gained his inspiration for building his floating fishing chair. Apparently, the rafts they constructed were not particularly stable and usually disintegrated in about three feet of water. It sounds a familiar story! Swimming lessons were also arranged for the boys and the schoolmaster would pace up and down the beach with boots unlaced and jacket ready to throw off in case of a child getting into difficulty. Only once did he have to demonstrate his life-guard skills when a non-swimmer got out of his depth.

The local Gruting boys spent a great deal of their spare time in fishing, both in the sea and in fresh water. During the spring piltocks (young coalfish) were the main quarry and in summer the mackerel. These were mainly caught with piltock wands, lengths of bamboo cane, which were sold in all the local stores, equipped with a fixed line and hooks. These were either fished trailing from the back of a small boat or from a suitable point on the shore. Daily reports of the previous night's catches were frequent topics of the boys' conversations at school. At other times the boys would acquire a section of old herring net and set it out along the shore. This often kept their families supplied with piltocks, mackerel, herring, the occasional sea trout and, one occasion, three large skate. His most impressive catch in a net was a four foot shark, which he hauled aboard their small boat by its tail. He kept the shark for a while in a zinc bath to show off to his friends before releasing it back into the sea. His most thrilling form of fishing involved wading out with a bamboo cane with three cod hooks lashed to its tip to snatch a five foot conger eel. The unfortunate eel, thus impaled, not only provided a source of food but its skin was turned into a very useful gun case. With regard to brown trout fishing in the local burn and lochs, Magnus claimed that few boys bothered with this, although he recalled once catching seventy-two small brown trout from Gruting burn during the month of April, the majority of which he returned to the water. Presumably, the fish were caught on worm.

Although he was born and spent his formative years on Shetland, Magnus Peterson spent most of his professional life working as an engineer for Fairey Aviation in the south of England. However, he was a frequent visitor to Shetland and kept up a keen interest in the islands' affairs.

CHAPTER 21

Moray McLaren & the Simmer Dim

Over the years I must have read hundreds of accounts written by anglers of the capture of their first fish. The capture of a first fish is somewhat akin to a rite of passage in an angler's life and I vividly remember catching my first fish, a perch of around four ounces, on a local mill lodge in Lancashire. The perch greedily devoured a brandling freshly dug from my grandad's allotment and was caught on a rod made from an old tank aerial equipped with a small bakelite reel and red-tipped quill float. Many anglers, I suspect, started their angling careers in a similar fashion. Moray McLaren, however, was different. He caught his first fish in India. Although he was born in Edinburgh on the 24th of March, 1901, four generations of his mother's family had served in India and, at the age of six, McLaren went to live in India.

McLaren's fishing career began in 1911 at the age of ten when he caught his first fish from a well somewhere in Rajputana in north-west India. The well was one of three or four in a dried-up lake bed, which only filled with water after the rains came. The local villagers had sunk these wells as water preservers against the dry season. As the lake started to dry up as the dry season came on, the water retreated into the wells, which always remained full. He was taken on his first fishing expedition by one of the innumerable Indian servants who were employed by his parents. As the servant was beating his way through the thick trees on the way to the lake, he suddenly stopped, took out a catapult and fired at a white dove in a nearby tree. The stone from the catapult hit the mark and, as the hapless bird lay

fluttering on the ground, the servant proceeded to pluck it and tear the flesh from its breast. After enquiring the reason for this, the young McLaren was told by the servant that he had forgotten to bring along the bait and the dove's flesh would serve that purpose. After reaching the well, the Indian servant tore a morsel of meat from the dove's breast and threw it in. Immediately, the dark water boiled as the fish competed for their share of the meat. McLaren gingerly held out his bamboo rod for the hook to be baited, as he did not like the idea of touching the flesh of the still warm bird with his own fingers. He gently lowered his bait into the well whereupon it was immediately seized by a greedy little fish. McLaren struck and the fish flew some twenty feet up into the air before shedding the hook and plummeting back into the well. His second attempt was more successful and, on feeling a tug on his line, he struck and the fish landed on the dried mud behind him.

McLaren went on to catch numerous other fish that day, none of which weighed more than a quarter of a pound. He never found out the type of fish he caught, which were black, slimy and from six to ten inches long. They were voracious feeders and he had to be careful to avoid being bitten while unhooking them. He proudly carried his catch home only to learn that the fish were inedible!

At the age of eleven, McLaren, having 'outgrown the teaching capacities of a series of governesses', was sent back to relatives in Scotland to continue his education at Merchiston Castle School in Edinburgh. In the summer of 1913, he was taken on holiday to St. Andrews so that his elders could play golf. Whilst there, he discovered Ladebraes burn on the outskirts of the city, and it is there that he caught his first decent-sized trout. He had not yet learned how to cast a fly but, after digging up a few worms and dock or docken grubs, he made his way to the burn. It was just before he was due to return home for high tea when he cast his dock grub into a little run above a mill pool. He felt a tug on his line and struck into a lively fish, which, for a few minutes, led him a merry dance. At length, he managed to ease the fish to the edge of the stream and pull it on to land. It was by far the largest fish he had ever caught and weighed just over a pound.

From Merchiston Castle School McLaren went on to Corpus Christi College, Cambridge. After further study in Paris, he was appointed assistant editor of the *London Mercury*. In 1928, he joined the BBC and became first assistant editor of the *Listener*. Three years later he returned to Edinburgh to a post at Scottish

Broadcasting House, eventually becoming the Scottish Region's programme director. In 1935, he moved to Broadcasting House in London and was appointed assistant director of the Features and Drama department. In 1940, following the start of the Second World War, he resigned from the BBC and was attached to the Foreign Office as head of the Polish region intelligence department. After the war he returned to Edinburgh to live and write independently and in 1946 he married the Scottish actress Lennox Milne.

He first visited Shetland shortly after the war and was completely overwhelmed by the islands and the fishing to be found there. He was particularly glad that he had not visited the Shetland Isles in his early years 'so that they could come upon me with pristine perfection more fitly and later on in my life'. He was especially captivated by the exciting fishing for sea trout in the saltwater voes. Most of what we know of his time in Shetland comes from his two books, *A Singing Reel*, published in 1953 and *The Fishing Waters of Scotland*, co-written with William B. Currie, and published posthumously in 1972.

His first impressions of Shetland were not too encouraging as the airplane landed at Sumburgh through the greyness of a summer mist. The fourteen miles from Sumburgh to Lerwick were equally depressing. However, on reaching Lerwick, he was immediately enchanted by its narrow, winding streets with paving stones reaching right across from house to house. He was even more pleased to be staying in a house whose foundations were in the sea and whose bedroom gave a direct view across to the island of Bressay. It was late May when he arrived and that evening, as the mist rose, he was enthralled by the half light of the 'Simmer Dim' as he wandered through the still bustling streets of Lerwick at 11pm.

The following morning he had his first experience of fishing. He was taken to the Loch of Tingwall by his host and guide, whom he refers to by his initials R.M. (possibly Ronnie Mathieson, the then secretary of the Zetland Anglers' Association). The morning was grey, but not too grey, with an occasional glint of the sun and the wind was in the right direction for the loch. In fact, the fishing conditions were ideal and it wasn't long before he encountered the astonishing fighting powers of Tingwall trout. About fifteen minutes into the first drift, McLaren's conversation with his gillie was abruptly interrupted by a sharp tug on his line and he was into his first Shetland trout. Shortly after hooking him, he thought he had lost him as the line went slack. The fish, however, had run towards the boat, but, on reaching the boat, it immediately tore off, stripping line from his reel and putting a hoop in his 9½-foot Palakona cane rod. As the fish splashed on the surface, McLaren estimated its weight at three pounds. Suddenly, the fish jumped clear of the water and he realised his estimation had been grossly exaggerated. When eventually the fish was boated, it weighed in at an ounce or so under two pounds. Still, McLaren was delighted with his first Shetland trout and one of the first fish he had caught since the end of the war. His gillie was less impressed by the size of his fish and constantly minimized the size of fish caught, estimating this one to be around three-quarters to a pound in weight, before the scales put him right. That first day on Tingwall produced a memorable basket of brown trout, some of the most sporting fish he ever had on the end of his line.

McLaren's descriptions of his encounters with hard-fighting fish are some of the best I have ever read but his most dramatic prose is reserved for his battles with the justly famed Shetland sea trout. He returned to Shetland in September 1949 and one morning he was taken by R.M. to a loch (probably Vidlin Loch) in the northern end of the mainland of Shetland, a loch connected to the sea by a short burn. In addition to holding sea and brown trout, the muddy floor of the loch was home to small flounders. The loch was round and quite sizeable, two to three hundred yards in diameter. McLaren and his companion started to wade the loch in different directions, keeping as far apart as possible. After catching three small herling (young sea trout), he found himself waist deep in the middle of the loch when he hooked into a fresh-run sea trout. The fish immediately ran out his line and, at the end of it, leapt out of the water. Another run and aerial display followed. Fortunately, there was no open sea for him to run to and the loch had no weeds or other obstructions. After playing the fish out and bringing him to his side, McLaren realised that he had only his small net with him, which was more suited to landing small brown trout. He had broken the clip on his sea-trout net a day or two earlier and had left it behind. He managed to lure the fish head-first into the little net and lift him. The fish continued to struggle and the hook pulled out. McLaren thrust his rod under the arm holding the net and put his other hand over the fish to press him against the mesh and secure him. It was then that another problem presented itself. His feet were almost stuck fast in the muddy bottom and, as he managed with great difficulty to extricate them, he almost fell over. In fear of losing both his life and the fish, he eventually managed to wade gingerly a hundred and fifty yards to the shore. On reaching the shore and safety, he flung the net, rod and fish on to the bank as far away from the water as possible. R.M., with his customary minimisation of the fish's weight, estimated it at a pound and a half. Later that evening, however, McLaren had great pleasure in telephoning him to say that he was two pounds out and that the fish weighed 3½lb!

Later that same day, he caught an even larger sea trout and although in later years he caught others of a greater weight he never caught a more sporting fish or one that gave him such protracted and varied excitement. After leaving the loch where he had caught his 3½-pounder, R.M. had to go back to Lerwick and McLaren decided to try his luck on the Laxo burn, famed for its sea trout, where he had been given permission to fish by Mr Robert Bruce. After meeting up with his wife at the keeper's house, he commenced fishing by the bend of the pool above the bridge on the Laxo burn. The name Laxo is derived from the Old Norse 'laks', which refers to a game fish, salmon, trout or sea trout and the burn had probably been fished with nets or traps by the Vikings centuries earlier. He was using a cast equipped with one fly, a Greenwell, the same fly on which he had caught his fish that morning, and was fishing it wet. He was soon into a fish, which turned out to be a small dark-coloured brown trout. After throwing it back, he was concerned that he might have disturbed the pool and put the fish down. He need not have worried. As he was idly casting, he was taken off guard by a boiling rise. He promptly struck and found himself attached to a very lively sea trout.

    The fish put on a terrifying display of its power in the confines of the pool. It tore up and down, jumped repeatedly and made the reel screech incessantly. Fortunately, the fish was freshly up from the sea and seemed unaware of the geography of its surroundings. If it had headed back down to the sea or upstream towards the rocks in the pool above, McLaren would not have been able to control it. Instead, the fish, in its terror, relied on its sheer strength and power to try and rid itself of the hook in its jaw. Eventually, after a battle of over ten minutes, the fish began to tire and McLaren was now faced with the prospect of trying to net it in his small landing-net. He made four vain attempts at landing him and almost slipped down the bank into the pool himself. His wife, who was also an accomplished angler, now came to the rescue. She took the net, climbed down the slope of the bank, and slipped the net beneath him until the mouth of the mesh was directly below his nose. McLaren slackened his line, the fish plunged nose first into the net, while his wife heaved. In an instant all three of them, McLaren, his wife and the fish, were lying on the shelving bank. As the fish was still thrashing about, he managed to place his hand under its gills and pull it to safety. That fish weighed 5½lb and, as it was landed, it had shed the fly, a Greenwell that he never used again. He reckoned it deserved a long rest!

    Although he fished on Shetland a number of times afterwards, he never forgot his encounter with that sea trout and the story of its capture is re-told, in a somewhat less dramatic form, in his book co-authored with Bill Currie, *The Fishing Waters of Scotland* (1972). This book, as its title implies, is written more in the form of a guide for the visiting angler.

In his later years, McLaren fished extensively throughout Scotland and further afield. He died on the 12th of July, 1971, aged seventy. Nowadays, he is perhaps best remembered for his literary and dramatic works and as a book reviewer for the *Glasgow Herald*.

CHAPTER 22

The Brown Trout Era

When Moray McLaren fished on Shetland shortly after World War Two he was surprised by the attitude of his host towards brown trout fishing. He found him, and other Shetland anglers whom he met, so preoccupied by the excellence of the sea trout fishing that they were unable to spare much enthusiasm for the brown trout fishing. They found it difficult to believe that an angler from Scotland would venture so far north in the months of May and June purely to fish for brown trout. McLaren was not so predisposed towards sea trout and believed the brown trout fishing in Shetland to be the equal of any to be found on most of the famous preserves in Scotland and he claims it would be difficult to find gamer fish than the brown trout he caught on the Loch of Tingwall on his first morning in Shetland.

His host's attitude towards brown trout fishing is reflected in the literary accounts of fishing in Shetland that have survived from before the Second World War and even into the 1950s and early 1960s. Most of these accounts focus on the excellence of the sea trout fishing, especially in the salt water voes, a type of fishing for which Shetland was justly famous and which attracted anglers from all over the country and beyond. Although brown trout fishing does feature in some of these accounts, it definitely plays second fiddle to sea trout fishing and, even though there are references to large baskets of small brown trout being taken, there are few accounts of large specimens being captured. All that was to change in the later decades of the twentieth century.

As we saw in Chapter One, as early as the 1960s the writing

was on the wall for sea trout and John Peterson, in a couple of articles in *The New Shetlander* (Spring and Summer 1964), was warning of the steady decline of these sporting fish. When Major R. V. Garton, author of *Lure of the Lochs* (1972), fished in Shetland in the 1960s he fished mainly for brown trout. On one occasion in July 1967, while fishing the Loch of Houlland near Eshaness, he found himself being dive-bombed by a number of Arctic terns, whose nests he had disturbed and, as he was casting, he accidentally hooked one and cast it into the loch. After witnessing this event, the Arctic terns attacked with renewed fury and he was only saved by the assistance of his wife who fended the birds off with his wading staff, while he managed to net the unfortunate bird and release it. David Street, author of *Fishing in Wild Places* (1989) was similarly attacked, this time by a great skua or bonxie, when he was trout fishing on the Loch of Grunnavoe during the early 1960s. Although Street had come to Shetland primarily in search of sea trout, he found he had more success with the brown trout. While fishing the Loch of Grunnavoe, before the bonxie attack, he had what he could only describe as a 'visitation from the spirits'. After setting up his rod and catching a few brown trout, he was suddenly overwhelmed by a sense of serenity and well-being brought about by the remote beauty of the place. Street's experience certainly gives credence to the old saying, 'there is more to fishing than catching fish', and nowhere is that saying more applicable than in Shetland.

It was during the 1980s that the sea trout fishing in Shetland declined to such an extent that in some years fewer than ten fish were caught by anglers. Fortunately, the decline in sea trout coincided with a rise in the popularity of reservoir trout fishing, primarily for rainbow trout, further south. Large waters such as Rutland, Grafham and Pitsford were opened up to fishing and fly fishermen were developing new flies, tackle and techniques to cope with the conditions on these waters. The fly fishing magazines were full of articles devoted to flies and tactics suitable for reservoir fishing, including float-tubing, and Shetland

The Brown Trout Era

A fine Shetland brown trout caught by Paul Bloomer on Papa Stour.

The Loch of Houlland and the remains of a broch.

anglers were not slow to realise that similar tackle and tactics could be employed on the wild lochs of Shetland and that big brown trout could be caught by design rather than by accident. Competition fishing, too, was becoming increasingly popular and new fly patterns and tactics were being developed by anglers to give them the edge. Anglers were also becoming more knowledgeable regarding the ecology of the waters they were fishing and the diet of the trout within. It is, perhaps, no coincidence that the first annual trout festival, designed to promote the excellent brown trout fish that Shetland has to offer, was first held in 1992.

When Malcolm Greenhalgh and Oliver Edwards were invited to the trout festival as guests of honour in 1993 and 1994, they were delighted by the quality of wild brown trout fishing in Shetland. Malcolm, in his autobiography *Casting a Line* (2014), was particularly impressed by the fishing on Spiggie:

> *We fished several lochs in our two visits, and had a great time float-tubing on one loch that produced trout well in excess of the pound mark (wild brown trout, not stocked fish). But I think our favourite loch was Spiggie.*

On the first occasion they fished the loch, it was a wild and drizzly day and the visibility was so bad that they could barely make out the outline of the hills half a mile away. Their host, however, was undeterred, and was soon spotted wading out two hundred yards from the shore:

> *We too set out, and discovered that the bed of the loch was hard, almost flat sand, and the water depth was thigh deep in wave troughs, and almost top of chest-wader deep when a wave rolled past us. As for the trout, they swam everywhere and anywhere over this sandy plateau. So it was simply a matter of slowly wading hither and thither, back to the wind, and casting out the flies and then retrieving them. One thing that we did note was that the least efficient way of fishing was to cast out the flies*

and retrieve them whilst standing still. The most efficient was to cast the flies out and then wade backwards as we retrieved them so that they came back on a curved, not straight, route. The difference in catch rate between the two retrieves - straight with us standing still and curved with us slowly moving - was incredible; at least 10:1.

Malcom's advice is extremely valuable and applies to fishing from the bank just as much as fishing while wading and it is a technique I have adopted both on lochs and local reservoirs with some success. Malcolm was suitably impressed by the beautifully marked brown trout of Spiggie and, having fished it three times, he claims that it never let him down and had a special atmosphere about it:

Of the hundreds of lochs that I have fished, between these northernmost islands of the British Isles, south to the lochs of Galloway, it has the most outstandingly magical atmosphere as well as beautiful trout.

When the Shetland Anglers' Association published its 1998 guide to trout fishing in the islands, it is noticeable that it contained little information on sea trout fishing. The guide did, however, contain sections on the brown trout's environment and the trout's menu, which examined the food sources available to the trout in Shetland waters. Association member, Graeme Callander, even provided a table and graph showing the stomach contents of over a hundred trout that were examined over the course of a season. The guide also contained a selection of more modern flies, together with their dressings, designed to cover the trout's varied diet. The tradition of developing and designing flies suited to Shetland waters continues to this day and a large part of the Association's website is devoted to this.

The late Bruce Sandison, whose family hails from Unst, was one of Scotland's best-known angling writers and journalists, whose most recent book, *Secret Lochs and Special Places* (2015), contains an excellent chapter on Shetland. Bruce fished on the islands on many occasions and in May 1992 was one of the guests of honour at the inaugural trout festival. His book is essential reading for the angler visiting Shetland and contains a vast amount of information, not only regarding Mainland lochs, but also regarding the lochs on Yell, Unst, Whalsay, Fetlar and Bressay. He was not afraid to speak his mind, either, and laid the blame for the decline of the sea trout in Shetland squarely on the shoulders of the fish farming industry.

The Loch of Tingwall was one of Bruce's favourite lochs, which he first fished with his friend and SAA member, Rae Phillips. Fishing from a boat, his favourite drift was from the north-east corner down the shore for around 300 yards to an old dyke. Bruce was impressed by the exceptional quality and hard-fighting abilities of Tingwall trout. Connected to Tingwall by a short feeder stream is the Loch of Asta, and Bruce claimed that the best sport to be had on this loch was from the bank on the east shoreline. Like Tingwall, Asta is a limestone loch, which, on the right day, can produce larger fish than its neighbour. Other lochs favoured by Bruce were Spiggie, Benston, and those in the vicinity of Ronas Hill. Like most good fishing books, Bruce's contains the story of one that got away - on the Loch of Girlsta. Bruce fished on Girlsta with Rae Phillips and, as they drifted down the east shore, Rae managed to boat two fish, each weighing 1lb 8oz. As they were sitting by the shore eating their lunch, Bruce suddenly spotted a fish rising a few yards from the bank. Abandoning his coffee and sandwich, he grabbed his rod and cast out over the ring of the rise. His fly, a Black Pennell, was immediately grabbed and his rod (Bruce invariably used a cane rod) was almost wrenched out of his hands. The huge trout bored down to the depths and sent his reel screaming in protest. Shortly afterwards, the fly pulled free and Bruce was left reeling from his brief encounter.

Shetland clearly has a lot to offer the angler in search of wild brown trout and over the last thirty or forty years a whole generation of Shetland anglers has grown up who have dedicated themselves to studying the habits of these fish. Not content with fishing traditional methods and flies, they have developed a wide range of techniques and flies to suit their favoured lochs and, whereas the capture of a large brown trout of five pounds or over was once a rarity, nowadays much larger fish are reported every season. Shetland angler, David Pottinger, is a legendary catcher of big wild trout, whose innovative fly, the Potty Palmer, has accounted for well in excess of one hundred wild brown trout over five pounds in weight during the forty seasons since it first graced his cast.

Although recent years have witnessed an improvement in sea trout numbers, I suspect that if Moray McLaren were to visit Shetland today, his host would be far less dismissive of the superlative brown trout fishing to be found in these islands.

CHAPTER 23

Flies for Shetland : Past & Present
(Flies marked with bold numbers can be found illustrated in the colour plate section)

Most fly fishermen, and I am as guilty as any, carry around far too many flies and I have boxes and boxes full of weird and wonderful creations made out of fur, feather, and increasingly, synthetic materials. Even though I carry around hundreds of flies to lake, river or loch, the vast majority of them never grace the end of my line and I tend to rely on a few tried and tested patterns that have rarely let me down. It is only when desperation sets in that I tie on one of my more unusual creations. Since the establishment of the Fly Dressers' Guild in 1967, fly dressing has become a popular hobby, which helps to while away those winter months when the weather is too foul to go fishing. In many ways, I suspect, flies are designed to catch fishermen as much as fish and hardly a month goes by without the angling magazines carrying the dressings of a number of new creations, which are claimed to be irresistible to trout or salmon. I must confess to being taken in by some of these new patterns, which I think might work on my local rivers and reservoirs and I cannot resist dressing a number of them. Most of them, however, lie languishing in my fly box destined never to grace the end of my cast. Up until comparatively recently, most flies were created out of readily available materials such as fur and feather, although traditional salmon flies were an exception, many of which were created out of exotic and difficult to obtain materials. Many of the modern creations, which appear in the angling press, are increasingly made out of synthetic materials or a fusion of traditional and synthetic materials and I find it hard to keep up with the plethora of new materials that are regularly advertised in the angling press.

In addition to angling magazines, which regularly promote new flies, the internet has also become a forum for fly dressers to exchange their views and patterns, and video clips give the fly dresser step-by-step instructions on how to tie these latest creations. Competition angling, too, has spawned a host of new patterns as anglers seek to gain the edge and develop match winning creations. Devising a new fly pattern, however, is somewhat akin to re-inventing the wheel and few modern patterns can lay claim to being truly original, most are variations of existing patterns with the addition of some extra material such as a strand or two of *Flashabou* in the wing or tail.

It must be extremely difficult for a novice fly fisher, faced with a myriad of fly patterns, to decide on which ones to use for a particular river, lake or loch and seeking local advice is strongly recommended. When I first started fly fishing on a local lake around fifty years ago, life was much simpler. On the advice of my mentor, my friend's father, I acquired a small selection of traditional wet flies, which served their purpose admirably and they still serve their purpose today. Tried and tested traditional patterns such as the Mallard and Claret, Butcher, Soldier Palmer, Zulu, etc., have stood the test of time and are just as effective today as when they were originally invented a century or more ago. Sir Edward Grey, who fished for sea trout on Shetland during the closing years of the nineteenth century, eschewed the use of a multitude of patterns. Instead, he relied on four patterns dressed in a range of sizes: Soldier Palmer, Woodcock and Yellow, Black and Orange Spider and the Black Red Hackle Fly (see opposite). The dressings of these and some of the other patterns mentioned in this chapter are given in the Appendix. Paul Bloomer, a keen angler and fly dresser who edits the section on flies on the Shetland Anglers' Association website, always empties his fly boxes at the end of the season and picks out the best flies that have performed well, usually not more than a dozen or so, and puts them in a master fly box for future reference. His master fly box also contains flies given to him by other local anglers that are worthy of a future trial.

Sea trout flies from Fly Fishing *by Sir Edward Grey, 1899.*

Shetland has a long tradition of fly dressing and apart from the more traditional flies used throughout Scotland and the rest of Great Britain, a number of patterns have been devised specifically for use in Shetland itself.

Edward Charlton (1814-1874), one of the earliest anglers to write an account of fly fishing on Shetland, relied on a small number of patterns whose dressings are to be found in James Wilson's *The Rod and the Gun*, first published in 1840. James Wilson (1795-1856) was a friend of Charlton's and the two treatises on shooting and fishing, which comprise his book, had originally appeared as lengthy articles in the eighth edition of the *Encyclopaedia Britannica*. The flies used by Charlton on Shetland were the Green Mantle, the Grizzly King and the Professor, the latter fly devised by Wilson's brother, John Wilson (1785-1854), Professor of Moral Philosophy at Edinburgh University and a very keen angler who wrote under the pseudonym 'Christopher North'. James Wilson, too, visited Shetland briefly on a tour round the coast of Scotland and fished on Strand Loch, where he used the same flies that he recommended to

Patterns from The Rod and the Gun *by James Wilson, 1840.*

Charlton. On that occasion, he and his companions, including Charles Duncan, one of the most successful fly fishers on Shetland at the time, caught almost two dozen trout, the best being a freshly-run sea trout of around three pounds, which fell to the Green Mantle. An account of Wilson's visit to Shetland can be found in *A Voyage Round the Coasts of Scotland and the Isles* (1842).

John Tudor, who sometimes wrote under the pseudonym of 'Old Wick', fished on Shetland a number of times between 1875 and 1881 and, in a series of articles written for *The Field* in 1878, he recorded a number of flies commonly used at that time. One particular fly, which was recommended to him for sea trout fishing, bears no name and the dressing is as follows: Body - dark red mohair or pig's wool, Rib - gold twist, Shoulder Hackle - black-red (coch-y-bonddu), Wing - jay, from the fibres

FLIES FOR
SHETLAND
PAST & PRESENT

(These flies are all mentioned in Chapter 23 and dressings for most of them can be found in the Appendix on page 251)

(1) The Belmont

(2) Clousta Blue

The Trout Angler in Shetland

(3) Terror

(4) Demon

(5) Castle Kergord

(6) Castle Dunkeld

(7) Loch Ordie

Flies for Shetland : Past & Present

(8) Potty Palmer

(9) Potty TI

(10) Potty Nite-Brite

(11) Potty Sparkler

(12) Potty Bluebottle

(22) Ogrehunch White

(23) Ogrehunch Black

(24) Hadland's Sea Trout Killer

(25) Magenta Palmer

(26) Andy Pandy

(27) Louby Lou

Flies for Shetland : Past & Present

(28) Barclay's Sunburst

(29) Low Rider

(30) Tangerine Dream

(31) Dark Longhorn Caddis

(32) Norski Lad

(33) Black Pennell Muddler

THE TROUT ANGLER IN SHETLAND

(34) Claret Clan Chief

(35) Clan Chief Muddler

(36) Black Adult Midge

(37) Spring Black

(38) David's Grey Boy

(39) David's Emerger

from the butt of the long wing feathers. The gentleman who gave him this pattern insisted that it should not be dressed with a tail as sea trout often rise 'short'. Other flies recommended by Tudor include the Francis fly, devised by angler and author Francis Francis around 1858, the Red Palmer, Black Palmer, Quill Dun, Red Badger and the Professor. In his more extensive work, *The Orkneys and Shetland* (1883), he recorded a fly said to be 'deadly medicine' on the Loch of Belmont on Unst. This fly was subsequently christened The Belmont (**1**) and has since spawned a modern variant, partly dressed with modern synthetic materials. Both dressings are given in the Appendix.

The Clousta Hotel at Bixter, which opened in 1895 and subsequently burned down in 1907, was a popular destination for visiting anglers. Its name and the nearby Loch of Clousta have become associated with a fly devised in the late nineteenth century - The Clousta Blue (**2**). Until recently the dressing for this fly, which appeared in Hardy Brothers catalogues, was thought to be lost until a cased example recently turned up on eBay.

In 1901, C.J.H. Cassels published an *Angler's Guide*, primarily intended for anglers visiting the recently opened St. Magnus Hotel at Hillswick. With regard to flies for use in the area, the author recommended the following flies: Butcher, Zulu and the teal wing with different bodies. For sea trout standard sea trout patterns were recommended.

A much more comprehensive list of fly patterns for both trout and sea trout was given in the *Anglers' Guide for The Shetlands*, published by John Tait and Co., the following year. The best flies recommended for sea trout, to be dressed on sizes, 8, 9, or 10 Limerick hooks were: Soldier or Red Palmer, Alexandra, Jungle Cock, Green Mantle, Lord Saltoun, Zulu, Priest, Butcher, Woodcock and Gold, Woodcock and Red, Cardinal, Blae and Silver or Silver Doctor, Black Palmer, Teal and Red, Teal and Green, Teal and Yellow, March Brown, Mallard and Claret and Grouse and Claret. The author also recommended the use of Terrors (**3**) and Demons (**4**), three-hook lures, dressed in imitation of sand-eels, for use in salt water.

Typical Shetland flies from a Redpath & Co. catalogue.

For trout fishing on lochs, the author recommended the following patterns, dressed on size 9, 10 or 11 Limerick hooks: Red Tag, Coch-y-Bonddu, Black Beetle, Zulu, Red or Soldier Palmer, Orange Partridge, Green Mantle, Claret and Grouse, Claret and Mallard, Red and Teal, Green and Teal, March Brown, Saltoun, Red, Orange and Silver Sedges, Moths and Bustards (for evening fishing), Alexandra, Black Palmer, Grouse and Purple, Grouse and Orange, Watson's Fancy, Butcher, Badger, Coachman and Cow Dung.

For fishing Shetland burns the following patterns, dressed on smaller Round or Sneck Bend hooks in sizes 11, 12 or 13, were recommended: March Brown, Hare Lug, Saltoun, Professor, Priest, Red Spider, Black Beetle, Coch-y-Bonddu, Blue Dun, Wickham's Fancy, Silver Sedge, Red Tag, Red Sedge and Orange Partridge.

Virtually all the flies mentioned above would have been well known to the anglers of the day and are common wet and loch flies, many of which are still used by anglers today. Red flies such as the Soldier or Red Palmer and the Cardinal seemed to be very much in favour and an author who went by the name of 'Butcha', who wrote an article for *The Field* on fishing in Shetland, published on the 26th of July, 1923, stated 'at least one red fly should be on every cast. Red appears to attract better in the peat coloured water'.

With regard to Terrors and Demons (which sounds like the title of a Dan Brown novel), John Buchan and his son had great success with a three-hooked Terror with a long Eton-blue wing while fishing for sea trout on Unst in 1926 and C.J.H.Cassels caught a 5¼lb sea trout in Spiggie Voe on a triple-hooked Demon lure dressed with white hackles with black centres (badger hackles).

Pat Castle was one of the most experienced and successful of Scottish anglers, who caught his first trout, weighing half a pound, when he was a small boy. He fished extensively throughout Scotland and his best basket of fish was taken on Shetland in 1912, when he caught fifty-two sea trout with the fly on one day. During the 1930s and 1940s, he wrote a number of books on angling, including *Angling Holidays in Scotland: Where to Fish and Where to Stay* (1937). In this book he gives the dressings of two successful flies that he devised for fishing on Shetland. The Castle Kergord **(5)** was specifically designed for fishing for sea trout on the Kergord Burn, hence its name. His Castle's Dunkeld **(6)**, a successful pattern for both trout and sea trout, is basically a variant of the traditional Dunkeld fly.

James Coutts, author of *Game Fishing: A Guide to the Shetlands*, published in 1967, recommended a fairly traditional list of flies for both brown and sea trout. He claimed that the locally favoured patterns for brown trout were: Peter Ross, Teal and Green, Teal and Red, March Brown, Greenwell's Glory, Soldier Palmer, Blue Zulu and Black Pennell. He suggested that the visiting angler equip himself with a selection of these flies dressed in sizes from 8 to 12. For sea trout he claimed that standard flies used for sea trout elsewhere would serve just as well in Shetland although the local favourites were: Silver Butcher, Silver Cardinal, Peter Ross, Grouse and Claret, Invicta, Teal, Blue and Silver and all of the Zulu and Pennell dressings. He suggested that a selection of these flies in sizes from 8 to 10 with a few size 6 flies would serve the angler well. His most successful fly for brown trout fishing on Shetland was the Cinnamon and Gold and his favourite cast for Shetland waters consisted of a Dark Mackerel (size 8) on the top dropper, a Cinnamon and Gold (size 10) on the middle dropper and a Coachman (size 10) on the point.

One fly that has come to prominence in Shetland over the last thirty years or so is the Loch Ordie (7). The fly itself was invented in the United States by Edward R. Hewitt in imitation of a butterfly and originally consisted of two palmer-like bodies in tandem, dressed on single hooks with a tiny flying treble sometimes added. Hewitt christened the fly the Neversink Skater and used it in Scotland when the Duke of Atholl gave him permission to fish on Loch Ordie where the fly worked wonders. Not surprisingly, the fly became popular on Loch Ordie, from where it took the name by which it is now known. There is some debate as to how the fly was introduced to Shetland and both Hector Barclay and Willie Binns are credited with its introduction. Hector Barclay is believed to have used the fly on Shetland in the 1970s while Willie Binns is said to have introduced it over thirty years ago after coming across it in Caithness. Nowadays, the fly is dressed by simply cramming as many dark red/brown hackles on to the hook as possible followed by one or two white hackles at the front. It is an extremely versatile fly and is frequently employed on the top dropper although big fish expert David Pottinger is credited with catching a huge trout on a Loch Ordie fished on a Di7 line inched slowly along the bottom. It is particularly successful in windy weather, which is so much a feature of Shetland and the fly itself is almost certainly taken for a sedge. Although the fly has been superseded to a certain extent by the rise in popularity of Hedgehog/ Sedgehog patterns developed on Orkney during the 1990s, it is still a deadly fly and over the years it has spawned a number of variants with the addition of a red or orange tail or jungle cock cheeks. Another variation, popularised by Colin Wiseman is dressed with grouse hackles rather than hen hackles and can be deadly on a dark day in a big rolling wave.

In 1982, the Shetland Anglers' Association published its own guide to angling in Shetland - *A Guide to Shetland Trout Angling*, which contained some valuable advice on flies and their use. By the 1980s sea trout stocks had declined and the main focus of this guide was on fishing for brown trout. The guide advised the use of just two flies on a cast to reduce the risk of snagging. The recommended flies were divided into categories suitable for use in early, mid, and late season:

> *Early season patterns include any of the dark flies, often with a red tag, e.g. Ke-He, Palmer, Zulu, Butcher, Black Spider, or a heavily dressed March Brown. Mid-season flies include Greenwell's Glory, Black Spider, March Brown and Wickham's Fancy. Late-season, as mid-season, but usually heavier dressed - a Cinnamon and Gold also works well at this time of year. Some anglers favour varying the size of the fly rather than the pattern, from 8's and 10's in early season down to 14's in mid and late season; this system can also be used in varying weather conditions. Other successful patterns seem to vary annually, and in recent years have included Dunkeld, Connemara Black, Silver Butcher and Loch Ordie.*

With regard to loch fishing for sea trout, similar flies to those used for brown trout were recommended. For sea trout fishing in the voes, the guide suggested the use of larger flies and black, blue, red and silver lures.

A much more comprehensive guide to fishing in Shetland, prepared by the Shetland Anglers' Association was published in 1998 - *Trout Fishing in Shetland*. This guide contained a very useful section on basic entomology entitled 'The Trout's Menu', which considered the main food items of Shetland trout and arranged them into three basic categories: The Up-Winged Flies (Ephemeroptera), The Flat-Winged Flies (Diptera) and Flies with Roof-Shaped Wings (Trichoptera). A number of imitative flies were recommended under each category, complete with illustrations and dressings.

For Up-Winged Flies the following patterns were recommended: Greenwell's Glory, Rough Olive, Golden Olive.

For Flat-Winged Flies the suggested imitations were as follows: Daddy Longlegs (dry), Wet Daddy, Black Midge Pupa, Black Pennell, Connemara Black, Blae and Black, Teal, Blue and Silver, Coachman, Bloody Doctor, Bibio, Cowdung, Coch-y-Bonddu.

For Flies with Roof-Shaped Wings the following imitations were recommended: Invicta, Black Speckled Sedge, Gold-Bead Sedge Pupa, Wickham's Fancy, Green Peter, Loch Ordie.

The guide also listed a selection of traditional and modern patterns, complete with their dressings, that had proved effective on Shetland waters: Gold Invicta, Bruiser, Olive Dabbler, Amber Dabbler, Clan Chief, Extractor, Eddie's Favourite, Soldier Palmer, Black Zulu, Green Tag Zulu, Blue Zulu, Hutch's Pennell, Orange Ke-He, Black Ke-He, Red Spot Palmer, Oakham Orange, Kate McLaren, Poacher, Golden Olive Bumble, Claret Bumble.

Over the course of the last twenty or thirty years, talented fly dressers on Shetland have devised a plethora of new patterns designed to tempt the truly wild fish of these islands. In a chapter such as this it would be impossible to do justice to all these patterns and the reader is directed to the excellent website of the Shetland Anglers' Association, which contains photographs and dressings of a whole host of flies suitable for Shetland waters. One particular novel feature of the site is the 'Cast of the Month', in which local anglers recommend their favourite flies for a particular month of the fishing season. In the section that follows I have chosen to look at a number of patterns devised by contemporary Shetland anglers and the dressings for these flies are given in the Appendix.

David Pottinger, who has fished in Shetland for over sixty-five years, has accounted for more trophy trout than almost anyone alive and his fame has spread beyond the confines of these remote islands. As well as being an expert angler, David is also a very talented fly dresser who has devised a number of patterns that have accounted for numerous specimen trout. One of his most famous patterns is undoubtedly the Potty Palmer **(8)**, a fly with at least forty seasons under its belt. This fly is responsible for the capture of over one hundred wild brown trout over five pounds in weight. David prefers to fish this in the late evening on the surface but it is a fly that will catch fish at any time of day on any line density. For fishing at night, David ties in two mini green lights at the head of the fly, an addition he describes as 'lethal'. The Potty T.I. **(9)** (named after a good angling friend who visited on the first night of its tying) was tied with daddy long-legs in mind. The fly is designed to be fished wet when daddies are on the water. In its first season David witnessed a fish of 7lb 9oz bow wave at least ten yards to attack the fly. A week later, on a different loch, it accounted for a fish of 8lb 4oz on the third cast. The Potty Nite Brite **(10)** has proved a very successful fly over many years, fished in the fading light of late evening in both Shetland and Orkney. Wild brown trout close to the magical double figure have fallen for this fly when the light is so low that colours are indistinguishable. The Potty Sparkler **(11)** is a great catcher of big trout especially when fished on the top dropper from a boat using a fast sinking line with contrasting patterns on droppers and tail. This pattern is allowed to sink to the bottom then stripped back and stopped just below the surface. It is heart stopping when a giant brown trout lunges up from the depths to engulf it. The Potty Blue-bottle **(12)** had its first outing on Shetland's Tingwall Loch in early season with great success. It is especially successful when house flies are visible, although not necessarily. The inspiration for the Potty Blue Jay **(13)** came from a pattern purchased by David in Norway in 1971. It is a deadly fly when fished in the sea and brackish water for salmon and sea trout. Brown and rainbow trout, including those of Rutland Water, have also fallen for its charms. It is a fly to try on one of those difficult days when nothing else seems to work.

Like David Pottinger, Colin Wiseman is a very experienced angler and prolific fly dresser who has helped many of the younger generation of Shetland fly dressers to hone their skills. His flies are well proportioned, beautifully tied and blend the colours associated with the great Celtic tradition of fly tying: clarets, magentas, olives, greens and browns. He constantly experiments with new patterns and variations on old patterns to suit the conditions of Shetland's lochs. One of his most enduring patterns is Colin's Beetle **(14)**, a simple but deadly fly suggestive of a number of creatures such as a snail, aquatic beetle or cased caddis. It is an excellent fly for the early season and should be fished slowly around the shallower margins. I can personally testify to the efficacy of this fly and it has caught me a number of trout, both brown and rainbows, on English reservoirs. In 1982, members of the Shetland Anglers' Association were given a complimentary set of two flies dressed by Colin Wiseman. The flies, which were responsible for the two biggest brown trout landed in 1981, were a Loch Ordy (Ordie) **(15a)** and a Black Zulu **(15b)**. Willie Binns caught a brown trout of 6lb 6oz on Girlsta Loch on the 30th of August, 1981 on a Loch Ordy (Ordie) while Dodie Irvine landed a specimen brownie of 9lb 4oz on the Loch of Huxter, Whalsay, on the 8th of April that same year on a Black Zulu.

Paul Bloomer is a relative newcomer to Shetland. He arrived in 1997 and has lived and worked on Shetland ever since. Paul has always been an angler and cannot remember a time when he did not fish. Growing up in the West Midlands, his earliest angling memories are of catching small roach and perch on local canals. Shortly after arriving on Shetland he caught his first trout on the Loch of Mousavord and has been a confirmed trout angler ever since. It wasn't long before he learned to dress flies and over the years he has caught thousands of trout, many on flies of his own creation. Paul is an artist as well as an angler and an article in the *Shetland Times* (12th June, 2009) shows him surrounded by boxes and boxes of neatly dressed flies. His artistic talents are clearly not confined to painting and print making but can clearly be seen in his creative flies. One of Paul's best brown trout to date was a magnificent and beautiful looking specimen of 7lb 9oz, caught on one of his own patterns, a Sticklecat **(16)**.

Another of Paul's creations is a fly christened Priscilla **(17)** by his ballet-dancing neighbour who caught him tying flies during the middle of what should have been a working day. He was experimenting with magenta hot spots in flies since he had been catching well at night on opaque black muddlers with magenta tails. He was looking for a fly that would get down a little deeper and, as a result, he tied a number of bead-headed Montana inspired nymphs. On her first outing on a notorious big fish loch, Priscilla accounted for a magnificent trout weighing 9lb 15oz.

Billy Reid is a fisherman by profession and has lived on Shetland all his life. He is a very keen angler and has been actively involved with the Shetland Anglers' Association for over twenty years, his current role being competition secretary for the bank fishing league. He enjoys competition angling and in recent years has twice been the Bank League champion. He particularly enjoys top of the water angling with a team of three ginked-up Hedgehog/Sedgehog flies. He modestly claims not to be an innovative fly dresser but his Hedgehog patterns have appeared in *Fly Fishing & Fly Tying* magazine (Spring 2012) and his Dunkeld Muddler **(18)** is a highly effective fly, which does particularly well in bright conditions and coloured water. With this fly Billy has managed to combine the elements of different traditional patterns into one killing fly that is highly regarded by local anglers.

Mark Sandison is a primary school teacher who has lived in Shetland all his life apart from a five-year spell in Aberdeen while training to be a teacher. Like many anglers, present author included, Mark had a break from fishing during his twenties when football took priority. However, since coming back to the fold he has become a more fanatical angler than ever. All his fishing is done from the bank and he likes to adopt a roving approach to his angling and, when the fish are unresponsive in one loch, he will simply move on to another. Over the years he has devised a number of successful flies for fishing in Shetland. Two of his most successful flies include the Fluorescent Orange Palmer Muddler **(19)** and the Pearly White Cat **(20)**. His biggest fish to date came from the Loch of Cliff on Unst and proved too heavy for his 7lb spring balance. It was not a particularly memorable fish and, coming from a loch containing salmon cages, he did not even bother to photograph it. His most memorable fish, a beautifully marked brown trout weighing 4lb exactly (see colour plate section opposite p56), was taken from a remote loch in the North Isles a few years ago.

Rae Phillips is the elder statesman of the Shetland Anglers' Association who lived through the halcyon days of sea trout fishing. He has fished since the age of seven and enjoys fishing for both brown and sea trout. He likes to fish light and for most of his fishing he uses a 9-foot rod equipped with either a floating or intermediate line rated AFTM 5. Over the course of his long angling career he has caught numerous trout in the 4-5lb bracket, especially from Lochs Benston and Strom. His favourite flies are two patterns of his own devising: the Widerbirse **(21)** and the Ogrehunch **(22 & 23)**. The latter pattern he prefers to dress 'anorexic' style and is a great pin fry imitation, which he describes as 'absolutely lethal', especially for sea trout. Rae still enjoys competition angling and during the annual trout festival in May 2010, he landed a magnificent brown trout of 4lb 12oz on a Bruiser fly from Benston Loch, which won him a prize for the best fish.

John Hadland was the former owner of the Rod and Line fishing tackle shop on Harbour Street, Lerwick and, under his management, the shop was a magnet for local fly fishermen where they could not only buy their fly tying materials but also flies dressed by his wife. Before he left Shetland he gave a selection of the flies he had developed to the Shetland Anglers' Association. Hadland's Sea Trout Killer **(24)** was one of John's favourite patterns for sea trout and is aptly named. His Magenta Palmer **(25)** is a rather garish fly to look at and no doubt raised a few eyebrows when he first tied it on to his cast. Nevertheless, John is a highly skilled fly fisherman and on its day this fly can be a killer, especially in coloured water.

When I was still in short trousers I remember watching the lunchtime TV programme *Watch with Mother*. Each day a different series was shown, which included Bill and Ben (my favourite), the Woodentops and Andy Pandy and I assume it was this latter programme which inspired Brian Watt to name two of the flies he developed, Andy Pandy **(26)** and Louby Lou **(27)**, after the two main characters in the programme. Brian Watt is an expert angler who is credited with changing the way people fish in Shetland with the tactics and flies he developed and refined. Both of these patterns are over twenty years old and they still catch as many fish today as they did when first tied. The Louby Lou recently accounted for a 6¼lb fish in one of the Northern Isles' big fish lochs. One of Brian Watt's patterns, the Green Palmer has the distinction of appearing in Stan Headley's book, *Trout and Salmon Flies of Scotland* (1997). Stan claims the fly proved devastating on Loch Harray and accounted for a number of large brown and sea trout on the Loch of Stenness in Orkney.

The Hedgehog, a pattern developed by Orcadian Sandy Nicholson in the early 1990s and its variant the Sedgehog, have proved extremely popular flies and have superseded Loch Ordie flies on the casts of many of today's anglers. I, too, have had considerable success with these patterns on my local reservoirs and tarns. The Barclay's Sunburst Stingy Bee Half Hog **(28)**, or BSSBHH for short, is described on the Shetland Anglers' Association website as a 'one off fly from a one off guy'. Leslie

Barclay is a very experienced and successful competition angler and this fly has been one of the main weapons in his armoury for the last couple of seasons. It contains all the active ingredients of a top of the water attractor and excels among surface active fish. It has consistently outfished more established patterns in this role in a wide variety of locations.

Graeme Callander is another angler whose innovative fly patterns regularly feature on the Association's website. When fish are taking the adult sedge, excellent sport can be had with his Low Rider **(29)**, a fly designed to sit in the water surface rather than on it and it is recommended that the hackles are clipped below the hook. Orange seems to be a very effective colour for flies in a number of situations and Graeme's Tangerine Dream **(30)** is an effective lure when fished as the top dropper on a fast sinking line.

Some good hatches of the dark longhorn caddis occur in Shetland lochs and Robert Sandison has designed an excellent fly, the Dark Longhorn Caddis **(31)**, in imitation of these flies. The fly, which is roughly dressed, is a simple but effective dry fly. It is dressed with black Antron, which has excellent floating properties even on windy days. The fly is best fished as a single dry fly and Robert recommends its use in the weedy margins of the smaller Shetland lochs that are unfishable with conventional flies.

Stephen Breivik is an outstanding fly dresser and very keen competition angler, who has caught his fair share of large trout. His most famous fly is the Norski Lad **(32)**, a fly that has spawned a whole family of variants such as the Olive Norski Lad and the Double Peach Norski. His flies are a firm favourite with competition anglers. Another successful fly from Stephen's vice is the Black Pennell Muddler **(33)**. The traditional Black Pennell, originally devised by Harry Cholmondeley-Pennell over a century ago, is one of the first flies I ever learned to dress. It is one of the most dependable patterns ever created and during my fifty years as a fly fisherman it has caught me hundreds of fish. I had never thought of dressing it as a Muddler pattern but, after seeing Stephen's pattern, I shall certainly dress a few and try them out. I feel sure that it is a fly that would do well on my local waters.

The Clan Chief is often to be seen gracing the top or middle dropper of a Shetland angler's cast and is an extremely successful fly for wild brown trout. Not surprisingly, this fly too has spawned a number of variations and one of the most successful of these is Terry Laurenson's Claret Clan Chief **(34)**. Terry is one of the most successful catchers of big trout in Shetland today. His success is down to a mixture of dedication, knowledge of Shetland waters, and a tried and tested selection of flies. The Clan Chief Muddler **(35)** is another very popular variant of this dependable fly and features in Tony Li's cast of the month for March 2016.

Alastair Jamieson is a very experienced angler who has represented Shetland against Orkney on many occasions. He enjoys fishing from both boat and bank and has an encyclopaedic knowledge of traditional fly patterns. Like Brian Watt, he has the distinction of having one of his flies, the Allie Hardy, included in Stan Headley's *Trout and Salmon Flies of Scotland* (1997). He is most at home with tiny imitative patterns and his Black Adult Midge **(36)** is an excellent pattern fished on the top dropper. His Spring Black fly **(37)** is often fished on the middle dropper and is a good all-round black fly imitation, which I have found useful on my local reservoirs.

David McMillan junior is one of Shetland's up and coming younger generation of anglers. As well as being a skilful fly fisher he is also a very competent fly dresser who has devised a number of patterns that have proved extremely successful on Shetland's numerous lochs. David's Grey Boy **(38)** is an excellent suggestive nymph pattern, which is best fished dead drift across the breeze on the point position of a floating line from the bank. Another good point fly from David's vice is David's Emerger **(39)**, which fishes well when trout are bulging just under the surface. He recommends fishing the Emerger, with the deer hair and seal's fur thorax treated with floatant, on the point with buzzers on the droppers.

It is impossible in a chapter such as this to include all the successful flies developed by Shetland anglers over the course of the last thirty or forty years and to those anglers whose flies I have omitted I pass on my apologies. However, it is clear from my researches that Shetland has a thriving and knowledgeable community of anglers who are not content just to accept traditional fly fishing wisdom but are prepared to go out and experiment and to modify existing fly patterns or to invent new ones to suit their particular favoured lochs.

*A tourist fishing for sea trout at the Houbans, Sullom, 1900.
Courtesy of Shetland Museum & Archives.*

CHAPTER 24

Piscator Non Solum Piscatur

Piscator non solum piscatur is the motto of the prestigious Fly-fishers' Club in London and loosely translates as 'there is more to fishing than catching fish'. And nowhere is this statement more appropriate than in the beautiful islands of Shetland. When I go on holiday I like to spend a day or a couple of evenings fishing and my holidays have seen me wet a line in some remote and beautiful locations, including Canada, Alaska, Norway and Northern Sweden, where I fished for perch through a hole drilled in a frozen lake. Nearer to home my holidays have taken me to numerous Scottish islands and I have cast a line on Mull, Skye, Arran, Islay, North Uist, Orkney and Shetland. There is something about wild and remote places that I find immensely attractive and I would much prefer to spend my time in such places rather than on a sun-drenched beach in southern Spain or Greece. I have a number of friends who go on fishing holidays. They flog the water from breakfast till dinner for days on end - 'endurance fishing' I call it -, yet they never see the world beyond the river. They catch more fish than I do but that sort of fishing holiday is not for me. I much prefer to have a holiday which includes the occasional day's fishing, rather than to thrash the water endlessly. Such have been my holidays on Shetland.

Part of the pleasure of going on holiday, especially a holiday which is going to involve some fishing, lies in the anticipation and preparation. Shetland is a true paradise for anglers who are interested in archaeology and natural history as well as fishing. Before embarking on a recent holiday to these remote islands I read all I could about the place, including the excellent website of the Shetland Anglers' Association. I promptly sent for a map giving details of over seventy lochs controlled by the Association, which are available to the visiting angler. For the princely sum of £30 a visiting angler has access to all these lochs for a full twelve month period. What a bargain when you consider you can pay more than that for a single day on some of the trout fisheries in England! As well as finding out about the fishing I dressed a number of the flies featured on the website including the Belmont, the Clousta Blue, Sedgehog and Colin's Beetle in addition to some of my old favourites such as the Black Pennell, Zulu and Invicta.

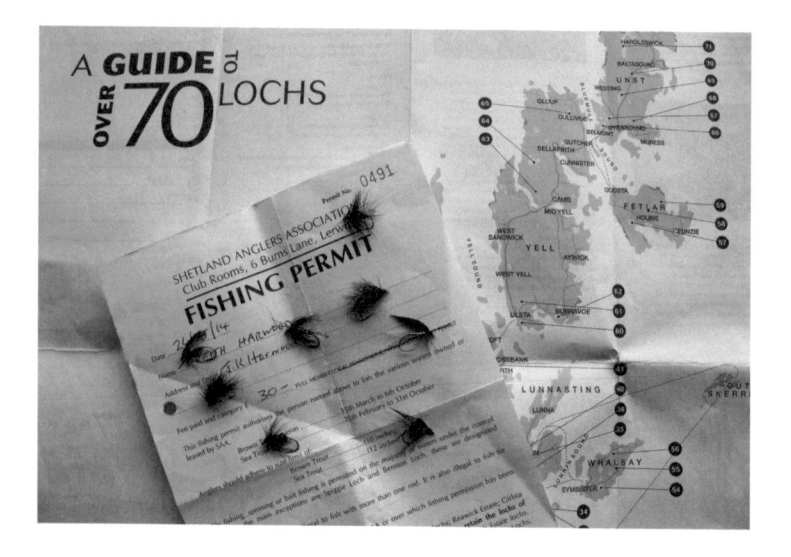

The journey from Lancashire to Aberdeen proved uneventful and my wife and I duly embarked on the overnight ferry, the *M.V. Hjaltland* (an Old Norse name for Shetland) bound for Lerwick via Orkney. I was glad we had booked a cabin since the crossing proved a little choppy and we retired early to our bunks. On arrival in Lerwick we quickly checked in at our accommodation and set out to explore the south of the island. One of our first stops was at Scatness, the site of an Iron Age broch. There are a number of brochs on Shetland, strange fortified tower-like buildings reminiscent of electricity cooling towers. As we parked the car by the side of the road overlooking the sea I spotted an otter swimming and searching the bladder-wrack immediately in front of us. Our binoculars quickly came out and we sat entranced, watching the creature for nearly half an hour as it worked its way along the shoreline. From there we moved down to Jarlshof, a complex archaeological site that I had studied but never seen. Jarlshof (the name was coined by Sir Walter Scott in his adventure yarn *The Pirate*, set in nearby Sumburgh Head) is one of the most important archaeological sites in Shetland with a history of uninterrupted habitation dating from 2500 BC to the 1600s AD. The recently restored Sumburgh Head Lighthouse designed by Robert Stevenson, grandfather to Robert Louis, is an iconic landmark and sits on the southernmost tip of mainland Shetland and is well worth a visit. On our drive back from Sumburgh Head we were brought to a standstill by gates across the runway at Sumburgh Airport. The main road crosses the runway and when a plane is coming in to land or taking off, level-crossing-like gates descend across the road until

Jarlshof.

the plane has passed. It seemed rather surreal as a plane came in to land as we sat in the car adjacent to the runway!

The following day we explored the north of the island, taking in the dramatic coastline around Eshaness, one of the most striking areas in Shetland. As we drove around the island there seemed to be a dramatic view or a loch around every corner. The highlight of the day, however, was the sighting of a pair of red-throated divers on a lochan near Stenness. The red-throated diver is a beautiful rare bird which breeds on remote lochs and is known in Shetland as the 'rain goose'.

On the Monday we ventured south again to St Ninian's Isle to view the remains of an old chapel dating back to the twelfth century and sitting on top of an even earlier structure, dedicated to St Ninian, probably built in the sixth century. In 1958 a local schoolboy, assisting on an excavation, discovered a wooden box on the site filled with silver objects, twenty-eight in total and comprising altar silver, brooches and sword fittings, replicas of which are on display in the museum at Lerwick. The objects appear to date from the ninth century and may have been buried for safe-keeping during a Viking raid. St Ninian's Isle is connected to the Mainland by a tombolo (a sand spit of shimmering white sand). While we were crossing the tombolo I was delighted to get my first sighting of the much rarer great northern diver searching for fish in the turquoise blue sea. I had been hoping to get a sighting of one of these beautiful birds while in Shetland and it made my day.

After an early evening meal I made my way to Tingwall Loch for the first of three fishing sessions during my week-long stay on the island. I chose Tingwall, (Old Norse for 'field of parliament' and site of the *lawthing*, Shetland's earliest parliament) for its proximity to Lerwick and because it was highly recommended on the Shetland Anglers' website. I parked by the boathouse where a local angler was just beaching his boat. He had caught two nice trout while boat-fishing on the loch although he claimed that sport had been slow due to the cold weather. I asked his advice about where to fish on this rather

Tingwall Loch.

The author into a lively Shetland trout on the Loch of Voe.

large loch and as the northerly wind was quite blustery he suggested fishing the south bank of the loch near the local golf course. He even gave me two of his flies to try, a Bibio Muddler and an ordinary Bibio. He suggested the Bibio Muddler for use on the point. When fishing somewhere unfamiliar I always find it helpful to speak to local anglers and invariably I have found them more than willing to part with their advice. After driving my car down to the golf course I tackled up with a team of three flies - the Bibio Muddler on the point, a Belmont on the middle dropper and a Zulu on the top dropper. As I approached the southern end of the loch the wind was becoming stronger as evidenced by the whirring of four wind turbines on top of a hill overlooking the loch. Casting was difficult and I had to time my casts between gusts of wind while my heavily ginked Zulu on the top dropper was being swamped by the waves. However, I persevered and worked my way round to the eastern shore which was a little more sheltered. As I fished my way along the shore I had a splashy rise to the Zulu but the fish failed to connect and that was it for the evening. I fished on until the light started to fade and then packed up slightly dejected. It was rather cold for the end of May and there was little fly life about.

I did not fish on the following day. Instead, we took a short boat trip over to the island of Mousa to visit the magnificent broch, which at 13m high is the best preserved broch still standing. The island itself is an RSPB bird reserve and is home to colonies of Arctic terns and great skuas, locally known as 'bonxies'. We did a circular walk of the island before venturing to the wonderfully preserved broch with its double skinned walls, a magnificent feat of engineering when you consider it was built around the time of Christ. The view from the top of its walls was magnificent.

On Wednesday the chill wind had abated and the temperature began to rise. We visited the splendid Shetland Museum in Lerwick, an absolute must for any visitor to the island. The gorge hooks and wooden otter boards on display bear witness to the fact that people have fished for trout in these islands long before the arrival of angling tourists during the Victorian era. On Wednesday evening I decided to try my luck again on Tingwall Loch. After parking at the golf club, I began fishing along the southern shore of the loch, but again without result, although the wind had dropped and I was able to cast out a decent line. After an hour or so with no luck I decided to cross over the narrow strip of land separating the Loch of Tingwall from the Loch of Asta and fish the latter. Another angler was fishing the western shore of this loch and he recommended putting a bushy fly on the top dropper. I duly tied on a Sedgehog and fished along the western shoreline, wading out into the shallow water. Again, there was nothing doing and no sign of any fly life on the water and so I returned to Tingwall for the last hour. I was fishing near some skerries at the south of the loch by the golf course when a fish rose at the Sedgehog and well and truly hooked itself. After a brief struggle I managed to bring my first Shetland brown trout to the net. Although it was not a big fish it was beautifully marked and after taking a quick photograph I gently slipped it back into the water. It's surprising how one fish can lift an angler's spirit and confidence! Shortly afterwards I rose another fish but failed to connect. As the light began to fade I noticed the odd fish rising a little distance to my left. I carefully waded over and cast out. Almost immediately I rose a fish, which made a grab at the top dropper but failed to connect. A few casts later I hooked another fish, which took my Black Pennell on the point, and this time I managed to land it. Well satisfied with my evening's efforts I decided to go back and partake of a well-earned beer!

   The following morning saw me fishing the Loch of Voe, a much smaller loch situated about fifteen miles north of Lerwick. This loch, too, was singled out for attention on the Shetland Anglers' map as being of easy access with good wading from the bank, while the fish were reported to respond to bushy flies. It was a bright, sunny morning with a blue sky and light wind and while perhaps not ideal fishing conditions it was good to be out in such idyllic surroundings. I tackled up and waded out into the shallow water at the southern end of the loch. I noticed that the water was more peat stained than the other lochs I had fished and was the colour of a good pint of bitter. On the third cast a fish rose to my bushy Sedgehog on the top dropper and a spirited fight followed before I carefully netted it. A couple of casts later and another fish rose at the fly but this time I failed to connect. I thought I was in for a bonanza! However, such are the vagaries of angling that the fish promptly went off the boil and I decided to move and fish the eastern shoreline. The water here was a little deeper and the wading a little more difficult due to underwater rocks. I fished this shoreline thoroughly without raising a single fish. After moving back to the shallower water near the southern end of the loch I was soon into another fish, which took the Black Pennell on the point. I continued fishing and was surprised when an Arctic tern swooped down at my Sedgehog on the top dropper, only veering away at the last moment. I was mightily relieved as I did not fancy an aerial tussle with a lively bird! As lunchtime approached and I was about to call it a day another beautiful trout grabbed the Sedgehog and was promptly landed. I suppose three fish is not bad for a morning's total but that early fish had upped my expectations and I went away a little disappointed.

    The last two days of our holiday were spent walking, bird watching and generally exploring the island. On the final afternoon we returned to St Ninian's Isle and undertook a circular walk of the island taking in the spectacular cliffs and watching the fulmars, skuas, Arctic terns and puffins as they went about their business. I was pleased to see that the great northern diver was still feeding in the area. I am not sure whether I believe in reincarnation but I remember thinking, if I am allotted another life span, I wouldn't mind being born again on Shetland so that I could fully explore the fishing potential of these remote and magnificent islands. One thing I knew for sure, though - it wouldn't be long before I'd return for another holiday.

And return I did - the following July/August and this time for two weeks. On this occasion Helen and I boarded the *M.V. Hrossey*, the *Hjaltland's* sister ship, at Aberdeen, and set sail on a glorious evening with the sea as tranquil as a mill pond. After a leisurely meal and a couple of drinks in the St Magnus Lounge, we retired to our cabin and awoke refreshed in Lerwick at 7am the following morning. After breakfast in a local café, we explored the familiar streets of Lerwick before making our way to our accommodation. One of our first ports of call was the Sumburgh Head lighthouse. It was a glorious day with a slight chill in the air but perfect for walking up to the lighthouse and taking in the scenery. The cliffs were ablaze with oxeye daisies and the puffins were milling around their burrows before departing to spend the long winter out at sea. The birds were not deterred by the presence of humans and I managed to take some wonderful photographs of 'tammie norie' as the puffin is referred to locally. At the lighthouse itself the authors (Paul Harvey and Rebecca Nason) of the recently published *Discover Shetland's Birds* (2015) were signing copies of their beautifully illustrated book and I could not resist buying a copy of this essential guide to Shetland's rich bird life.

A day or two later we ventured down to one of our favourite spots on Shetland, St Ninian's Isle, in the hope of spotting the great northern diver, which we had seen the previous summer fishing in the turquoise waters of the bay. This time we were disappointed, but undeterred, we crossed the white sandy tombolo and completed a circuit of the island stopping at various vantage points to watch the puffins and tysties (black guillemots) bobbing about on the sea below the cliffs. However, the following week, while exploring Burra, I was delighted to see a great northern diver hunting in the waters off the pretty village of Hamnavoe.

On our previous visit to Shetland we had confined ourselves to exploring the Mainland but this time I wanted to explore some of the other islands in the archipelago and our first port of call was the island of Bressay, just a short ferry ride from Lerwick. One of our reasons for visiting Bressay was to drive across the island and explore the National Nature Reserve of Noss. Unfortunately, we never managed to make Noss since, on the two occasions when we tried, the sea was too rough for the boat to take us across. They say that every cloud has a silver lining, and our failure to visit Noss meant that I had time to fish the Loch of Brough, conveniently situated by the side of the road. According to the information in the *Guide to over 70 Locations*, the Loch of Brough holds some good fish up to more than three pounds, though the average is around twelve ounces. Nymph patterns were the recommended flies and I tied a Gold-Ribbed Hare's on the point of my cast, a Black Pennell on the middle dropper and a Claret Buzzer on the top dropper. Unfortunately, on the two occasions that I fished this loch I never even saw a fish let alone caught one. However, to be fair, on each occasion the sun was quite bright and the conditions were not ideal for fly fishing. I suspect that had I fished the loch in the 'simmer dim', I would have fared much better. Although the fish were not playing the game, I did hear the piping sound of a pair of golden plover as I was fishing the western shore of the loch. I quickly made my way back to the car for my binoculars and camera and over the next hour or so I managed to get closer to the birds, which obviously had a nest nearby on the rough moorland, and took a number of photographs. I was particularly pleased to see these attractive looking birds which are quite rare in my part of the world.

At the time, I was researching a book on John Buchan and angling and I very much wanted to visit Unst, where Buchan had stayed and fished with the Rev. Charles Dick, minister of Uyeasound Church (see Chapter Seventeen). After a couple of short ferry crossings and a drive across Yell, we finally made it to this most northerly inhabited island in the British Isles. Although we visited Uyeasound and managed to photograph the places associated with John Buchan, no visit to Unst would be complete without visiting its famous furnished bus shelter and the remains of the Viking longhouse, which lies beyond. From there we drove up to the summit of Saxa Vord, the site of a former RAF station, which closed in 2006, and gained a fine view of the dramatically located Muckle Flugga lighthouse. Sadly, our day on Unst was all too short and I did not get the opportunity of wetting a line on the Loch of Cliff or any of the other of its fine trout lochs.

On returning to Lerwick I did manage to squeeze in a fishing trip to the Loch of Tingwall, which I had fished the previous year. Making use of the experience gained from my previous visits I tied a Sedgehog on the top dropper, a Spring Black on the

The famous furnished bus shelter on Unst.

middle dropper and a Black and Claret Buzzer on the point of my cast. Wading the south-east shoreline, it wasn't long before I connected with a lively fish of around ten ounces. Several more fish soon followed, all of which took my point fly. I had a couple of rises to the fly on the top dropper and one trout leapt clear of the water right over it but all of them failed to connect.

During our stay I particularly wanted to visit Fetlar in order to see the red-necked phalaropes, which are rarely encountered in the British Isles outside of Fetlar. After travelling from Lerwick and across Yell, we eventually boarded the ferry for Fetlar only to find that the birds had already set out on their long migration to spend the winter in the Galapagos Islands. We did, however, visit the excellent Fetlar Interpretive Centre, where the lady in charge was very helpful in answering my questions regarding Sir William Watson Cheyne's attempts at improving the fishing on the island's lochs. On our way back to the ferry we made a slight detour to view Papil Water and I wished I had time to fish this water, which is reputed to contain some fine trout. Although we did not see any trout rising, we did see plenty of bonxies, which were not too happy at our approach.

As every visitor to Shetland is aware, the weather can change at the drop of a hat and I spent two or three wet mornings in the archives at the Shetland Museum in Hay's Dock. It is almost certainly the best small archive and museum I have ever visited and I managed to glean a great deal of information about the history of angling on Shetland, which appears elsewhere in this book. The museum and castle at Scalloway are equally impressive and on another wet morning we paid a visit to the former capital of Shetland. I was fascinated by the museum's exhibit relating to the 'Shetland Bus' during the Second World War.

Unfortunately, our fortnight's holiday ended all too soon and I did not spend as much time fishing as I would have liked, nor did I have time to explore Whalsay or the Out Skerries or Foula or . . . I could go on and on, but it goes to show that on Shetland 'there is more to fishing than catching fish'. Still, there is always next time!

APPENDIX

Selected Fly Dressings

In the alphabetical list of flies that follow, I have not included the dressings of the more traditional flies, which can be found in any of the standard reference works on flies, particularly Stan Headley's *Trout & Salmon Flies of Scotland* (1997) or Courtney Williams' *A Dictionary of Trout Flies* (1949). In most dressings I have not included hook size or makes, as these are very much a personal choice.

ALLIE HARDY (not illustrated)
Alastair Jamieson
Thread - Brown.
Tail - A tuft of fluorescent phosphor yellow floss (Glo-Brite No. 11).
Body - A mix of fiery brown and dark olive seal's fur.
Hackle - One fiery brown and one olive cock hackle of equal size. Two turns each at the head, then both palmered back down the body.
Rib - Gold wire.

ANDY PANDY (26)
Brian Watt
Thread - Black.
Tail - Magenta Glo-Brite.
Tag - Magenta ostrich herl.
Rib - Silver wire.
Body - Magenta peacock herl.
Hackle - Furnace hen palmered.
Wing - Bronze mallard, top and bottom.
Hen - Black deer hair, shaped like a bullet.

BARCLAY'S SUNBURST STINGY BEE HALF HOG (28)
Leslie Barclay
Thread - Fluorescent pinky orange.
Butt - Flat gold tinsel.
Body - 2/3 claret seal fur followed by 1/3 olive seal fur.
Rib - As tying thread.
Wing - Olive deer hair.
Head - Sunburst sea fur dubbed over.

BELMONT (1)
from Rev. John Russell
Body - Peacock bluish-green silk.
Rib - Fine gold tinsel.
Hackle - Ginger/red.
Wing - Peacock sword feathers over landrail.
A modern variant of this fly uses blue-green SLF dubbing for the body and red twinkle instead of landrail.

BLACK ADULT MIDGE (36)
Alastair Jamieson
Thread - Black
Body - 4 or 5 strands of crow herl.
Rib - Fine silver wire.
Wing - White hackle point.
Thorax - Black midge dubbing.
Thorax Cover - Crow.
Hackle - Black hen.

BLACK PENNELL MUDDLER (33)
Stephen Breivik
Thread - Black.
Tail - Golden pheasant tippets dyed red.

Body - Black tying thread or black floss.
Rib - Fine silver wire.
Head Hackle - Black Hen.
Head - Deer hair muddler style with 'V' clipped out to reveal body.

CASTLE DUNKELD (6)
Pat Castle
Thread - Black.
Tail - Golden Pheasant topping.
Body - Flat gold tinsel.
Rib - Gold wire.
Hackle - Magenta hen.
Wing - Bronze mallard.

CASTLE KERGORD (5)
Pat Castle
Thread - Black.
Tail - Red floss.
Body - Flat silver tinsel.
Rib - Silver wire.
Hackle - Black hen.
Wing - Peacock sword feathers with golden pheasant topping over.

CLAN CHIEF MUDDLER (35)
Tony Li
Thread - Black.
Tail - Glo-Brite red No. 5 and yellow floss.
Body - Silver tinsel with black and red cock hackles over.
Cheeks - Yellow goose biots.
Head - Deer hair muddler style.

CLARET CLAN CHIEF (34)
Terry Laurenson
Thread - Black.
Tail - Glo-Brite No. 4 with sunburst marabou over.
Body - Claret seal fur.
Body Hackle - One red and one black cock hackle palmered together.
Rib - Medium silver wire.
Head hackle - Straggly claret hen.

Wing - Slips of electric blue goose biots.
Cheeks - Jungle cock.

CLOUSTA BLUE (2)
Traditional Shetland pattern
Tail - Golden Pheasant topping.
Body - Flat silver tinsel.
Rib - Silver wire.
Hackle - White or possibly light blue. *(Only one surviving example of this fly is known and the hackle may originally have faded from a light blue colour to white).*
Wing - Blue mallard.

COLIN'S BEETLE (14)
Colin Wiseman
Hook - B175 size 12-8 with lead wire wound on.
Thread - Black.
Tag - Glo Brite 10.
Body - Black Chenille
Head Hackle - Black Hen.

DARK LONGHORN CADDIS - DRY (31)
Robert Sandison
Thread - Black.
Body - Black thread.
Wing - Black Antron, tied so that when fished static it remains at right angles to the body of the fly.
Head - Dark red nail varnish to represent the distinctive eyes.
Feelers - Partridge feather.

DAVID'S EMERGER (39)
David McMillan junior
Thread - Black.
Body - Sparse black seal fur.
Rib - Clear buzzer wrap.
Wing - Sparse deer hair.
Thorax - Claret seal fur well brushed out with sparse tuft of deer hair in front.
Hackle - Grizzle cock.

Cheeks - Medium Mirage.

DAVID'S GREY BOY (38)
David McMillan junior
Thread - Black.
Tail, body, thorax cover and beard - Bronze mallard.
Rib - Silver wire.

DUNKELD MUDDLER (18)
Billy Reid
Thread - Red.
Tail - Glo-Brite floss No 11 & 12 mixed.
Body - Flat gold lurex.
Body Hackle - Orange cock.
Rib - Gold wire.
Head - Deer hair muddler style.

FLUORESCENT ORANGE PALMER MUDDLER (19)
Mark Sandison
Thread - Fire orange.
Tail - Equal mix of Glo-Brite No 7 & 11.
Body - Fluorescent orange SLF or similar.
Body Hackle - Furnace cock.
Rib - Oval gold.
Head - Deer hair tied muddler fashion with a few tips left as a collar.

GREEN MANTLE
from James Wilson
Thread - Black.
Body - Green wool, rough and picked out.
Wing - Grey mallard flank.

GREEN PALMER (not illustrated)
Brian Watt
Thread - Black.
Tail - Bunch of olive green hackle fibres.
Body - Green seal's fur.
Rib - Narrow flat pearl Mylar.

Body hackle - Olive green hennycock.
Head Hackle - Longish olive green hen hackle.

GRIZZLY KING
from James Wilson
Thread - Black.
Tail - Slip of red feather slip.
Body - Dark green wool.
Body hackle - Badger, tied palmer fashion.
Rib - Fine oval gold.
Wing - Barred teal flank.

HADLAND'S SEA TROUT KILLER (24)
John Hadland
Hook - Stainless steel long shank, sizes 6-12.
Thread - Black.
Tail - Orange or red cock hackles.
Butt - Red floss.
Body - Pear Mylar.
Wing - White bucktail over-layered green, yellow, olive bucktail and a few fibres of flash added in.
Throat hackle - Orange or red cock.
Head - Built up of thread with eyes painted on.

LOCH ORDIE (7)
Edward R. Hewitt
Thread - Black.
Hackles - Hen or henny-cock hackles, tied in to slope backwards down the hook shank. The colour sequence is black, dark ginger, white. On Shetland dark red/brown hackles fronted by one or two hackles is popular. Some variants have the addition of a red or orange tail or jungle cock cheeks. Another variation developed by Colin Wiseman uses grouse hackles rather than hen hackles.

LOUBY LOU (27)
Brian Watt
Thread - Black.
Tail - Magenta marabou with silver side flash.
Body - Black seal fur.
Rib - Medium flat silver tinsel.
Wing - Black marabou with silver side flash.
Head - Black deer hair.

LOW RIDER (29)
Graeme Callander
Thread - Black.
Tag - Green ostrich herl.
Body - Peacock herl.
Rib - Oval gold tinsel.
Palmered Hackle - Dark brown cock.
Wing - Dark brown deer hair.
Shoulder Hackle - Dark brown cock.
Hackles should be clipped below the hook so that the fly sits in the water.

MAGENTA PALMER (25)
John Hadland
Thread - Black.
Tail - Glo-Brite 1.
Body - Pearl over Glo-Brite 1 thread.
Rib - Clear monofilament line.
Hackle - Non-fluorescent magenta cock.

NORSKI LAD (32)
Stephen Breivik
Thread - White.
Tail - Black marabou with a few strands of something silvery or flashy over.
Body - Flat silver.
Wing - Four or five strands of Angel Hair under black marabou.
Head - Spun white deer hair with some fibres left as collar hackle.

OGREHUNCH (22 & 23)
Rae Phillips
Thread - Black.
Tail - Two strips of spurdog tail trimmed or pearlescent tinsel or similar as substitute.
Body - Flat silver tinsel or Mirage.
Rib - Silver wire.
Cheeks - Strips of spurdog tail down either side of body or substitute.
Collar Hackle - Strands of fluorescent pink synthetic dubbing tied round the hook.
Head - Small deer hair muddler head (black for coloured water and white for clear water and sea trout). If the spurdog is left to 'steep' for a few days in saltwater it takes on a luminous hue, which trout find irresistible.

PEARLY WHITE CAT (20)
Mark Sandison
Thread - Fire orange.
Tail - Tuft of white marabou.
Body - Mirage (or pearl Mylar over silver holographic).
Rib - Silver wire.
Wing - White marabou (not too thick).
Throat - Fluorescent green Glo-Brite yarn.
Head - Built up of tying thread.

POTTY'S BLUEBOTTLE (12)
David Pottinger
Hook - Kamasan B170 size 10-12.
Thread - Black.
Tag - Three turns Gutermann blue CA02776 or blue wire.
Body - Black chenille.
Rib - Gutermann blue CA02776.
Hackle - Black.
Wing - Paired blue jay.

POTTY BLUE JAY (13)
David Pottinger
Hook - Kamasan B175 size 8-12.
Thread - Red.
Body - Flat silver tinsel.
Rib - Silver wire.
Wing - Paired blue jay.
Head hackle - Red hen.

POTTY NITE BRITE (10)
David Pottinger
Hook - Kamasan B170 size 8-10.
Thread - Black.
Tail - Glo-Brite magenta floss 1 and 2 mix.
Body - Peacock herl.
Rib - Glo-Brite magenta floss.
Head - Brown cock hackle with white cock hackle in front.

POTTY PALMER (8)
David Pottinger
Thread - Fluorescent orange thread built up into a prominent hot spot behind hook eye.
Body and Tail - Peachy orange wool (Robin Double Knitting, Product code 4006, Shade 163).
Rib - Flat silver UNI Mylar overlaid with 6lb clear fluorocarbon for strength.
Body Hackle - A peachy/golden olive cock hackle.
Head Hackle - Greenwell hen.

POTTY SPARKLER (11)
David Pottinger
Hook - Kamasan B800 size 6-10.
Thread - Orange.
Eyes - Silver bead chain tied below hook shank.
Tail - Anglian water gold and silver mix.
Body - Anglian water gold and silver mix.
Wing - Anglian Water gold and silver mix.
Whisker - A few strands of red cock.
Head - Orange ostrich herl.

POTTY T.I. (9)
David Pottinger
Hook - Partridge 01 Single Wilson salmon size 10.
Thread - Brown.
Body - Two fairly large brown hen hackles wound not too closely together.

PRISCILLA (17)
Paul Bloomer
Hook - B175 with black metal bead at head.
Thread - Fluorescent magenta.
Tail - Black marabou with a few strands of pearly sparkle material.
Body - Peacock herl dyed magenta.
Rib - Red wire.
Thorax - Fluorescent magenta dubbing.

PROFESSOR
Professor John Wilson
Thread - Black.
Tail - Red feather slip (optional).
Body - Yellow floss silk.
Rib - Fine oval gold.
Hackle - Light ginger hen.
Wing - Grey mallard flank.

SPRING BLACK (37)
Alastair Jamieson
Thread - Purple.
Body - 4 strands of crow herl.
Hackle - Cock pheasant blue neck.
Rib - Fine silver wire.

STICKLECAT (16)
Paul Bloomer
Thread - Black.
Eyes - Chain bead.
Tail - Medium or dark olive marabou.
Body - Pearl UV straggle fritz.
Wing - Medium or dark olive marabou with strand or two of crystal flash.
Thorax - Scarlet seal fur.

TANGERINE DREAM (30)
Graeme Callander
Thread - Fluorescent orange.
Tail - Glo-Brite 7 & 8.
Body - Dubbed Glo-Brite 7 & 8.
Rib - Gold wire.
Wing - Sooty olive marabou.
Head - Red Glister.

WIDERBIRSE (21)
Rae Phillips
Thread - Black.
Body - Olive hackles tied 'Loch Ordie' style, from lighter olive hackles at the base to darker olive at the head. The scruffier and bushier this fly is tied the better.

Bibliography

Aston, Sir George - *Mostly About Trout*, George, Allen & Unwin Ltd, 1921.

Brennand, George - *Halcyon*, Kineton: The Roundwood Press, 1968.

Brunton Blaikie, J. - *I Go A-Fishing*, Edward Arnold & Co., 1928.

Buchan, John - *Memory Hold-The-Door*, Hodder and Stoughton Ltd., 1940.

Buchan, Susan - *John Buchan by his Wife and Friends*, Hodder and Stoughton Ltd, 1947.

Cassels, C. J. H. - *An Angler's Guide to the Lochs that can be fished from St. Magnus Hotel, Hillswick, Shetland*, Rosemount Press, Aberdeen, 1901.

Charlton, Edward - *Travels in Shetland 1832-52*, The Shetland Times, 2007.

Coutts, James - *Game Fishing: A Guide to the Shetlands*, Highlands and Islands Development Board, 1968.

Daa, Aald an Freends - *Aest An Wast Da Hill*, Sangirt Publications, 2004.

Farson, Negley - *Going Fishing*, Country Life Ltd, 1942.

Fraser, Duncan - *Angling Sketches from a Wayside Inn*, Andrew Baxendine, Edinburgh, 1911.

Garton, R. V. - *Lure of the Lochs*, Friary Press, Dorchester, 1972.

Greenhalgh, Malcolm - *Casting a Line*, The Medlar Press, 2014.

Grey, Sir Edward - *Fly Fishing*, J. M. Dent & Co., 1899.

Harwood, Keith - 'In Ultima Thule', *Waterlog* magazine, No. 88, Summer 2014.

Harwood, Keith - *The Angler in Scotland*, The Medlar Press, 2015.

Headley, Stan - *Trout & Salmon Flies of Scotland*, Merlin Unwin, 1997.

Headley, Stan - *The Loch Fisher's Bible*, Robert Hale, 2005.

Hendry, Colin - *Scottish Poaching Equipment*, HMSO, Edinburgh, 1982.

Hutton, Guthrie - *Old Shetland*, Stenlake Publishing, 2009.

McLaren, Moray - *A Singing Reel*, Hollis and Carter, 1953.

McLaren, Moray & Currie, William B. - *The Fishing Waters of Scotland*, John Murray, 1972.

Peterson, John - *Shetland: A Photographer's Notebook*, Lindsay Drummond, 1948.

Russell, John, the Rev. - *Three Years in Shetland*, Alexander Gardner, 1887.

Sandison, Bruce - *Trout Lochs of Scotland*, revised third edition, Collins Willow, 1994.

Sandison, Bruce - *Secret lochs and Special Places*, Black & White Publishing, 2015.

Schiel, Liv Kjorsvik & Moberg, Gunnie - *The Shetland Isles*, Colin Baxter, 2006.

Shetland Anglers' Association - *A Guide to Shetland Trout Angling*, Shetland Anglers' Association, 1982.

Street, David - *Fishing in Wild Places*, Golden Grove, 1989.

Tait, John & Co - *Anglers' Guide for the Shetlands*, John Tait & Co., 1902.

Tudor, John - *The Orkneys and Shetland: Their Past and Present State*, Edward Stanford, 1883.

Tulloch, Bobby - *Bobby Tulloch's Shetland*, The Shetland Times, 1993.

Tweedsmuir, Lord - *Always a Countryman*, second edition, Robert Hale, 1971.

Wilkinson, Roderick - *Fishing the Scottish Islands*, Swan Hill, 1994.

Index

Aberdeen Journal, The 51, 84, 90, 179
Aberdeen Weekly Journal 91
Airv House Inn 97
Anderson Institute, the 183, 200
Anderson, John of Hillswick 104
Anderson, Mr Gideon 76
Angling Sketches From a Wayside Inn 143
Archer flight 187
Archimedian minnow 81
Arthur, Charles 25
Asta, Loch of 34, 218, 245
Aston, Sir George 5, 127, 129, 133
Aytoun, Professor William 102

Baltasound 62, 145, 146, 149, 155, 156, 157, 160, 161, 169, 170, 178, 180
Baltasound Voe 170
Barclay, Hector 228
Barclay, Leslie 235, 251
Beer, Jon 23
Belmont, Loch of 147, 225
Benston, Loch of 52
bergset 32
Binns, Willie 228, 232
Bixter 130, 225
Black-Beetle 5, 135, 137, 139, 141
Blaikie, Doctor James Brunton 121
Bloomer, Paul 6, 20, 48, 57, 215, 222, 232, 255, 256
Blue Mull Sound 147
Boddam 99, 100
Breivik, Stephen 236, 251, 254
Brennand, George 167
Bressay 12, 31, 51, 74, 76, 184, 208, 218, 248
Bressay Lighthouse 184
Bridge of Walls Hotel 35
Brindister, Loch of 72
Brough, Loch of 76, 248
Brouster 16, 40, 87, 89, 97, 98
Brouster, Loch of 16, 40, 97, 98
Bruce, Mr Robert 210
Buchan, John 41, 64, 121, 168, 173, 174, 175, 176, 178, 179, 180, 181, 227, 249, 257
Buchan, Susie 176, 178
Burns Lane 47, 54
Burra Firth 147, 148, 156, 157, 160, 169, 170

Burraland, loch of 102

Callander, Graeme 6, 217, 236, 254, 256
Cassels, C.J.H. 59, 225
Casting a Line 216
Channerwick 100
char 15, 23, 24, 25, 102
Charlton, Edward 5, 34, 73, 75, 77, 79, 81, 223
Cheyne, Sir William Watson 18, 41, 250
Cholmondeley-Pennell, Harry 236
Clarke, Barry Orde 54
Clickimin 29, 99
Cliff, Loch of 26, 145, 148, 149, 169, 170, 171, 234, 249
Clingswater 53, 199
Clingswater, Loch of 53
Clousta Hotel 35, 130, 225
Clousta, Loch of 196, 225
Clumlie, Loch of 72
Constable, Andrew 36, 37
Coutts, James 66, 227
Cullivoe 74, 75
Cunningsburgh 21, 100, 180, 181
Cunningsburgh Church 180, 181

Dales Voe 90
Dawn, Chris 53
Devon minnow 186
Devon, the 64, 128, 139, 186, 198
Dick, Reverend Charles 175, 181
Dounreay Angling Club 50
Duncan, Mr Charles 34, 76
Dunrossness 99
Dutch herring 'busses' (boats) 31

Earl of Zetland 35, 84, 102, 155, 168, 175
Easter Quarff 99
Edinburgh Evening News 116
Edinburgh Saturday Angling Club 143
Edwards, Oliver 216
Eela Water 60, 104, 196
Eshaness 60, 214, 242

Falkus, Hugh 191
Farson, Negley 5, 9, 41, 191, 192, 193, 194, 195, 197
Fetlar 12, 18, 41, 67, 68, 75, 136, 218, 250

[259]

Field, The 40, 93, 104, 224, 227
fish farms 15, 21
Fishing Gazette, The 35, 135, 155
Fishing in Wild Places 214, 257
Fishing the Scottish Islands 71
Fishing Waters of Scotland 208, 211, 257
Fladdabister, Loch of 100
Fly Fishing 113
Foula 75, 250
Fraser, Duncan 143
Funzie, Loch 18

Game Fishing - Guide to the Shetlands 66
Garton, Major R. V. 214
Gaskell, Mr 5, 105, 107, 109, 111
Geirhildr 196
German merchants 31
Girlsta, Loch of 15, 23, 45, 102, 196, 218
Glenmorangie 53, 54
Gloup Voe 75
Going Fishing 191, 195, 196, 257
gorge 28, 244
Greenhalgh, Malcolm 216
Grey, Sir Edward 5, 38, 113, 114, 115, 116, 117, 119, 121, 222, 223
Grunnavoe, Loch of 214
Gruting 200, 203, 204
Guide to Shetland Trout Angling, A 68, 229, 257
Gutcher 12, 173

Hadland, John 234, 253, 254
Halcyon 167, 234, 257
Hamilton, Sir Robert 49, 167, 196
Hamnavoe 21, 248
Hanseatic 31
Hardy Altex 186
Hardy, Allie 237, 251
harpoons 28
Headley, Stan 235, 237, 251
Heather Moss 5, 155, 157, 159, 161, 163, 165
Helga Water 79, 80
Henderson family 36
Henderson, Mr John of Gloup 74
Hewitt, Edward R. 228, 253
Highlands and Islands Enterprise 53
Hill, Ronas 14, 68, 162, 218
Hillswick 59, 76, 77, 79, 80, 81, 104, 142, 225, 257
Hillswick House 76
Houbie Burn 41

Houlland 29, 214, 215
Houlland, Loch of 214, 215
høvi 18, 19, 30

Irvine, Dodie 17, 56, 232

Jamieson, Alastair 237, 251, 255
Jarlshof 190, 241
John Tait & Co. 60, 61, 62

Kergord 52, 227, 252

Laurenson, Terry 237, 252
Laxfirth Voe 45, 96, 188
Laxo burn 196, 210
Lerwick 9, 10, 12, 13, 16, 33, 35, 38, 43, 44, 45, 46, 47, 51, 60, 61, 62, 72, 73, 74, 76, 79, 80, 81, 89, 90, 95, 96, 99, 100, 102, 108, 109, 112, 130, 135, 142, 145, 149, 155, 156, 164, 165, 168, 173, 175, 180, 181, 183, 184, 190, 195, 200, 208, 210, 234, 240, 242, 244, 245, 247, 248, 249, 250
Lerwick Angling Club 38, 43, 45
Leslie, John 5, 183, 185, 187, 189, 190
Levenwick 188
Li, Tony 237, 252
Lunna House 116, 117

Magnus Troil 73, 74
Manson's Almanac and Directory 46
Marine Harvest 22
Mathieson, Ronnie 208
McLaren, Moray 5, 9, 205, 207, 209, 211, 213, 219
McMillan, David 237, 252, 253
Mepps lures 67, 68
Miller, Alec 6, 47, 55
Moatt, Captain 88
Mostly About Trout 127
Mousa 100, 244
Muckle Flugga 177, 178, 180, 249
Muckle Flugga lighthouse 177, 180, 249

New Shetlander, The 19, 24, 183, 186, 202, 214
Nicholson, Sandy 235
North Roe 60, 160, 161, 162, 164, 165
Northmavine 59, 60, 75, 79, 102

Old Scatness 30
Old Wick 5, 93, 95, 97, 99, 103, 224

Ollaberry 60
Olna Firth 80, 85, 194
Orkneys and Shetland: Their Past and Present State, The 15, 93
otter boards 39, 40, 64, 101, 244
Our Boys Athletic Club 183
Out Skerries 86, 250

Papa Stour 12, 75, 215
Papil Water 250
Peterson, John 19, 20, 199, 202, 214
Peterson, Magnus Fraser 203
Peterson, Professor J. 199
Phantom Minnow 60, 64, 148
Phillips, Rae 218, 234, 254, 256
piltock wands 32, 203
Pottinger, David 6, 19, 58, 219, 228, 231, 232, 254, 255
Punds Water 60, 77, 79, 80, 102, 103, 104

Queen's Hotel, Lerwick 35, 90, 155
Queen's Hotel, Unst 35, 145
Queyfirth Loch 60
Quill minnow 186
red-necked phalaropes 250
Regan, Tate 24
Reid, Billy 233, 253
Rivers and Lochs of Scotland: The Angler's Complete Guide 71
Robertson, Mr Alexander 74
Roer Water Burn 60
Russell, John 5, 83, 85, 86, 87, 89, 91, 251

Sandison, Bruce 22, 54, 71, 217
Sandison, Mark 6, 48, 57, 234, 253, 254
Sandison, Robert 236, 252
Sandy Loch 72, 99
Sandy Water 162, 165
Saxa Vord 55, 180, 249
sea lice 21, 22, 158
Secret Lochs and Special Places 217
Shelton, Dr Richard 41
Shetland Anglers' Association 6, 7, 11, 15, 18, 23, 25, 41, 46, 47, 48, 52, 53, 55, 56, 57, 58, 60, 68, 69, 72, 190, 217, 222, 229, 230, 232, 233, 234, 235, 240, 257
Shetland Bus, The 117, 250
Shetland Life 16, 20, 203
Shetland Times, The 10, 43, 44, 45, 104,

116, 233, 257
Silver Devons 139
Singing Reel, A 9, 208, 257
Spiggie Hotel 35, 36, 100
Spiggie Voe 151, 153, 227
Spiggie, Loch of 8, 35, 151
St Magnus Hotel 35, 38, 59, 60, 61, 104, 151
St Ninian's Isle 242, 247
Stewart tackle 65, 67, 137, 138, 152, 158, 163
Strand, Loch of 22, 45, 51
Street, David 214
Sulma Water 90
Sumburgh 9, 12, 74, 95, 99, 181, 208, 241, 247
Swan, Dr M. A. 24

Tait, Dr Ian 6, 175
Tait, Magnus 96
Tait, Michael 16
Tallack, Malachy 48, 57
Three Years in Shetland 87, 90, 91
Tingwall, Loch of 10, 34, 49, 51, 81, 208, 213, 218, 245, 249
Toby lures 67, 68
Tod, Mr. E. M. 138
Toft 12, 173
Trebister, Loch of 72
Trout and Salmon Flies of Scotland 235, 237
Trout Festival 48, 53, 58, 216, 218, 234
Trout Fishing in Shetland 5, 15, 69, 135, 137, 139, 141, 213, 214, 216, 230
Trout Fishing on Unst 70
Trout Lochs of Scotland 71
Tudor, John 15, 35, 40, 93, 104, 224
Tulloch, Mr J. S. 24
Twageos 184
Twin Brethren 167, 169, 170, 171

Ulsta 12, 173
Unst 5, 12, 26, 30, 35, 55, 56, 59, 64, 67, 68, 70, 75, 136, 143, 145, 146, 147, 148, 149, 161, 167, 168, 169, 170, 171, 173, 174, 175, 176, 178, 179, 180, 196, 217, 218, 225, 227, 234, 249
Unst Angling Club 55, 70, 143
Up-Helly-Aa 20
Urafirth Loch 60
Urafirth Vadals 60

Urafirth Voe 60, 79
Uyeasound church 176, 177, 179, 180, 249

Vaila Sound 98, 111
Vatsetter, Loch of 72
Vibro lures 67, 187
Vidlin Loch 209
Vikings 30, 210

Wadbister Voe 81
Wagtail spinner 168
Walls 35, 87, 96, 97, 98, 108, 111, 124
Watley, Loch 146

Watt, Brian 54, 235, 237, 251, 253, 254
weels 28
Whalsay 5, 12, 17, 50, 55, 56, 68, 83, 84, 85, 86, 87, 89, 90, 91, 218, 232, 250
Whalsay Anglers' Association 56
Whitelaw Loch 52
Wilson, James 77, 78, 82, 223, 224, 253
Wilson, Professor John 82, 102, 255
Wiseman, Colin 58, 229, 232, 252, 253
Woore, Thomas 33

Yell 12, 18, 21, 48, 67, 68, 74, 75, 136, 142, 173, 218, 249, 250